Nasty Business

Nasty Business

The Marketing and Distribution of the Video Nasties

Mark McKenna

EDINBURGH
University Press

Edinburgh University Press is one of the leading university presses in the UK. We publish academic books and journals in our selected subject areas across the humanities and social sciences, combining cutting-edge scholarship with high editorial and production values to produce academic works of lasting importance. For more information visit our website: edinburghuniversitypress.com

© Mark McKenna, 2020, 2022

First published in hardback by Edinburgh University Press 2022

Edinburgh University Press Ltd
The Tun – Holyrood Road
12 (2f) Jackson's Entry
Edinburgh EH8 8PJ

Typeset in Monotype Ehrhardt by
IDSUK (DataConnection) Ltd

A CIP record for this book is available from the British Library

ISBN 978 1 4744 5108 6 (hardback)
ISBN 978 1 4744 5109 3 (paperback)
ISBN 978 1 4744 5110 9 (webready PDF)
ISBN 978 1 4744 5111 6 (epub)

The right of Mark McKenna to be identified as author of this work has been asserted in accordance with the Copyright, Designs and Patents Act 1988 and the Copyright and Related Rights Regulations 2003 (SI No. 2498).

An earlier abridged version of Chapter 8, 'Whose Canon is it Anyway? Subcultural Capital, Cultural Distinction and Value in High Art and Low Culture Film Distribution', appeared in Jonathan Wroot and Andy Willis (eds) (2017), *Cult Media – Re-packaged, Re-released and Restored*, London: Palgrave Macmillan: pp. 31–47.

Contents

List of Figures vi
Acknowledgements vii
List of Abbreviations ix

1 Introduction: It was the Best of Times, it was the Worst of Times . . . 1
2 A Very Nasty Business: Complicating the History of the Video Nasties 7
3 Tracking Home Video: Independence, Economics and Industry 31
4 Historicising the New Threat 54
5 Trailers, Taglines and Tactics: Selling Horror Films on Video and DVD 70
6 Branding and Authenticity 97
7 'Previously Banned': Building a Commercial Category 121
8 The Art of Exploitation 144
9 Conclusion: The Golden Age of Exploitation? 168

Appendix I 174
Appendix II 177
Appendix III 180
Appendix IV 182
Bibliography 188
Index 200

Figures

2.1	National Viewers' and Listeners' Association promotional poster	28
3.1	Derann Super 8mm abridged release of *The Texas Chainsaw Massacre*	41
5.1	*The Evil Dead*'s promotional competition to win a year's supply of red meat	88
5.2	The video sleeve for the second 'Not Guilty' release of *The Evil Dead*	89
6.1	A selection of artwork used for Redemption's video releases	104
7.1	Vincent Damien (V. D.) O'Nasty, *Viz*	132
7.2	*Headcheese and Chainsaws* Fanzine	134
8.1	Screengrabs from VIPCO's DVD release of *City of the Living Dead*	151
8.2	Arrow Video's release of *City of the Living Dead*	159
8.3	Arrow Video's 2016 release of *The Driller Killer* using the original VIPCO artwork	165

Acknowledgements

I began the research for this book in 2010, collating what was originally intended to be a history of the distributor VIPCO for my website vipcosvault.co.uk. This early work went on to form the basis of my PhD thesis, which gradually shifted from a project that considered VIPCO exclusively into a project that explored the entire industry, from the early 1980s right up until the present day. The reason for this shift was in part because Mike Lee, the managing director of VIPCO, proved impossible to find and it was only recently that Jason Impey managed to locate him where everyone else had failed. Because of this, the project looks very different from how it began, but I would first like to thank the people who gave up their time to be interviewed in this early incarnation of the project. Rob Bewick, Allan Bryce, Barrie Gold, Graham Humphreys, Craig Lapper, Martin Myers, Nigel Wingrove, Stephen Woolley and Jay Slater, I thank you all for your time, knowledge and enthusiasm, and although this project evolved into something quite different, I hope that this book in some way reflects our conversations. I would also like to thank the British Board of Film Classification and the Albert Sloman Library at the University of Essex for supporting my requests to view their archives, and I would like to thank Angus Wark from the National Library of Scotland his support in the final stages of the research.

I consider myself incredibly fortunate to have developed this research at the Centre for Research in Media and Cultural Studies at the University of Sunderland. Not only did the University fund the research that forms the basis of this book, but the Centre provided an exciting and vibrant research community in which I could develop my ideas. While I thank all of the staff for their support and advice during these formative years, I would especially like to thank Andrew Crisell for creating an energetic forum in which we could debate our ideas. I would like to thank Martin Barker and Julian Petley for their support and generosity when I was first beginning this project, and I would like to thank Kate Egan for her kindness before I knew her personally, and for her continued advice and support since we have become friends. I would like to thank James Chapman for his enthusiastic response to the research forms the basis of this book and for his continued support throughout the book's development. Thanks go to Justin Battin, Paul Benton, Louise Buckler, Steve Cannon, Ewan Cant, Silvia Caramella, Oliver Carter, Lise Dilling-Nielsen, Rosie Ferries, Steve Jones, Lianne Hopper, Russ Hunter, Keith Hussein, Neil Jackson, Rob Jewitt, Stephanie Jones, Lisa Richards, Adrian Smith, Iain Robert Smith, Dan Kilvington, Shaun Kimber, Giovanna Maina, John Mercer, Alexandra Mondin, Marc Morris, Tim Noble, Jamie Sexton, Michael Shaftoe, Andrew T. Smith, Sam Summers, Calum Waddell, Ashley Wallington, Dan Ward, Tom Watson, Andy Willis, Trish Winter, James Woolley, Jonathan Wroot, Federico Zecca all of who have contributed to my completion of this work in some way. My thanks to John Paul Green who was always happy to lend an enthusiastic ear to discuss my project, and who, along with Kevin A. Hall, was kind enough to offer feedback on earlier iterations of this book, thank you both. Thanks also to Johnny Walker and Billy Proctor for their continued advice and encouragement. I would like to thank Luke Scott and Staffordshire University for supporting the development of this book, and I would like to thank all of the staff at Edinburgh University Press for their support with its production: Gillian Leslie, Richard Strachan, Rebecca Mackenzie, Eddie Clark, and their copy-editor Stephanie Pickering, thank you all for making this a straightforward and pleasurable experience. This book would not have been possible without the support of my family. To my mother Sylvia, and to my sister Kelly Ann, I thank you for your love and encouragement always, but particularly through the many years that it took to develop this project. Last but by no means least, there are two people without whom this book would have never come to fruition. To Martin Shingler, I thank you for your knowledge, patience and insight. I will forever be indebted to you. To my wife Sarah, this book would not exist were it not for your belief in me, thank you for your unwavering support, for your reassurance and for your love. To anyone I have forgotten to name individually, this is not a reflection on you or your input but rather of my failing memory, my apologies and my thanks.

Abbreviations

ASA	Advertising Standards Authority
BBFC	British Board of Film Classification (formerly British Board of Film Censors)
BFI	British Film Institute
BVA	British Video Association (formerly British Videogram Association)
CLD	Catholic Legion of Decency
DPP	Department of Public Prosecutions
DVD	Digital Versatile Disc
HoC	House of Commons
HoL	House of Lords
IDA	Indecent Displays Act 1981
MPAA	Motion Picture Association of America
MPPDA	Motion Picture Producers and Distributors of America
NVLA	National Viewers' and Listeners' Association
OPA	Obscene Publications Act 1959
OPS	Obscene Publications Squad
VCR	videocassette recorder
VHS	Video Home System
VPRC	Video Packaging Review Committee
VRA	Video Recordings Act 1984

For my father,
'Sir' Charles Kelly McKenna (1940–2012),
and Elias whom he would have loved so much

CHAPTER 1

Introduction: It was the Best of Times, it was the Worst of Times . . .

> Home video recorders first came on the market in the late '70s and the so-called 'video nasties' arrived very soon afterwards. While the major studios dithered about whether or not to put their recent blockbusters out on tape, enterprising distributors filled the shelves of the newly opening rental shops with lurid shockers that would never have stood the remotest chance of getting a cinema release. In fact in the early days the only movies you could rent on video were low budget sex and horror titles. For fans of exploitation cinema, it was a Golden Age!
> Allan Bryce

For anyone who is unfamiliar with the period, the moral panic that accompanied the arrival of video nasties must seem an odd and implausible moment in British history. In 1982, just as home video was finding a foothold, alarm erupted over the publicity materials that were being used to promote a disparate group of horror films that had just been released into the newly established marketplace. One tabloid journalist dubbed these films the 'video nasties', and the name stuck, quickly becoming a colloquial term that would be used to describe what was believed to be a new wave of extreme horror films entering the UK from the US and Europe. Concern soon began to build about these video nasties and the effect that they might be having upon society, with some keen to suggest that the videos were the root cause of a variety of social ills. This concern quickly escalated into a moral panic and a campaign that sought to 'Ban the Sadist Videos', with the tabloid press leading the charge that resulted in a series of prosecutions that targeted consumers, retailers and distributors alike. By 1984, the hysteria was over, passing almost as quickly as it had arrived, but in its wake, it left an indelible mark on British society, a slew of prosecutions, and the Video Recordings Act (VRA) – a system of censorship that still governs films released to the British market today.

The alarm raised by the advent of the video nasties is an important moment in the history of British censorship and is most frequently discussed in those terms. However, as draconian as the legislation was, the moral panic played an equally important role in the formation of cult communities, and the period is increasingly remembered as a golden age for exploitation movies. This is the perspective that informs Allan Bryce's *The Original Video Nasties: From Absurd to Zombie Flesh-eaters* (1998), from which the passage at the head of this chapter is taken. It captures perfectly the dominant narrative of the introduction of home video to the United Kingdom, and it conjures up the romanticised image of a lawless period in British history in which, for a short time at least, transgressive films were released unchallenged into the conservative British marketplace and to an audience who were hungry for uncensored tales of sex and violence. Bryce's account shares many similarities with other accounts of the period, and it is precisely because of these similarities that it is a useful place to begin deconstructing how a romanticism for the period has often worked to limit critical discussion and obscure an industrial history.

The video nasties are often presented as an external threat, arriving in Britain from somewhere else and having little in common with the established traditions of cinematic horror. This is a notion that was central to the *Daily Mail*'s press campaign and which constructed the independent British video industry as immoral opportunists, and this is an idea that can be seen, albeit implicitly, in Bryce's suggestion that the video nasties 'arrived', as if from somewhere else. The belief that they were something new, foreign or different was one of the defining characteristics of the campaign against them and something that was repeated over and over again in accounts that sought to alienate and attack specific parts of the industry, and this idea is reiterated in Bryce's suggestion that these 'lurid shockers [. . .] would have never stood the remotest chance of getting a cinema release' (1998: 3). However, while this was undoubtedly the rhetoric of the press, as tempting as it is to imagine Britain's conservative values under threat by this invasion of unknown controversial horror films, the idea that these films were entirely new to the British marketplace simply does not hold up to scrutiny. Thirty-one of the seventy-two videos targeted by the Department of Public Prosecutions (DPP) as video nasties had already received a theatrical release in the United Kingdom in the years prior to being condemned on home video. Of the remaining forty-one films that became categorised as video nasties, only six were ever refused a theatrical certificate outright, while a further thirty-five were never submitted to the British Board of Film Classification (BBFC) for consideration. While it is entirely likely that had they been submitted, some of this number would have been refused a certificate, that still does not alter the fact that almost half of the films on the DPP's list had already received nationwide circulation prior to their release on home video. While this might seem inconsequential, it is enough to muddy any real sense that these films should be understood as something new, foreign or different and presents a challenge to the invasion narrative that dominated the tabloid press. Bryce's suggestion that 'the major studios dithered about whether or not to put their recent blockbusters out on tape' repeats another element that is common to most histories of the video nasties, which, while having a basis in fact, does not attempt to map the marketplace in any meaningful way, interrogate the motivations and investment of the major studios or scrutinise what their entry into the British video market might have meant for the independent sector (many of whom were distributors of the video nasties) when they eventually did join the market. Instead, Bryce reiterates the popular narrative that this was a 'golden age of exploitation', with shelves filled to bursting point with challenging and transgressive films, until the Video Recordings Act cleansed the industry in a wave of censorious action.

To be clear, these challenges to Bryce's narrative are not intended as a criticism of him personally. Bryce's work on the video nasties – both in his books *The Original Video Nasties: From Absurd to Zombie Flesh-eaters* (1998) and *Video Nasties 2: Strike up the Banned: A Pictorial Guide to Movies that Bite!* (2001) and in the magazines *The Darkside* and *Video: The Magazine* – is incredibly valuable and he has been a hugely significant figure in the history of the video nasties. I have begun with Bryce's account because it illustrates the romanticism that informs histories of the video nasties; and because, on a fundamental level, it is no different to other popular accounts of the video nasties, all of which celebrate the 'golden age of exploitation' and capitalise on a sense of the distributors as illicit, dangerous or disreputable. Kim Newman speaks of 'the plague years', a term he similarly employs to invoke 'a golden age' (1996: 132), while Francis Brewster, Harvey Fenton and Marc Morris talk of 'The Outlaw Years', in an account that conjures up an image of pastoral Britain, before the 'malevolent influence' of the 'video nasties spread across a previously innocent land' (2005: 4). While none of these accounts is wholly inaccurate, each hyperbolically reworks the rhetoric of the tabloid press campaign to appeal to a readership who are invested in the golden age of exploitation and the idea that the video nasties were the illicit product of a disreputable industry. In doing this, these accounts mirror the tabloid reports, in which distributors were not enterprising, they were unscrupulous; they were not entrepreneurial, they were opportunistic; and they were not independent, they were self-serving. And while this narrative served a clear purpose within the campaign, presenting the independent sector as sleazy opportunists and as immoral, duplicitous and exploitative dealers, likening the effect of their products to the effect of drugs, the narrative's continuation beyond the 1980s in fan and cinephile discourse is largely due to the value that this image continues to have in the contemporary marketplace. The sum effect of this has reduced the dominant image of the early video industry to little more than a caricature. If we are to begin to think critically about the early video industry, then we need to start by first recognising that much of our current understanding about that industry is derived from an image that was originally conceived, constructed and circulated by the media discourse of the tabloid press, and that this is an image that has been perpetuated by the communities invested in exploitation film.

While it is not my wish to absolve the video industry of any blame, there does need to be greater transparency about what they are being blamed for, and analyses and histories should begin by dispensing with inherited moral judgements about that industry that are largely derived from the tabloid press. This book seeks to complicate the common perception of what has been otherwise seen as a 'thoroughly corrupt' industry by instead exploring a new economic sector that was struggling to self-regulate in the face of overwhelming adversity, considering how the popular perception of the industry in public discourse, and in some cases their own marketing efforts, served only to destabilise these attempts. It will chart the evolution of the video nasties as they moved from media moral panic into profitable distributive commercial category and will simultaneously examine the evolution of the independent home entertainment sector as it moved from an industry of generalists, producing products designed to appeal to as broad a demographic as possible, into specialists, capitalising on the notoriety of the moral panic and focusing on a narrower range of products that were designed to appeal to niche or cult audiences. By examining the video nasties over more than thirty years, it becomes possible to see how promotional strategies evolved, and how, as the industry has evolved, ideas of value and authenticity associated with these films has begun to change.

This book comprises nine chapters. Following this introduction, and as means of orienting further discussion, Chapter 2, 'A Very Nasty Business', provides a historical overview of the moral panic, presenting a potted history of the video nasties campaign as it unfolded in the press before then complicating the established narrative by presenting the image of an industry attempting to negotiate regulation in the face of overwhelming economic, political and social adversity. This emphasis on industry reveals that what is often thought of as being a quintessentially British phenomenon has many parallels with the implementation of broader legislative frameworks governing film globally in the American marketplace. This reconceptualisation is explored in Chapter 3, 'Tracking Home Video', which maps the emergence of the videocassette recorder (VCR) in the late 1970s and documents the economic boom that followed by examining the opportunities that were made available to the independent sector through their early adoption of video technology and considers the significant independent players and the important, profitable genres. It then traces how the development of the moral panic facilitated the suppression of the independent sector, and how this coincided with the major labels finally committing to the market. Chapter 4, 'Historicising the New Threat', scrutinises the invasion narrative that was central to the press campaign against the video nasties and analyses how the British market for exploitation cinema relates to the American marketplace, exploring the differences evident in the kinds of promotion used across the different territories. The purpose of this chapter is to historicise the marketplace for exploitation cinema in the United Kingdom but also to highlight possible differences between these markets that could account for the reaction that followed. Chapter 5, 'Trailers, Taglines and Tactics', offers a detailed analysis of what is widely credited as the catalyst for starting the moral panic, the promotional strategies of distributors. However, rather than giving a blanket acceptance of these materials as sensationalist and therefore problematic, this chapter locates this kind of promotion within contemporary practice and draws parallels between the marginal products of the independent industry and the mass-market appeal of the mainstream film industry. This leads to a consideration of other contemporaneous forms of publicity and promotion, as a means of challenging traditional readings of the video nasties as having no precedent in the British marketplace. Chapter 6, 'Branding and Authenticity', looks at how the companies' own branding practices evolved from the earliest days of the independents in 1979 through to the late 2000s and the consolidation of the sell-through markets that were formed in the early 1990s. This chapter traces the economic positioning of the distributors, assessing how an industry of generalists became an industry of specialists in a marketplace that was carved out largely by the moral panic, and examines how these branding practices began to move the video nasties from journalistic rhetoric or media moral panic into a distributive commercial category, an epithet that could be sold by distributors and understood by consumers. Chapter 7, 'Previously Banned', continues this perspective by considering the gentrification process that the video nasties have undergone since the term was first coined in 1982, examining how distributors, cultural intermediaries and fans have all added to the category, incorporating films based upon a collective notion of excess. Following this, Chapter 8, 'The Art of Exploitation', looks at ways that the decline of analogue technology and the advent of digital platforms such as DVD, Blu-ray and, more recently, digital download, has triggered a process of reappraisal that even now is reshaping the contemporary market for the video nasties. It explores how this reappraisal is not based upon earlier conceptions of the video nasties as archetypes of excessive exploitation cinema but has been complicated by the idiosyncrasies and expectations of these digital platforms. This chapter foregrounds how earlier ideas of authenticity are being negotiated and often neglected in favour of traditional concepts more commonly associated with the canonical film, and how these ideas are helping to elevate the video nasties as important filmic texts and valuable artefacts in their own right. Chapter 9, 'Conclusion: The Golden Age of Exploitation?', considers how the aesthetic of video is being mobilised in contemporary media as a mode of nostalgia that functions as a visual shorthand for the 1980s; drawing parallels between this generalised sense of nostalgia and the genre-specific nostalgia based around horror and the video nasties, it considers how the legal status of the video nasties in the 1980s contributed to a sense of a golden age of exploitation that was imagined to exist outside of the commodification processes of the industry, before exploring how today's marketplace might be better understood as a 'true' golden age of exploitation, with established markets ensuring that more films are available than ever before. Over its nine chapters, the book will detail the evolution of the independent video industry in the UK and will explore how the market has changed for the video nasties. The book highlights the ways in which a desire to challenge the dominant narrative of the video nasties as an explicitly moral issue and as an issue of censorship, while absolutely necessary, has limited critical discussion that has obscured the role that commerce and industry played in both the formation of the category and the continued evolution of the video nasties.

CHAPTER 2

A Very Nasty Business: Complicating the History of the Video Nasties

The history of the video nasties has been recounted many times (Barker 1984; Barker and Petley 1997; Egan 2007; Petley 1984a, 1984b, 2011) and the films that caused offence have themselves been endlessly examined (Dickinson 2007; Jackson 2002; Maguire 2018; Mee 2013; Petley 2005; Starr 1984; Szulkin 2000; Waddell 2016). However, the industry that gave rise to the category has received scant attention. While earlier histories have tended to emphasise issues of censorship that offer only glimpses of an underexplored industrial history, this chapter, and indeed this book, aims to address this oversight by focusing explicitly on an industry that is still portrayed in heavily caricatured terms; that is frequently presented as immoral or corrupt and is still understood through the rhetoric of the tabloid press, as 'merchants of menace' (Sun Reporter 1982: 5).

The first part of this chapter presents a short contextual history drawn from the tabloid press, the intention of which is to provide a historical overview, outlining key moments in the campaign against the video nasties while also outlining the ways in which distributors were discussed in the press. This narrative account will provide the basis for the second part of the chapter which seeks to complicate the established story of the video nasties and position the reaction to them, something that is often discussed as being a quintessentially British phenomenon, within a broader tradition of the legislative frameworks governing film globally. From this, a picture begins to emerge that emphasises a narrative of industrial control, rather than a narrative of societal concern, and begins to complicate conventional readings of both the films and the industry that produced them.

Towards an Industrial History of the Video Nasties

In almost every account, the catalyst that begins the chain of events that leads to the introduction of the Video Recordings Act in 1984 is the same: *Television and Video Retailer* magazine reporting on a number of complaints made to the Advertising Standards Authority (ASA) about the nature of the advertising being used to promote three videocassettes: *The Driller Killer* (1979), *SS Experiment Camp* (1976) and *Cannibal Holocaust* (1980). This unease over the artwork first appears in the February 1982 issue of the magazine and predates any anxieties over content by a matter of months.

By May of 1982, it was estimated that over 1.5 million homes in the United Kingdom had already adopted home video, with predictions indicating that this figure would rise to over 3 million by the end of that year (Renowden 1982). The technology was being embraced at such an exponential rate, with little outward sense of regulation, that James Ferman, the secretary of the British Board of Film Censors (BBFC), felt compelled to intervene, voicing his anger at the lack of a regulatory body governing video by exclaiming that 'they are watching shocking scenes which we would never allow in a cinema, even under an X-certificate' (Graham 1982).[1] Gareth Renowden, editor of *Which Video?* and video columnist for the *Daily Mail* (two roles that did not necessarily fit comfortably together) expressed similar concerns at the lack of a regulatory body or classificatory system governing video in a piece for the *Daily Mail* entitled 'The Secret Video Show'. The article makes reference to a survey conducted by Scarborough school teacher Richard Neighbour and details Neighbour's anxiety that his research into teenagers' viewing habits had 'revealed that their "top ten" videotapes included titles like *Scum* (1979), *Zombie Flesh Eaters* (1979), *The Exorcist* (1973), *Flesh Gordon* (1974), and *The Texas Chainsaw Massacre* (1974)'. Neighbour argued that video would give 'the children access to something that the parents may not be able to control' (Renowden 1982). However, and despite their apparent concern, both Renowden and Neighbour were quick to clarify that this was not a call for censorship, but merely a plea for stricter parental controls in lieu of an industry sanctioned classificatory system. This article would prove significant in its emphasis on rhetoric centred on child protection, an aspect that would soon become a central feature of the campaign that was growing against the independent home video industry.

Renowden's warning to parents seemed to reverberate throughout the press and was soon reiterated in a piece that would prove to be instrumental in the ensuing panic. 'How High Street Horror is Invading the Home', by journalist Peter Chippendale, appeared in the *Sunday Times* on 23 May 1982, and while the piece was similar in tone to Renowden's, Chippendale's article would prove to be far more influential and far-reaching (Chippendale 1982). The article speaks of 'nasties', giving a name to what would soon become collective fears, with Julian Petley citing this as the first time the term appeared in the national press (2012: online). The article singles out titles like *Snuff* (1976), *SS Experiment Camp* and *The Driller Killer* as archetypes of what was being described as the 'catalogue of depravity' (see West 2010b) that the video nasties represented. Significantly, the latter two of the videos listed had already been targeted as a result of their packaging in the February issue of *Television and Video Retailer* and would continue to be cited as a cause for concern throughout the campaign. The article is also significant because it provides a template for the defining characteristics of what would henceforth be known as the video nasties, films released on video that revelled in 'murder, multiple rape, butchery, sado-masochism, mutilation of women, cannibalism and Nazi atrocities' (Chippendale 1982).

As tensions were growing, Conservative MP for Fareham, Peter Lloyd was presenting a bill to the House of Lords to amend the existing Cinematograph Act 1909 (House of Lords 1982). The 1909 Act had become the catalyst for the creation of the BBFC in 1912[2] and Lloyd's bill was presented with the aim of tightening the censorship governing films screened in cinema clubs. However, with the current concerns about the video nasties believed to be beyond the scope of the proposed amendment to the bill, Lloyd conceded that this 'Bill deals with the problems of last year, but these video sales and rentals will be the problem of next year and the year after that' (Martin 2007: 14). In spite of the apparent limitations of his own bill, Lloyd was keen to offer a solution in the form of the Obscene Publications Act 1959 (OPA), believing it would be 'adequate if it was enforceable', but ultimately, he felt that 'the police [did] not have the man-power' to govern video in this way (Chippendale 1982).

Throughout this period, as concern over the problem of video grew, video shops were increasingly being raided and the films that were deemed to be problematic confiscated and then destroyed. Lloyd's solution would be tested the following month when on 9 June raids were conducted on the premises of the three video distributors that were most closely associated with what were now universally known as video nasties. Headed up by the newly appointed operational head of the Obscene Publications Squad (OPS), Superintendent Peter Kruger, and using the tabloid press as intelligence,[3] the OPS conducted raids on the premises of Astra Video Ltd, Go Video Ltd and VIPCO Ltd, seizing *I Spit on Your Grave* (1978), *SS Experiment Camp* and *The Driller Killer* respectively. With forfeitures totalling 1000 films, these confiscations were pending the preparation of a report for the Director of Public Prosecutions to determine whether prosecutions could be brought against the three companies under the terms of the OPA (Author unknown 1982a). This raid represents a significant turning point in how the police were approaching 'the problem' of the video nasties – shifting their emphasis away from the prosecution of retailers and consumers in an effort to stem the tide at the source by removing the product entirely at the point of distribution. Chippendale followed up his article by interviewing Kruger, who expressed his own anxieties over the inherent functionality of the videocassette recorder. He was concerned that its ability to play film in slow motion, freeze-frame, pause and rewind was of as much concern as the content of any of the films that were being released (Martin 2007: 14), and these same technological concerns would become a fundamental part in the argument that was building, with anxieties over the ability to watch scenes out of order, and therefore out of context, paramount.

As the campaign gathered momentum, the tabloid press found an ally in veteran moralist campaigner Mary Whitehouse, the president and founder of the National Viewers' and Listeners' Association (NVLA). The NVLA was a pressure group developed to target media content that it deemed harmful or damaging to society and since its formation in 1965 it had directed its attention at a variety of diverse programming. From the seemingly innocuous, such as Tom Baker's 1975 incarnation as *Doctor Who*, described by Whitehouse as 'teatime brutality for tots' (Hayward 2006), to the ostensibly educational, such as *Panorama*'s coverage of the liberation of the Belsen concentration camp, described by Whitehouse as 'Filth' and 'bound to shock and offend' (Pearson 1994), Whitehouse had a history of taking a hard line on programming that she felt to be a morally corrupting force, and the video nasties were no different.

Adding some credibility to the idea that early video distributors actively courted the controversy that followed is the fact that Whitehouse only became aware of the video nasties when in 1982 the managing director of Go Video Ltd, Des Dolan, sent her a copy of the company's latest release, *Cannibal Holocaust* (1980). Dolan assumed, correctly, that Whitehouse's sense of indignation and moral propriety would function as a no-cost advertising campaign and provide the company with some much-needed publicity for its latest release (Gregory 2005). It did precisely that, though perhaps not in the way that Dolan had hoped or expected. The unexpected gift from Dolan rallied the NVLA, with Whitehouse becoming an instrumental figure in the campaign that would eventually lead to the censorship of video.

From May 1982, when the first articles began appearing, to the August of the same year, there was a visible increase in the number of articles citing concern over the problem that the video nasties posed; in what would seem to be an effort to quell any further political fallout, Norman Abbott, director general of the British Videogram Association (BVA), was reported as saying that 'it is a competitive situation, and everybody was trying to outdo each other and be more outrageous. But now the publishers have decided to put their own house in order' (Martin 2007: 14). In an attempt to address these concerns, the BVA announced the formation of a working party in conjunction with the BBFC with the express aim of tackling the issue of video nasties head-on (Dawe 1982: 7). However, concern quickly turned into blame when on 31 August 1982, a test case was successfully brought against the distributor VIPCO under the OPA at Willesden Magistrates Court in North West London. The prosecution insisted that the videocassettes that were seized from VIPCO's offices (Abel Ferrara's *The Driller Killer* and Tobe Hooper's *Death Trap* (1976)), were 'an extravaganza of gory violence, capable of depraving and corrupting those that watched' them, and required that they forfeit 590 copies plus the master tapes to prevent any further reproduction (West 2010a). When this was reported in the press, the presiding judge was quoted as saying that this should send a 'clear warning' to other distributors and that if the DPP were to seek prosecutions under Section 2 of the Act, there was every likelihood of fines and/or imprisonment. Prosecutor Stephen Wooler felt that while the case was 'exceptional', it was an 'attempt to discover where the law stood' and that based upon the findings of the case, in all likelihood distributors would be prosecuted in the future (Sun Reporter 1982: 5). This ruling would prove to be hugely significant as it provided a legal precedent for the prosecution of cases like this and gave credence to the rhetoric of the tabloid press that these films were, in fact, obscene, and that they did have the ability to deprave and corrupt an audience. Perhaps most significant is that this test case marks a move from press rhetoric that was broadly one of concern to the beginning of rhetoric of blame. The vilification of the independent video industry can be seen to begin here, and following the success of this case, as the DPP continued to target distributors and retailers in further prosecutions.

The video nasties quickly became an all-purpose explanation for moral decline, and the reporting of this decline oscillated between an emphasis on the supposed detrimental effect that these films were having on society and attacks on the industry that produced them. Early headlines foregrounded issues of child protection, such as 'Sadism for Six-year-olds' (Miles 1983c), 'The Rape of our Children's Minds' (Author unknown 1983b), with one mother even attributing her own son's violent rape of two women in Hounslow to the effect of 'video nasties' (Miles 1983a). However, following the successful prosecution of the company VIPCO in Willesden Magistrates Court, the emphasis can be seen to shift toward targeting the distributors and their business practices. Headlines such as 'The

Men Who Grow Rich on Bloodlust' (Harding 1983) named and shamed producers and distributors, while the article 'Fury Over Video Nasties: The Merchants of Menace "Get Off"' (Sun Reporter 1982) documented Mary Whitehouse's feeling that the ruling at Willesden Magistrates Court had not gone far enough. Distributors were increasingly presented as the villainous scourge of society, to such a degree that even a donation to a children's charity from Astra Video (the company that had released *I Spit on Your Grave* and *Blood Feast* (1963)) was reported as nefarious. While the donation was most likely an attempt by managing director Mike Behr to rehabilitate the company's image, it was reported in the press as the 'Charity Shock from the "King" of the Nasties' (Miles 1983b). The donations had been accepted by Dr Barnardos, National Children's Homes, Save the Children Fund, the Sunshine Fund for Blind Babies and Children and Mencap, through a scheme in which £1 from every sale of their popular videocassette *Adventures of Choppy and the Princess* (1982) would be donated to the charities. Revd Michael Newman, Vice Principal of the National Children's Homes, claimed that they 'would not have accepted the money had they known of the company's involvement in so-called "video nasties"' (ibid.).

Shortly after this, the Conservative MP for Luton South, Graham Bright, was approached by Mary Whitehouse who suggested that he propose a private members' bill that would tackle the problem of the video nasties directly and at a governmental level.[4] The Bright bill, as it became known, was proposed in 1983 and would require that all commercial video recordings released in the United Kingdom carry a classificatory certificate, designating the British Board of Film Censors as the organisation that would provide that classificatory certificate. The bill was given added credence when a group calling themselves the Parliamentary Group Video Enquiry published a report entitled 'Video Violence and Children'. Conducted by sociologist and theologian Revd Dr Clifford Hill, the report claimed that four in ten children had seen a video nasty, and though Hill's report was later debunked as methodologically flawed and fraudulent, it would be instrumental in providing a pseudo-scientific basis for the headlines, giving credibility to the cries that video should be censored. This more than anything else helped to propel Bright's bill through Parliament, in the hope that the Video Recordings Act that it proposed would begin to address the concerns that the report had raised. However, the government were reluctant to become directly responsible for the video industry, and the bill named the BBFC as the organisation responsible for the certification of video, thereby ensuring that control of the industry fell to an organisation with a long history of censoring and classifying film.

The prosecution of distributors continued, culminating on 3 February 1984, when the managing director of World of Video 2000, David Hamilton Grant, was sentenced to eighteen months in prison for being in possession of over 200 copies of an obscene article for publication for gain. Grant had released the film *Nightmares in a Damaged Brain* (1981), a film which had previously been granted a certificate for theatrical exhibition by the BBFC, and which he had previously released theatrically. Grant was prosecuted on the basis that the version he had released on video was marginally longer than the BBFC certificated release, and this resulted in him serving twelve months of the eighteen-month sentence, and his company World of Video 2000 (and its parent company April Electronics) being put into liquidation. This is perhaps the most extreme example resulting from the extension of the Obscene Publications Act to cover home video; however, there were also two major consequences that arose as a result of the introduction of the Video Recordings Act 1984. The first was that from that day forward, any distributor hoping to release a film to the UK market on video would be required first to submit the film to the BBFC for categorisation and often censorship. The second was that, although many persevered, when faced with the prohibitive costs associated with certificating their entire back catalogues, the vast majority of independent distributors were forced to cease trading, with the Act effectively decimating the independent video industry.

Complicating the Established Narrative

There is a tendency within established histories of the video nasties to overstate the disreputability of the independent sector and to exaggerate the degree to which the distributors themselves could and should have been held directly responsible for the events that followed. This is not to say that the distributors did not play a part, but by continually framing the distributors as disreputable, earlier accounts have simply removed the need to confront the claims made against the industry, thus eliminating the need to scrutinise how these practices might have related to standard promotional practice seen in other sectors in the same period. In doing this, many of these accounts have failed to properly historicise or contextualise the marketing methods employed in the promotion of the video nasties, and because of that have often simply reinforced established histories, neglecting industrial perspectives that would serve to complicate the established narrative significantly. While later chapters explore the promotional strategies in more detail, this section presents a parallel history, which, rather than simply present an opportunistic industry unburdened by concern, instead, presents the image of an industry struggling to self-regulate in the face of almost universal condemnation, vilification and criminalisation.

Prior to the complaints that appeared in *Television and Video Retailer*, there had been no visible outward sign of concern about any of the advertising being used in the promotion of horror films on video, although other genres had raised concerns. John Martin's account suggests that the complaints made against the video nasties first appeared in the February issue of the magazine in response to an advert for *SS Experiment Camp* that had appeared on the back cover of the January issue. However, on re-examination, although the advert does appear on the back cover of the January issue, there is no letters page in the February issue, and the letters page in the March issue does not make any mention of the film or the advertising methods used in the promotion of the film. The film does warrant a mention on the letters page of the July issue of 1982, though this is in the form of a letter from the London and Home Counties Sex and Horror Video Appreciation Society that defends the video nasties (Wark 2017). There is one complaint in the letters page of the March issue of the consumer magazine *Television and Home Video* that expressed the 'disquiet' of a customer who felt that some of the advertising being used in the promotion of the *Electric Blue* series of adult titles 'would not be out of place in a hard-porn magazine' (Wilson 1982: 59). Similarly, in April 1981, *Video Review*'s letters page featured a letter asking why the magazine carried so many adverts for sex films. The magazine's response is revealing, clearly stating that their reason was twofold; firstly, it suggested that these titles accounted for a large portion of the industry and that, because many distributors carried adult titles, these advertisements were simply reflecting the product that was available in the marketplace; secondly, they suggested that 'there [was] not very much money being spent on advertising by the "major" distributors as many of them [were] still not selling enough tapes to justify heavy advertising' (Nicholson 1981: 67). What is significant here is that even as late as April 1981 the majors have still not established a foothold in the market and that in both of the complaints, the advertising that was causing concern was of a sexual nature, and did not relate to horror films at all.

Given these inconsistencies, it seemed prudent to query the alleged catalyst for the moral panic, namely, the initial complaints that were made to the Advertising Standards Authority (ASA) over the nature of the artwork used in the promotion of horror videocassettes. Although reported extensively across numerous media outlets and a firmly established aspect in the history of the video nasties campaign, on further scrutiny it would seem as if this too may also be unfounded. Despite keeping meticulous records, the ASA had no record of any complaints made against the advertisements for *The Driller Killer*, *SS Experiment Camp* and *Cannibal Holocaust* in *Television and Video Retailer* or, for that matter, in any other magazine. Their records are extensive, containing hundreds of thousands of entries going back to the organisation's incorporation in 1962. These records are catalogued against a variety of criteria such as advertiser name, complaint type, media type, issue/code rule and complexity. However, despite numerous attempts to cross-reference the catalogue, the ASA were unable to locate a record of any complaint against any of the advertising used against any of these films, suggesting perhaps that there were no such complaints. However, in January of 2017, Matt Wilson, the press officer for the ASA, found a statement in the 1982–3 annual report that did make reference to the video nasties moral panic (Wilson 2017):[5]

> The Authority has noted the action being taken by the British Videogram Association, in conjunction with the British Board of Film Censors, to establish standards and a classification for video tapes. The Association is rightly anxious about the standard of much of the packaging and many of the advertisements. The BVA sent us several complaints against advertisements for videos so revolting (as, for example, those entitled 'SS Extermination Camp' and 'Driller Killer') that we were appalled by their publication and took stern action to prevent a repetition. The Authority is pleased that the video trade is making efforts to ensure compliance with BCAP and will continue to use the full range of sanctions at its disposal to repress breaches of the Code. In addition, the Authority has welcomed the statement by the CAP Committee that it will expect the standards of BCAP to be observed by all advertisements carried on video tapes.[6]

What this seemingly innocuous report reveals is potentially of great significance in establishing the source of the initial complaints and has far-reaching implications that problematise the entire received history of the video nasties. All accounts of the video nasties begin in the same way, with a series of complaints made to the Advertising Standards Authority about the advertising being used to promote certain horror videocassettes. The British Videogram Association then responded to these complaints publicly, concerned that 'everybody was trying to outdo each other and be more outrageous' but also suggesting that distributors had 'decided to put their own house in order' (Martin 2007: 14). To assist in this, the BVA announced the formation of a working party with the British Board of Film Censorship and began to develop a classificatory system to help govern video. In this version of events, the BVA pitched themselves as intermediaries and mediators endeavouring to advise their members on best practice and the best way to respond to these issues.

However, what the annual report reveals is that the ASA had not been approached directly and this was not the result of a public outcry, but this was instead the BVA, the trade body designated with representing the needs of the industry, reporting on sectors of their own industry. It is possible that the ASA had other records related to the video nasties, and that they were subsequently archived, but had the general public shown any concern about these videos then this would have undoubtedly shown up in the annual report. Instead, it appears that while the BVA was publicly presenting a face of concern for the entire industry, in private, they were conspiring against the industry that they claimed to represent. Certainly, in an interview given in 2005, Norman Abbott, director general of BVA, was more than happy to perpetuate the image of a binary industry of 'responsible', 'orthodox', 'mainstream' distributors, who had found themselves in competition with small-time companies, 'often with limited resources, most of them not British, who had made . . . films of a much more extreme nature and were only too happy to find a British market for them' (Gregory 2005). In this interview, Abbott explicitly states that the mainstream distributors were concerned that their product risked being contaminated by association, with the suggestion that on the shelves of retailers you could find *Mary Poppins* (1964) next to *The Texas Chainsaw Massacre* (1974), and the people who produced *Mary Poppins* weren't too happy with that juxtaposition (ibid.).

Given that the ASA's report incorrectly lists *SS Experiment Camp* as 'SS Extermination Camp' it would seem that these issues were not necessarily the priority that they would later become for the BBFC or the BVA, though they did claim to be taking 'stern action to prevent a repetition'. Without wanting to speculate too much upon the BVA's motivation to report on pockets of their own industry, this does seem to be demonstrative of a division in the industry, even then. The BVA had made early attempts to be named as the organisation charged with governance of video. They had proposed a voluntary system of classification that had failed to gain traction and then was not widely adopted. Then as the Bright bill moved through Parliament, they were increasingly sidelined in favour of the BBFC, an organisation that already had a long history in classifying and certificating films.

While these attempts to be named as the organisation charged with the governance of video may perhaps appear inconsequential, it is important to acknowledge the remuneration that these companies could expect to receive, were they named as the official body chosen to classify video in the UK. The current tariff for the submission of a film released on video (DVD/Blu-ray) for classification by the BBFC stands at an £80.90

submission fee, plus £6.40 per minute of footage, with all content, trailers and advertisements liable for that cost (BBFC 2019: online). At current rates, this equates to a figure of £656.10 + VAT for a standard ninety-minute film, not including any additional trailers or advertisements. That figure is then drawn from distributors for every film released in the United Kingdom, with theatrical distribution, and video on demand (VOD) services liable for their own costs. Clearly, the BVA stood to benefit considerably were they to become charged with the classification of home video. Demonstrating resolve against the unsavoury elements of the industry could be born out of genuine concern for the shape of the industry or motivated by a desire to steer public opinion and take control of the industry themselves; this remains unclear. What is clear is that the director general of the BVA, Norman Abbott, reported these complaints throughout the press as a consumer complaint, and this then becomes the trigger for the moral panic that in turn reshaped the industry. This begins a chain of events that results in suppression of certain parts of the industry through the imposition of a system of governmentally sanctioned censorship enacted through the Video Recordings Act.

Stephen Woolley, the managing director of Palace Pictures, a company whose early success was built upon the back of the video nasty *The Evil Dead* (1981), is unequivocal in what he believes was the ultimate goal of the VRA. He has commented that 'on the one hand it was partly a censorship thing, but [. . .] more importantly it was how the majors wrested control again [. . .] it was a way of suppressing in many respects, the importance of the independents' (quoted in Gregory 2005), and although this is difficult to prove, this perspective could have some basis in fact. It is a widely known fact that there was a great sense of trepidation from the major distributors about the introduction of home video and the potential threat it posed to the established revenue streams they derived from the cinema. Because of this, the majority of the major Hollywood distributors were incredibly late in joining the industry, and it was this reticence that had initially opened up a space for the independent sector to thrive (something which is explored more fully in the next chapter).

Though it is difficult to imagine now, especially given the revenue generated for the film industry, first by video and then subsequently by DVD and Blu-ray, upon its launch it was believed that home video would bring about the downfall of the entire film industry. In a speech addressing a house judiciary subcommittee of the ninety-seventh meeting of Congress in 1982, Jack Valenti, the long-time president of the Motion Picture Association of America (MPAA), warned that 'We are going to bleed and bleed and haemorrhage unless this Congress at least protects one industry

... [an industry] whose total future depends on its protection from the savagery and the ravages of this machine ... I say to you that the VCR is to the American film producer and the American public, as the Boston Strangler is to the woman alone' (Valenti 1982). Deliberately provocative and hyperbolic, this statement from such an important and influential figure in the American film industry carried weight, and it was intended to lead to the suppression of the sale of video by suppressing the sale of blank cassettes. Valenti and the MPAA felt that if they could establish that the recording of copyrighted television programming without the permission of the copyright owner constituted an infringement under the Federal copyright law, they would have a chance of suppressing the technology that he believed would spell the end of the American film industry. However, Valenti's concerns would later prove to be unfounded when quite the opposite happened, and video eventually became a hugely valuable secondary income stream that would vastly outweigh the revenue derived from traditional theatrical screenings. Nevertheless, it is important to acknowledge the power struggles that were in play then, and that corporations on both sides of the Atlantic were invested in the suppression and/or control of home video. Indeed, only by understanding the investment of all of these interested parties might we understand what was at stake for the established film industry with the introduction of video; but in order to do that, it is first necessary to consider a historical precedent from the days of Hollywood' s infancy.

Established in 1922 by the film studios themselves, the MPAA was founded with the express aim of ensuring the viability of the American film industry by attracting investment and managing its public image at home and abroad. Known then as the Motion Picture Producers and Distributors of America (MPPDA), by the end of the decade, and following a series of high profile tabloid newspaper scandals (most notably the alleged rape and murder of actress Virginia Rappe by the comedian Roscoe 'Fatty' Arbuckle), the organisation was increasingly the public face of an industry that was attempting to put its house in order. The industry quickly became the focal point for moralists who were concerned that the promiscuity, gambling and alcohol that seemed to typify the Hollywood lifestyle was having a negative effect on society, and the MPPDA were forced into action, first implementing a code of conduct for Hollywood's actors, in the hope that they could govern their behaviour off-screen, and secondly, through the institution of a code to govern the content of the films that Hollywood produced – the Motion Picture Production Code. Until that point, local authorities, progressive reformers and a variety of religious and civic organisations had experienced only limited success is suppressing the industry that they believed was having a detrimental effect on society (see Vaughn 1990: 40). It is widely accepted that this concern over the destructive force that film was believed to be having on society triggered a moral panic that resulted in the censorship of the film industry.

Under increased pressure from these moralist campaign groups, the MPPDA accepted the recommendations of two figures who were prominent in the Catholic community: Martin Quigley, publisher of the trade paper *Motion Picture Herald*, and public relations officer Joseph Breen. Together, they devised a code of standards to which the film industry would be required to adhere and in 1929, presented it to the Catholic hierarchy and corporate film executives, both of which welcomed the recommendations (Smith 2005: 38). The code was drafted by Father Daniel Lord, a priest, professor of dramatics and editor of a popular Catholic youth publication, who was himself particularly concerned about the negative effect that film was having on children. Ruth Vasey suggests that the widespread belief that 'children would learn "sophisticated", violent, or antisocial behaviour from watching motion pictures' played a fundamental role in the Production Code being accepted, and that the 'Code was largely designed to assuage these anxieties, which had been exacerbated by the introduction of sound' (Vasey 1997: 5). Stephen Prince suggests that the resulting document 'enshrined the ideals of family and marriage, religion and country and abhorred behaviours that were sinful to the religious mind' (Prince 2003: 21); while Gregory Black suggests that it was felt that entertainment films 'should reinforce religious teachings that deviant behaviour, whether criminal or sexual, cost violators the love and comforts of home, the intimacy of family, the solace of religion, and the protection of the law. Films should be twentieth-century morality plays that illustrated proper behaviour to the masses' (1996: 39). After much negotiation, the terms of the Code were agreed upon with all parties agreeing to abide by them. However, by 1934 it was apparent to the Catholic organisations leading the charge that very little had changed, at which point the organisations banded together to form the Catholic Legion of Decency (CLD) as a means of addressing their concerns. The CLD's primary objective was to highlight problematic films to their members throughout the country, and in doing so, pressurise Hollywood by threatening to blacklist and boycott any movies that they deemed to be unsuitable for public viewing. In an attempt to appease these quarters, prominent Irish Roman Catholic layman Joseph 'Joe' Breen, the same man who had co-authored the original Code, was appointed as the head of the Production Code Administration in a bid to ensure that stipulations of the Code were followed to the letter (see Prince 2003). This ushered in what Robert Sklar has referred to as Hollywood's 'Golden Age of Order' after a perceived 'Golden Age of Turbulence' (1975: 175).

This is the accepted version of that history, in which the motivation to censor film was as a solution to the perceived moral decline and corrupting force of the Hollywood film industry. However, Richard Maltby has argued that the motivation to censor Hollywood was infinitely more complex than this traditional narrative of moral panic would have us believe. He has suggested that 'Hollywood was, is, and always shall be a cinema censored by its markets and by the corporate powers that control those markets' (2012: 237), and argued that that the introduction of the Act was about more than merely controlling the content of individual films, but rather, its overarching concern was with 'the cultural function of entertainment and the possession of cultural power' (1995: 41). In an overview of this revisionist history, Maltby suggests that:

> the issues and motivations behind 'self-regulation' were more complex and were determined more by economic considerations than by matters of film content [. . .] the events of July 1934 are best seen not as the industry's reaction to a more or less spontaneous outburst of moral protest backed by economic sanction, but as the culmination of a lengthy process of negotiation within the industry and between its representatives and those speaking with the voices of cultural authority. (1993: 40)

In these interventions, what Maltby argues for above all else is an acknowledgement of power, asking questions such as who controls the industry? And who stood to benefit from the imposition of these sanctions? These are simple questions that have the potential to reveal much about the systems and processes that governed film and that surrounded and protected the possession of cultural power during the enactment of the Motion Picture Production Code in the United States. Similarly, though in a different country and almost fifty years after the introduction of the Production Code, these same questions have the potential to reveal much about the systems and processes that governed video and that surrounded and protected the possession of cultural power during the enactment of the Video Recordings Act in the United Kingdom. There are undoubtedly parallels that can be drawn here, irrespective of the temporal or geographical distance between the markets, and when considered side by side, the similarities are indeed striking. Both pieces of legislation were introduced following concern over the perceived threat that a new technology posed to the moral fabric of society; both campaigns used the figure of the vulnerable child centrally in rhetoric that propelled the campaign forward in the public consciousness. In both cases this rhetoric is seen to result in a moral panic, and that moral panic is then marshalled chiefly by organisations connected to the church: in the case of the Motion Picture Production Code it was the CLD and the installation of Joe Breen in the office of the MPPDA; in the case of the Video Recordings Act it is through the Parliamentary Group Video Enquiry, an independent research group led by the Revd Dr Clifford Hill that produced research to expedite the video recordings bill through Parliament, and through Mary Whitehouse and the NVLA, a pressure group that espoused Christian values. Both pieces of legislation allowed the dominant players in the industry to retain control of the governance of film through a body that had been founded by the industry itself and, as I will now argue, in both cases it ensured that control of the film industry remained in the hands of the major studios.

Prior to 1984, there was a competitive and diverse film market in the United Kingdom with a wide array of companies distributing a huge assortment of films from a variety of international film markets. As already demonstrated, in the early days of video Hollywood had for the most part resisted the technology, fearful of the effect it would have on their industry and their lucrative theatrical takings and concerned that video as a technology was prone to copyright infringement, meaning that they would struggle to prevent the unlawful viewing of their films. However, this is not to say that majors did not venture into home video in the United Kingdom at all. Twentieth Century Fox, Columbia Pictures (through RCA/Columbia Pictures), Warner Bros and Walt Disney all established a presence on home video, while Paramount Pictures and Universal Pictures both released content through the CIC video label (Cinema International Corporation). But these were tentative steps into a marketplace that the industry's most visible representative, Jack Valenti, hoped would disappear, warning anyone who would listen about the threat that video posed to Hollywood. As head of the MPAA, the American trade association designed to protect the interests of the six major film studios of Hollywood, it is safe to assume that Valenti was representing the views of these companies, at home and abroad. This is hugely significant because while it may be entirely possible that the major studios would have always inevitably taken over the industry, if for no other reason than simply through a demand for their product, in 1982, Valenti was still trying to suppress the technology. No doubt, had the technology been suppressed, then Hollywood would have retreated from that industry, and the home entertainment revolution might have been curbed or even blocked altogether. However, it is dangerous to speak in absolutes here, especially when speculating on what might have happened had legislation found in favour of Valenti and the studios. What it is possible to do unequivocally is to consider the marketplace in the United Kingdom before and after the introduction of the Video Recordings Act and ask similar questions to those Maltby asked around the introduction of the Motion Picture Production Code – who controls the industry? And who stands to benefit from the imposition of these sanctions?

Prior to 1982, the independent sector in the United Kingdom was largely unchallenged. Video had been adopted at a phenomenal rate, and the reticence of the major studios to adopt and adapt to the new technology had opened a space for independence to thrive. Distribution companies were quickly established to meet the growing demand for content, and aware that they were unlikely to convince mainstream Hollywood studios to licence their films, distributors began approaching companies outside of the control of Hollywood, licensing low-budget independent film from the United States and Europe. Companies appeared overnight to meet the demand, and many set up shop beside their cinematic counterparts on London's film district on Wardour Street. Astra Video, Go Video, VIPCO, VTC and Intervision all established a foothold on video in the UK, while companies that were previously successful in the Super 8mm market, such as Derann, made a move into the increasingly profitable home video market. The industry had grown so quickly that independent distributor VIPCO Ltd had seen pre-tax profits in its first year (1979) of £78,000, which quickly rose to £293,000 in its second year and a massive £1,500,000 in its third year (Impey 2019). But the bubble was about to burst, and by 1982, the British video market was already changing and what had previously been the sole domain of the independents was increasingly populated by the major film studios, slowing the boom that had catapulted the independent distributors into prosperity. Recognising the need to adapt to the competitive environment, some distributors believed that the key to continued success lay in provocative marketing (Dolan 1982: online).

The major distributors began entering the market in the winter of 1981 and early 1982, concentrating primarily on releasing films from their back catalogue over new releases, but the popularity of these films would nevertheless present a challenge to the market share of the independents. However, more challenging than the competition was the press campaign that was steadily building against the independent sector, which, significantly, began in earnest just as the major distributors entered the market. This campaign led directly to the introduction of the Video Recordings Act 1984, which was implemented on 1 September 1 1985. However, it would take a further three years to classify the sheer volume of cassettes that were now on the market.

By September 1986, one year after the implementation of the Video Recordings Act, the British Videogram Association's membership consisted of precisely thirty full members (BVA 1986). Included in this were all of the established Hollywood studios, recognisable from what would have historically been understood as the 'Big Five' and the 'Little Three', the studios that shaped the industry in the formative years of cinema: Warner Bros; MGM (having recently merged with United Artists to release their works through the imprint MGM/UA); Paramount and Universal Studios (distributing through the imprint Cinema International Corporation (CIC)); 20th Century Fox (who merged with the CBS Corporation to form CBS/Fox); Columbia (who licenced their catalogue to Granada Video through the imprint of The Cinema Club), and Walt Disney, who joined the market in November 1982 with the release of *Pete's Dragon* (1977), a film that was at that point already five years old. Outside of the established film studios, many companies that were established in other areas also began to enter the market. Music producers such as A&M Records, Chrysalis, Polygram, Virgin or Picture Music International (PMI), a division of EMI, were all making inroads into the video market into what was being touted as a hugely profitable industry. However, what the membership of the BVA reveals more than anything else is that the overwhelming majority of the film companies that held full membership with the British Videogram Association in 1986 were either established distributors associated with major studios, mini-major studios, the imprints for national television stations moving into the video arena, or the result of multinational record producers extending into the video market. There are two conflicting conclusions that can be drawn from this: firstly, that the independent distributors that had initially established the marketplace and developed the networks and infrastructure had disappeared, and the market was now the sole domain of the established companies and major studios. In this version of events, the independents are imagined as opportunists who were put out of business by the Video Recordings Act, and the legislation had succeeded in its goal of cleaning up these problematic elements from video market in the United Kingdom – this is the widely accepted narrative. Or, secondly, and the more likely scenario, that an independent sector did survive, but they were not members of the BVA at this time and were therefore not represented in this list. I would suggest that while the first version is the popular version of that history, the second version is the closest to the truth.

With the costs associated with certification estimated at £1000 per film, the majority of the independent companies found the process to be prohibitively expensive and simply chose to not certificate their back catalogues through the BBFC. While it is widely believed that these companies ceased trading altogether and the market quickly became dominated by the major studios, this only presents part of the picture. What happened in many cases is simply that distributors chose to fold their existing companies, removing any association with their back catalogues, often only to restart again under another name. Personnel often moved around. One example of this is Des Dolan, formerly of Go Video. After Go Video, Dolan went on to form Mogul Video and All American, both of which operated in the post-certification period. Similarly, Mo Claridge of Atlantis Video was associated with Pyramid and Capricorn Video in the 1980s before going on to run Anchor Bay UK, a company responsible for re-releasing numerous horror and exploitation films, in the 1990s and early 2000s. While many moved on to form new companies, it was also common for personnel to move around; for instance, Martin Myers began his career at his father's company, Miracle Films, before forming Merlin Video. The company released seventeen films between 1982 and 1984, including the video nasty *Zombie Creeping Flesh* (1980), and then disappeared shortly after the introduction of the Video Recordings Act. However, Myers would go on to become the Director of Sales, Marketing and Acquisitions at Vestron Pictures, the company responsible for releasing *Dirty Dancing* (1987), the first film to sell over a million copies on video. This process of reformation was by no means instantaneous, and it took a little while for the independent sector to lick its wounds and begin to re-emerge into the marketplace, and by that time the major distributors had already started to reshape the market in their own image.

Returning to Richard Maltby's idea, and as a means of establishing who controlled the industry and who stood to benefit from the introduction of the VRA, it is perhaps more useful to focus on how this was achieved rather than the effect it had upon the independent sector. Directly echoing Maltby's observations about the introduction of the Motion Picture Production Code, I would suggest that the motivations to censor the video nasties were more complex than the narrative of moral panic would have us believe and were determined more by economic considerations than by any concern over the content of the films. The Video Recordings Act, just like the Motion Picture Production Code before it, can be seen as the culmination of a lengthy process of negotiation between representatives of the industry and those speaking with the voices of cultural authority. In the case of the VRA, the voices of the Conservative Party, the British Board of Film Classification, the British Videogram Association, the Parliamentary Group Video Enquiry and the National Viewers' and Listeners' Association all joined together in harmony to condemn the independent sector as a deviant and corrupting force in British society; while the some of this may have been informed by genuine, albeit misguided concern, particularly in the case of Mary Whitehouse and the NVLA, this concern disguised the fact that all of these organisations stood to benefit either financially or politically from the introduction of the Act.

For the Conservative government, the moral panic provided a valuable and convenient piece of political theatre. Their image had been tarnished after a series of high-profile public relations disasters. Their economic policies had contributed to an industrial downturn that had led to the loss of over 2 million manufacturing jobs between 1979 and 1981. There had been numerous inner-city riots that famously culminated in the Toxteth and Brixton riots, and during the Falklands conflict there had been the Battle of Goose Green, and the divisive decision to sink the vintage Second World War Argentinian battleship the *Belgrano*, and by doing so, overrule the Royal Navy's own rules of engagement and needlessly kill 323 sailors. Home video presented an opportunity for the Conservatives to demonstrate resolve in the face of a largely fictitious problem. When Bright's bill was read before the House of Lords in June 1984, Lord Houghton of Sowerby highlighted the fact that when MP Gareth Wardell had attempted to progress a similar bill through the house in December 1982, he was discouraged from doing so by the then home secretary, Willie Whitelaw. Whitelaw had believed that 'there was a great deal more work which needed to be done on the matter before they could contemplate legislation' (House of Lords 1982) and remained steadfastly committed to the introduction of a voluntary scheme through which the industry could govern itself. Houghton still remained committed to the introduction of a voluntary scheme and suggested that the only thing that had changed in the intervening period was the Conservative Party's manifesto. With the General Election looming, the Conservatives had decided to 'brush aside the attempts of the trade to get a voluntary scheme' and to introduce government legislation instead (House of Lords 1982). Nevertheless, and in spite of Houghton's reservations, the bill passed through the House of Lords unchallenged and was given royal assent on 12 July 1984. The Act was slowly phased in from September of that year, coming into full force by 1 September 1988. This three-year grace period was given to allow the BBFC, the organisation that had been charged with categorising films that were released on video, enough time to censor and classify the huge amount of films that had already been released on video up until that point. Through this Act of Parliament, the BBFC's status moved from that of a voluntary organisation that simply made recommendations and could, and often would, be overruled at the level of the local council, to that of a governmentally approved statutory body. Along with this new statutory status came the assurance that the organisation would now receive payment for every film released on video in the UK. If that film received both a cinematic release and a release on video, then they would be paid twice, the suggestion being that the accessibility of video to a younger audience should invite stricter categorisation.

While BBFC secretary James Ferman had intervened expressing his concern over the types of film that were being released on video, it is not clear if this was entirely altruistic. The BBFC stood to benefit enormously from the introduction of the Act and the statutory status that named them as the body charged with the certification of video. This status would guarantee the organisation an income that would ensure its future. Similarly, it is also conceivable that the BVAs motivation to intervene was also born out of genuine concern, but it is important to acknowledge the fact that until the BBFC were named as the body that would classify video, the BVA was attempting to take control themselves. Added to this the fact that the BVA was already established as a trade body governing video, it is reasonable to assume that the BVA was seeking to protect the interests of their members, a membership that, as we have already seen, comprised largely of major distributors. That being the case, Stephen Woolley's belief that this was 'how the majors wrested control again' begins to have a greater degree of credibility, especially when considered alongside the fact that we now know that the BVA made the initial complaints against its own industry to the Advertising Standards Authority in 1982. Norman Abbott's statement on behalf of the BVA and his suggestion that it was a competitive situation with all of the distributors becoming more and more outrageous, combined with his assurance that the distributors had decided to put their own house in order, while being on the surface seemingly intended to placate concerned parties, also seems to contradict what was happening behind the scenes between the BVA and ASA.

Even the interactions of Mary Whitehouse, while well-meaning, can be seen to serve a broader political purpose. While there can be no doubting both her own and the NVLA's commitment to a path of moral conservatism, their cause only gained ground when it coincidentally served to benefit the Conservative government. The Conservative Party drew a large portion of their membership from Christian groups and social conservatives, and the visibility of Whitehouse and her stance against the corrupting force of video allowed the Conservatives to align themselves with a topic through which they could demonstrate resolve as a means of repairing some of the damage that their image had sustained in the PR disasters already discussed. This made Whitehouse a powerful ally to

Margaret Thatcher and the Conservative government and ensured that she was able to exert a degree of political influence throughout this period, but this does not necessarily mean that the underlying reason for the government's involvement came from the same place of concern and moral indignation as that of Whitehouse. More likely, it is simply that both parties stood to benefit. Whitehouse is often retrospectively cast as an interfering busybody and while this may be true, this perception of her fails to acknowledge what an effective political campaigner she was. That said, both she and the NVLA were not above using the aesthetic of exploitation as a means of attracting an audience to their conventions, as seen in the flyer for a three-day conference that she held in Blackpool to protest the sale of video nasties (Figure 2.1). The flyer is the same acid yellow as *I Spit on Your Grave* while the text 'video nasties' and 'how best to control them – will Mr Graham Bright's Bill do the trick?' was in blood red. 'Come and see', 'How bad are even LEGAL' even read like the tagline for an exploitation poster and the event, which ran for three days, clearly attracted a lot of attention. Despite the poster's reliance on the same language of titillation as the films that she was rallying against, there can be no doubting her belief that what she was doing was right and was informed by her own Christian beliefs.

Similarly, the Revd Dr Clifford Hill and the Parliamentary Group Video Enquiry (PGVE) can be seen to begin from a similar point of moral conservatism informed by their Christian beliefs. However, the fact that the research drew fraudulent conclusions to expedite the bill through Parliament only calls into question the motivation for conducting the research in the first place. Though the group had no official status within Parliament, the Parliamentary Group Video Enquiry was run by, and for, members of the House of Commons and the House of Lords, who had commissioned Hill to produce the report. It is not without significance that the only independent study to consider the audience did not consider the video nasties as representing a significant threat. In *Video Playtime: The Gendering of a Leisure Activity* (1992: 134), Ann Gray reflects on interviews she conducted with a cross-section of women from all social backgrounds, and suggests that while some of the women expressed concern about the possibility of their children accessing unsuitable videotapes, surprisingly few mentioned the video nasties by name, this despite the interviews being conducted at the height of the moral panic in 1984. Because of all of these factors, it is reasonable to suggest that the report and the group, although headed-up by a theologian, does not begin, as Mary Whitehouse does, from the point of social conservatism informed by her Christian beliefs but rather from the point of political strategy informed by the needs of members of the House of Commons and House of Lords that made up the group.

> **The Most Topical FRINGE Of All!**
>
> **COME AND SEE**
> [Short Extracts Only!]
> **HOW BAD ARE EVEN LEGAL**
>
> **'VIDEO NASTIES'**
>
> **MARY WHITEHOUSE**
>
> **ON**
>
> **HOW BEST TO CONTROL THEM**
> – Will Mr Graham Bright's Bill Do The Trick?
>
> 'FRINGE MEETINGS'
> in
> The Prince William Suite, Clifton Hotel,
> Talbot Square, Blackpool.
>
> 11th, 12th, 13th, October   12.45 p.m. and 5.45 p.m.
>
> Lunch/Sandwiches Available At The Hotel
>
> Turn left out of the WINTER GARDENS and the
> CLIFTON HOTEL is 5 minutes walk
>
> MOREAU PRINTING SERVICES
> Tel. Colchester (0206) 231040

Figure 2.1 National Viewers' and Listeners' Association promotional poster. Reproduced courtesy of the Albert Sloman Library, University of Essex.

This process clearly marks the beginning of attempts to take control of the video industry and leaves the question of *who* was trying to take control as yet unanswered. As already illustrated, all parties stood to benefit from the imposition of these sanctions: Mary Whitehouse and the

NVLA as a moral victory, a victory for social conservatism and a victory that provided them both with a platform from which to exert a greater degree of political leverage, Revd Dr Clifford Hill and the PGVE possibly as a moral victory but more likely as a political strategy that benefited the other members of the group and their links to the government. While the standard narrative of social conservatism argues that the moral panic was wholly a reaction to the videos that were now stocking the shelves of video shops up and down the country, this narrative only gains ground when it fulfils a broader political purpose for the Conservative government of the period. However, since they were not interested in the governance of films themselves and quickly passed control of those negotiations to the BBFC and the BVA, then the question becomes, whose needs did they represent? And how did they stand to benefit? While these organisations served a purpose for the Conservative government, being named as the statutory body governing video in the UK brought its own financial remuneration and it is clear that both organisations provided an economic function to the industry that they served, an industry whose power still lay in the hands of its most influential organisations, the major studios.

If one accepts Maltby's belief that 'Hollywood was, is, and always shall be a cinema censored by its markets and by the corporate powers that control those markets' (2012: 237), then it stands to reason that once Hollywood became interested in establishing a presence on video it would not simply leave it to chance but would begin to exert control through the corporate powers that controlled those markets. Furthermore, as with the case of the Motion Picture Production Code, 'the issues and motivations behind "self-regulation" were more complex and were determined more by economic considerations than by matters of film content', and

> the events of July 1934 [or of the mid-1980s] are best seen not as the industry's reaction to a more or less spontaneous outburst of moral protest backed by economic sanction, but as the culmination of a lengthy process of negotiation within the industry and between its representatives and those speaking with the voices of cultural authority. (Maltby 1995: 40)

It is reasonable to assume that the Video Recordings Act follows a similar trajectory, and that the issues and motivations behind the regulation of the home video industry were more complex than is typically believed, and that they too were determined more by economic considerations than by matters relating to the content of videos. That the events of 1982–4 were not merely the result of a spontaneous outburst of moral protest backed by economic sanction but were the culmination of a lengthy process of negotiation within the industry between its representatives and those speaking with the voices of cultural authority. The video nasty moral panic may be better understood as the way in which the major studios took back control of an industry that it was increasingly clear they would not be able to suppress. Home video was here to stay; the only question was, who was going to control it? The next chapter will consider how this development of the home video marketplace allowed the unbridled adoption of the technology in the UK and will consider the window of opportunity that this afforded to the independent sector. It will examine what kinds of film were popular and how the market share of the independents was affected once the major labels began to embrace video.

Notes

1. At that time, the BBFC's existing purview, even theatrically, was only one of recommendation, functioning primarily as an advisory body that could still be overruled at a local council level.
2. For more information on the institution of the BBFC refer to Edward Lamberti's *Behind the Scenes at the BBFC: Film Classification from the Silver Screen to the Digital Age* (2012).
3. Kruger has since admitted that at that time, neither he nor his staff knew anything at all about video. He himself became aware as a result of concerns raised in the media and after obtaining copies of *The Driller Killer*, *Cannibal Holocaust* and *I Spit on Your Grave* he approached the Director of Public Prosecutions who in turn gave permission to apply for a warrant under the Obscene Publications Act 1959 (Gregory 2005).
4. In years since the moral panic, Bright has become a figure of fun, having famously claimed in an interview that research was taking place that would prove conclusively that videos such as the video nasties were not only damaging to children but were also detrimental to dogs (see West 2010).
5. This information only came to light after numerous attempts to cross reference the database of the ASA. Earlier correspondence had found no record of the video nasties at all though Wilson later suggested that if there had been any complaints it is possible that they could have been archived off. Nevertheless, the annual report reveals that the original source of the complaints was BVA and not the general public.
6. In 1983, BCAP stood for the British Code of Advertising Practice. CAP is an abridged version of that.

CHAPTER 3

Tracking Home Video: Independence, Economics and Industry

In traditional histories of the video nasties, much is made of the window of opportunity afforded to the independent sector in those early days of video by the reluctance of the major studios to join the market. It is into this space that the first video companies emerge, and it is here that the video nasties are born. However, despite the importance of this moment to that history, in traditional accounts of the video nasties very little attention has ever been paid to how and why this window of opportunity appeared in the first place, or indeed, what impact it would have on the independent sector when that window eventually closed. Where the previous chapter was primarily concerned with the ways in which the window of opportunity was closed by those acting on behalf of the industry, this chapter looks at how that window was opened, exploring what this development meant to the major studios – the companies that had fought long and hard to establish film as a viable and lucrative form of entertainment, and who for the first time since the advent of film, were not in control of the format that was quickly becoming the most popular way to consume their core product.

An over-acceptance of the narrative of moral panic has meant that while traditional histories of the video nasties often begin from a point at which the major distributors are reticent to join the market, these histories rarely, if ever, return to complicate the narrative by considering just how threatened the industry was by the format or the implications for the independent sector when the majors eventually did join. Instead, the two sectors are often presented as operating independently of each other, with the decline of the independent sector often attributed to problematic marketing strategies, low-budget product, or worse, the inevitable conclusion of a market that was being flooded with high-quality big-budget film produced by the major distributors. While all of these elements are contributing factors, they would be better understood as symptoms rather than the root cause. Had this process taken a number of years then it is entirely conceivable that any one of these factors could have been the underlying cause of the disappearance of the independent sector; however, the fact that the market is systematically dismantled at the same moment that the major studios join the market cannot be dismissed as a mere coincidence. By complicating the economic history of the video nasties and considering what really was at stake for the major distributors, this chapter will offer an alternative history in which ideas of independence were distorted in an attempt to reshape the industry. By moving away from the dominant narrative of moral panic, and by pulling together what has hitherto been seen as unrelated histories, this chapter considers what established technological and economic histories can tell us about the moral panic and what they can then reveal of the underlying industrial motivation that was hidden behind the scare tactics of the tabloid campaign.

Beginning with a consideration of how the commercialisation of home video had taken the established film industry by surprise, this chapter will consider what action was taken by the major distributors when faced with the popularity of the new medium. It will present the attempts that were made to suppress the technology, and the simultaneous inroads that were being made into the market, presumably as fall-back strategy should the attempts at suppression fail. It will map the early video industry through a cross-section of the market from 1982 to 1985, assessing what kinds of film were popular and from which sector of the industry those films were coming. This chapter will illustrate the importance of the independent sector to the early video industry and will ask whether their disappearance was an inevitability, or the result of strategic moves on the part of major studios to gain control of an industry that they had hitherto neglected.

Tracking Home Video: Building an Industry

One of the most important things to understand about home video technology and the industry that it created is that it did not come from the film industry itself and that it was not developed with the consumer market as a main priority. Though the established film industry would go on to capitalise on video (and the subsequent formats that have superseded it), home video, and the industry that was built around it, pervasive as it is, has its origins in a far different, if no less ambitious goal. In September 1951, in Princeton, New Jersey, David Sarnoff – the chairman of the board of the Radio Corporation of America (RCA) and founder of National Broadcasting Company (NBC) was celebrating forty-five years with RCA. Sarnoff had been a pioneer in the world of radio and had played a pivotal role in the development of television but he was continuing to look to the future. The evening of his forty-fifth anniversary, Sarnoff requested that three gifts be developed and delivered to him on the event of his fiftieth anniversary, in five years. He requested: 'an electronic air conditioner, a true amplifier of light, and a television picture recorder that would record the video signal of television on an inexpensive tape' (Lardner 1987: 54). Sarnoff called the latter the 'videograph', and Stewart Wolpin has suggested that this technology would have solved a costly problem that was facing NBC, a subsidiary of RCA, on a daily basis. Because of time zone differences in the US, a programme broadcast live on the east coast would need to be filmed on 35mm or 16mm film, the film would then quickly be developed and then transferred to the west coast in a three-hour window to ensure that the programme was broadcast at the same local time. Known as telerecording or Kinescope, the process was fraught with problems and was incredibly expensive, with Wolpin suggesting that, '[f]ilming a half-hour show could cost as much as $4,000' and that 'by 1954 the American television networks were using more film than Hollywood' (1994: 53). While Sarnoff and RCA would not win the race to video, the industrial necessity of the technology ensured that Sarnoff's dream was eventually realised, though it would be almost two decades before the earliest viable commercially successful consumer-friendly version of the videocassette recorder came into being. However, when the technology was eventually developed, it was not by RCA, although they would go on to play a pivotal role in the success of the format, both in the US and in the UK.

In 1969, Japanese company Sony made a breakthrough when it introduced the Sony U-Matic, one of the first systems to house magnetic tape inside a plastic cassette. The U-Matic was the result of a collaboration between Sony, Matsushita Electric Industrial Co. (Panasonic), and the Victor Co. of Japan (JVC), with JVC agreeing to 'co-operate on the specifications of the machine' (Wasser 2001: 70), and sharing the patents between the partners for a technology that they had been developing independently. This decision would have dramatic implications for the future success of both Sony and JVC when following the production of the U-Matic, Sony and Matsushita broke away to develop their own machine (Rothman 2009). Realising the widespread adoption of the U-Matic as a successful home entertainment format was hindered by the prohibitively high cost of the cassettes, Sony decided to re-think the marketing strategy for the technology that they were developing as the successor to the U-Matic, the Sony Betamax. Marketing the Betamax machine primarily as a 'time-shifting device' (Wasser 2001: 71) and a 'complement to television' meant the Sony could encourage consumers to reuse the videocassettes, which were still prohibitively expensive, and in doing so make the machine far more attractive to consumers (Ascher and Pincus 2007). At the same time, Victor Co. of Japan (JVC) had already begun developing its own successor to the Sony U-Matic, built upon the same patents that it had shared with Sony and incorporating the skills and knowledge they had learnt in the production of the U-Matic. The release of the Video Home System (VHS) pitted JVC against Sony in the race to become the dominant commercial consumer video format on the market, a race that Sony was winning, simply by having made it to market first.

Suppressing Home Video: The Last Picture Show

While the technology giants fought it out in the marketplace, the major film studios were understandably concerned by home video and the potential damage that it could do to their existing theatrical revenue, and to some degree, they were right to be concerned. The UK cinematic market had been in steady decline since reaching its box office peak of £1.6 billion in 1946, a staggering figure that equated to 'every man, woman and child in the UK going to the pictures 33 times each' in that year (House of Commons 2012). Where the cinema of the 1940s had held a captive audience with entertainment options limited and only 0.3 per cent of households owning a television set in 1948, by the end of the 1950s, cinema was being forced to compete with the little box in the corner, and it was losing. By 1958 the number of homes that owned a television had risen to a massive 52 per cent, a figure that would continue to climb, reaching over 90 per cent by the end of the 1970s (Hamill 2000: 61). The increased demand for television meant that the audience that had previously been captivated by the cinema were increasingly choosing to stay at home. Michelle Pautz suggests that the North American market had seen a decline in weekly cinema attendance from 80 million people in 1930, which equated to approximately 65 per cent of the resident US population, to a weekly attendance of only 27.3 million people, equating to a mere 9.7 per cent of the US population in the year 2000 (2002: 1). While television had provided an audience with opportunities those opportunities had drawn them away from the cinema and by the 1980s many in the film industry were concerned that video had the power to do the same thing. Certainly, a report published by the House of Commons in 2012 ('Video Killed the Cinema's Star') perpetuates the idea that the decline of cinema in the UK during this period can be almost entirely attributed to the advent of video. A perspective is reinforced by the fact that in 1984, as the videocassette recorder was becoming more and more widespread, cinematic returns in the UK hit an unprecedented low, with only 54 million tickets sold, down from 138 million just ten years earlier (Author unknown 2019). However, and as already illustrated, broader statistics clearly illustrate the downward trend of an industry already in steady decline for over thirty years prior to the introduction of the videocassette recorder (VCR). While many were keen to attribute the decline in cinematic revenue to the uptake in video, the trajectory is not consistent enough to draw that conclusion. In the UK at least, in 1998, just as video was becoming an essential technology and ownership exceeded 84 per cent, cinematic returns unexpectedly spiked and continued to rise steadily alongside the sales figures of the VCR and then DVD player well into the next decade. Nevertheless this belief has persisted and certainly, in the late 1970s and early 1980s, it was still widely believed that video had the potential to decimate the film industry. Indeed if the figures followed the same downward trajectory that the film industry had seen with television it was entirely conceivable that video could spell the end of cinema-going altogether, and with that, the end of the Hollywood industry that had popularised and profited from film. After all, their core product was ostensibly the same, a film packaged for consumption in the home, and the film industry recognised this and was doing everything it could to ensure that this did not happen.

When Sony launched the Betamax format in 1975 it was met with immediate resistance from the film industry. The decision to market the platform to consumers primarily as a device through which they could record television had solved the major issue that the company were facing over the cost of videocassettes. However, while this decision had solved one problem, it created a whole new set of challenges for Sony when the Walt Disney Company and Universal Studios took legal action against them, arguing, correctly, that the machine technology had the potential to enable copyright infringement. The case challenged the 'legality of the manufacture, sale and home-use of VTRs (VCRs) to record copyrighted motion pictures from television broadcasts without compensation to the copyright owners' (United States Supreme Court 1984: 3), and Disney and Universal embarked on an aggressive and expensive eight-year court case with the express aim of suppressing video. Sony Corp. of America v. Universal City Studios, Inc. or the 'Betamax case', as it became known, was an embittered legal battle that saw the Disney Corporation and Universal Pictures pushing for a decision that would nullify the recording capabilities of the technology. In a case that would last for almost a decade, they argued that the Sony Betamax infringed existing copyright laws by allowing people to copy films and television programmes.[1] For Cætlin Benson-Allott, the 'specific phenomenology of video spectatorship ought to remind motion picture historians that the Format Wars were heated confrontations between international corporations for national consumer loyalties' (2013: 71).[2] Unlikely as it may seem, while these corporations were embroiled in a court case to suppress the technology, they were also hedging their bets and simultaneously making the first tentative steps into the burgeoning video market. Five years after the introduction of Sony's Betamax, Disney established its own video distribution arm in 1980, Walt Disney Telecommunications and Non-Theatrical Company (WDTNT), while Universal established MCA Videocassette, Inc. as a distribution arm through which they would release their films on video. However, it should be noted that these early releases typically consisted of older titles and, since court proceedings continued until 1984 and infringement of copyright remained a concern, it is possible that even if the court case was successful, they would re-evaluate whether they wanted to continue to invest in this technology. As it was, with the marketplace dominated by the independent sector, these movements are possibly better understood as the judicious and speculative movements of the major distributors establishing a presence on video without overly committing to the fledgling formats. If they could suppress the machines' ability to copy film, then it was conceivable, especially given the emphasis of Sony's marketing on that functionality, that the format would fail and, for the film studios, the potentially catastrophic problem of video would go away. But if it did not they had already made inroads into the market.

The problem did not go away, and while Sony was reeling from the first effects of the court case, JVC made it to market with their own videocassette recorder, the Video Home System (VHS). Though they had chosen not to collaborate with Sony in the development of Betamax, JVC was not averse to collaborating with other companies to ensure that their product was widely available, and in 1976 the company adopted an Original Equipment Manufacturer (OEM) model of dissemination, sublicensing its technology to parent company Matsushita Electric Industrial Co. (Panasonic), who in turn approached RCA to distribute the machine in the United States. Competitor Sony had already failed in its attempts to secure a distribution deal via RCA due mainly to its refusal to let RCA re-brand the machine as an RCA product, and being unable to reach an agreement on the cost per unit (Wasser 2001: 73). Paul McDonald attributes this to Sony's longstanding policy of avoiding OEM arrangements 'due to its distinguished record of product innovations' (2007: 35). RCA had also cited concerns to Sony regarding the limited recording time available on their cassettes, which at one hour (a limitation that was initially governed by the compact size of the Betamax cassette), was almost universally criticised as inadequate. Nevertheless, they remained steadfast in their resistance, feeling that to accomplish the extended tape length requested by RCA they would need to sacrifice the overall quality of the playback and that this would have a greater impact on sales. Ultimately the company's commitment to quality meant that they failed to secure a deal with RCA, and this decision would prove to have long-lasting effects that would cost the company dearly.

Unlike its competitor, Matsushita recognised the pivotal role a powerful US distributor could play in the success or failure of their product, and because of that, they agreed to let RCA rebrand their VHS machine as an RCA product. RCA's desire to increase the overall recording time of the cassettes, though rejected by Sony, was embraced by Matsushita, and this was another stipulation that would prove pivotal in winning the race to dominate the home video market. Since the VCR's primary function would be that of a 'time-shifting' device that would enable an audience to record television programmes they would otherwise miss, RCA felt that the running time of two hours afforded by the current VHS cassettes was insufficient, despite it being a full one hour longer than their competitor. They believed that for the format to be fully embraced by the consumer they would need to produce a longer videocassette that would enable customers to 'time-shift' televised sporting events, such as American football games. Matsushita agreed and introduced a four-hour cassette in 1977. Another factor that contributed massively to the adoption of the VHS machine was that, following discussions with JVC, RCA took the decision to competitively market the device at $300 cheaper than Sony's Betamax, which, priced at $1,300 was primarily being adopted by the higher income groups. By 1978, Zenith, the US Betamax distributor, adjusted its price to compete but by then the Sony Betamax had already begun to lose its market share, based mostly upon the price and the restrictions imposed by the length of the videocassette being offered.

By the time the format war entered the UK, the discrepancy in tape length was nominal: with Betamax at three hours thirty-five minutes compared to VHS's four hours. Instead, it was the prohibitive cost of the new technology that would determine the market in the UK. In 1978, a VHS video recorder cost £798.75, the equivalent of about £4,502.94 in 2018 (Bank of England). Consequently, given the economic downturn that the UK was experiencing, the industry would rely heavily upon a rental model to bring the new technology to market. High street rental stores, such as Radio Rentals and DER introduced the VHS to UK market in 1978 under a similar OEM model of distribution to the one that had proven so successful for RCA in the United States. As Radio Rentals and DER were subsidiaries of Thorn EMI, and Thorn EMI was partnered with JVC, it is unsurprising that they actively promoted their own product, JVCs VHS (see Hindley 1985). This was combined with the fact that JVC was quick to license the VHS format to other electronics manufacturers under similar OEM deals as they had done with RCA, ensuring that the market in the UK was dominated by the VHS format. Unsubstantiated reports persist that a decision by Sony to restrict pornography on the Betamax system became a major contributing factor that resulted in the defeat of Betamax in the format war (Gibbs 2015). While it is conceivable that this was the case in the US, pornography in the UK remained heavily regulated until the early 1990s. Therefore, a decision to restrict pornography on the Betamax would have had little effect on the popularity of the format in Britain. The remit of the Obscene Publications Act meant that hard-core pornography was far more likely to be accessed via the black market anyway, and through economies that were far out of the reach of any jurisdictive control that Sony may have tried to exercise.

Within a year, the number of videocassette recorders imported to the UK went from 30,000 units in 1977, to 260,000 in 1978, reaching almost 5 million by 1982. VHS accounted for 70 per cent of these sales, with the remaining 30 per cent divided equally between Sony's Betamax and a relative newcomer to the market, the Phillips V2000 system. The V2000 was an innovative system that employed a similar approach to audio cassettes, offering the ability to record on both sides of the tape. However, for all its innovation, it entered the market too late to make an impact, released in 1979 to a market that was quickly becoming the domain of JVC and the popular VHS system. In the years since the demise of Betamax, the format has become a cautionary tale, with 'Betamaxed' becoming a term used to describe a technology that is overtaken by an inferior, but a better-marketed competitor. 'Techies' can still be found expounding the superiority of Sony's pioneering machine, while Guardian columnist Jack Schofield offered an interesting perspective, arguing that the fuller picture is more complex than that and should be considered in marketing terms (2003: online). He suggests that:

> 'The core product' – such as a car, a computer, or a video recorder – is just the start. You have to add on all the things like reliability, service and support (the expected product), its expansion capabilities (the augmented product), and its potential for future development (the potential product) to get 'the whole product'.

Traditional arguments surrounding the decline of Betamax consider it a technical anomaly, understood through ideas of a superior 'core product' that somehow, against all expectations failed. However, and as Schofield suggests, this is a misunderstanding of what had actually happened, it was not 'the core product' that had failed. By most technological benchmarks

Sony's Betamax was a superior machine, but by 1978 that did not matter. Sony's unwillingness to compromise on the quality of their recordings by extending the length of the videocassettes and their refusal to enter into OEM deals that would have ensured the wider distribution of their product had all taken their toll, leaving the door open for JVC and the VHS system to succeed. By entering into numerous OEM deals with a variety of different companies, VHS became a more visible and attractive prospect. The visibility of the VHS at branches of Radio Rentals and DER, throughout the country, instilled a sense of 'reliability, service and support' – 'the expected product'. Video cameras were developed and sold alongside video recorders, indicating the possibilities that the machine had for expansion, or 'the augmented product'. The popularity of the format would increasingly mean that when faced with the prospect of having to buy a film on video twice, Betamax and VHS, video rental outlets would begin to align themselves with the format that outwardly appeared to have the greatest potential for future development – 'the potential product'. However, for all of these factors, the prohibitive price of both formats was the single biggest problem affecting the adoption of video worldwide, and the decision in the UK to make their VHS machines available through rental schemes on the high street through shops like Radio Rentals and DER was inspired. Where the prohibitive price point of the Betamax had limited the machine to an affluent consumer base, the VHS was now quickly becoming the number one working-class pastime, a factor that would not go unnoticed in the imminent campaign against the video nasties.

The Home Entertainment Revolution

While it is true that some of the major distributors were fearful of the harmful effect that video technology would have on their established business, this is not true of all of the major distributors. Toward the end of 1977, in a pioneering deal with 20th Century Fox, Magnetic Video became the first company to enter the US video market, releasing a series of films that had been sub-licensed from Fox's back catalogue. For Fox, these were tentative steps into the video market in a deal that guaranteed them half a million dollars a year and a royalty of $7.50 for every cassette sold (Wasser 2001: 95). While the deal was a hugely significant step for the legitimisation of home video, it also clearly demonstrates that Fox's priorities lay elsewhere and for them, video was only a tertiary concern. Fox insisted that any films licensed to Magnetic would need to be at least two years old, and crucially, that they would have already been aired on network television. For Fox, this would ensure the maximum theatrical return, followed by the maximum return for a film's release to network television. They would then finally consider a release into the as yet uncharted waters of home video, but only after all possibility for profit had been exhausted elsewhere. Though Fox is a pioneer in its willingness to embrace video, it is clear that this was only intended as a supplementary source of income. By entering into a deal with Magnetic Video, Fox could monitor the development of the industry without any real investment on its part (other than allowing access to its back catalogue), and without any real risk or cost to the company.

It inspired others, and in 1979 Columbia and Paramount soon followed the pioneering steps of 20th Century Fox, though they preferred to form their own home video divisions. Other major studios remained more cautious, with Disney, Metro-Goldwyn-Mayer (MGM) and Warner all starting home video divisions in 1980 and United Artists (UA) and MCA/Universal following in 1981 (Wasser 2001: 96). Nevertheless, these steps into video did not necessarily mean that the major distributors were immediately visible in the marketplace in the UK. Alliances continued to be formed: Columbia collaborated with RCA, creating RCA/Columbia Pictures in 1981; in 1982, United Artists (UA) leased foreign home video rights to Warner Bros and, following Metro-Goldwyn-Mayer's (MGM) acquisition of United Artists (UA), this new consortium formed the home video division MGM/UA. The same year, 20th Century Fox collaborated with the video arm of American commercial broadcast television network CBS to create CBS/FOX. These companies then began to emerge in the UK, but by the time they did there was already an established and thriving independent industry and infrastructure.

Some businesses had been well positioned to capitalise on home video having operated for many years in the Super 8mm film market. Prior to the advent of the VCR, Super 8mm was the mainstay of the film enthusiast, with companies like Derann and Iver Film Services supplying the demand for film in the United Kingdom (Figure 3.1). Derann was a small family-owned business that was formed in Dudley, England, by cinema projectionist Derek Simmonds and his wife, Anne.[3] The company began life in 1964, hiring out 8mm films from a bedroom at the Simmonds's home in Stourbridge, and quickly progressed to licensing feature films from major distribution companies. Derann approached MCA (the parent company of Universal Pictures) with a pioneering plan to release *Psycho* (1960) on Super 8mm in the United Kingdom under the Derann banner. When this proved a success, Derann cast their net wider, securing a deal with EMI to release an abridged version of *The Scars of Dracula* (1970) – a film that would become their most profitable release on the Super 8mm format, selling over 1,400 units. Over the next fourteen years, Derann added United Artists, 20th Century Fox and eventually Disney to its catalogue, although Disney was a relative latecomer to their roster, joining in 1978, just as the market was about to change.

Iver Film Services had been a film production company in their early days, before making the decision to shift the emphasis of the company and concentrate on distributing films on Super 8mm. This background meant that they were well placed to evolve and adapt to the development of video since they already had longstanding relationships with representatives from across the industry. Because of this, they were able to extend many of the licenses to films they already owned from Super 8mm onto VHS and Betamax, and significantly, it was out of these longstanding rela-

Figure 3.1 Derann Super 8mm abridged release of *The Texas Chainsaw Massacre*. Image courtesy of Paul Waines.

tionships that they were reportedly told that 'VCRs will record films from television for free, so why bother with pre-recorded tapes', a statement that ironically came from the representatives of Sony Europe and Phillips, the companies that developed the Betamax and the V2000 systems respectively (Hall 2019: online). Despite repeatedly being told that any such diversification was a foolhardy venture they remained steadfast and began building a catalogue of films that would be released on videocassette all the way up until 1984. However, in 1978, video was still in its infancy and it would be three or four years before the industry would really develop, with video rental shops appearing on every street corner. Iver initially began selling videos at Super 8 exhibitions, and they proved to be so successful that it inevitably led to the company moving away from Super 8 altogether and devoting the company's output entirely to video. Others quickly followed Iver, and by 1979 the sector was booming with independents like Hokushin, Intervision, IPC, Magnetic, VCL, Video Warehouse and VTX – both subsidiaries of World of Video 2000 – and VIPCO, a company that would become synonymous with the video nasties, all entering the market. The market grew quickly, although much of this period has gone unrecorded. The pre-cert database, while not exhaustive, lists only one pre-recorded videocassette released on video in the UK in 1978. Iver Film Services' *The Tiger Lily* (1975), a Paul Bernard film starring Diane Cilento, an actress who had previously been nominated for an Academy Award for Best Supporting Actress for her role in the 1963 film *Tom Jones*. The film is in many ways insignificant, but the video does represent a significant moment of crossover between the Super 8mm market and the market that would eventually become home video. These businesses were creating the industry, and without the later conventions around packaging that would become commonplace, they released the film in an adapted square Super 8mm box, later issuing an incredibly sought after release of *The Texas Chainsaw Massacre* in the same square box. By 1979, a further thirteen companies had joined the market, collectively distributing 466 films on video; by 1980 that figure had almost doubled to 866 films. This figure increased exponentially, and by 1981 there were 2173 films released on video by 143 distributors. Video was booming, and distributors were releasing all kinds of films, from all over the world to an enthusiastic British public.

However, despite distributors releasing a wide variety of different genres to the market, the dominant perception of the early days of video is that the platform owes its early success to its links with the pornography industry. Indeed, in his thorough exploration of the video industry, Frederick Wasser details the ways in which the early adoption of video technology in the US was intrinsically linked to the recognition of its value by early porn distributors, who in turn blazed a trail into the new market that video afforded. Wasser cites a report by Merrill Lynch that claims that towards the end of the 1970s, 'X-rated cassettes accounted for half of all pre-recorded sales', going on to claim that X-rated material 'created the infrastructure for video distribution' (2001: 95). While this is true of the US, similar claims have often been made about the marketplace in the UK, but these reports are only ever supported by anecdotal evidence. Because of the legal status of pornography in the UK, it is impossible to accurately assess the role that pornography might have played in the uptake in technology.

It was just such a report that appeared in *Television and Home Video* magazine in May of 1980 where it was estimated that between 60 and 80 per cent of videos distributed in the UK at that time were adult in nature (Wade 1980: 32). In fact, only ninety-two of the films released in 1980 could be categorised as pornographic, with a further fifty-six that might more broadly be classified as erotic in nature. Even when grouped together these releases account for only 17 per cent of the videos released in 1980, and not the massive 80 per cent of releases that was claimed by *Television and Home Video* magazine. However, perhaps even more significant is that the number of adult cassettes released would continue to fall year on year, usually equating to roughly 5 per cent of videos released in any given year. Kerekes and Slater address the skewed perception of the early industry with the observation that the 'estimated 60% of all pre-recorded videocassettes sold in 1978 were pornographic in nature wasn't so much down to this being the material that was most favoured by the general public, but more to do with there being little other product available' (2000: 14). A factor that has heavily contributed to the perception that the early video industry was almost entirely composed of pornographers was the fact that in the early days of video, very few distributors paid for advertising. The companies that were visible in advertisements in trade magazines and consumer magazines alike were often distributors specialising in pornography – these were companies that often worked on a mail-order basis and relied heavily on advertising to make customers aware of their product. The upshot of this was the widespread belief that video was dominated by pornography, a belief that even convinced leading companies within the adult industry that they should establish a presence on video, often with disappointing results.

Ann Summers was one such company and was perfectly placed to exploit the video boom in Britain fully. Formed in 1970, they would go on to become the socially acceptable face of the sex shop on the conservative British high street and in early 1980 the company was beginning to make a move into video. In an interview in 1981, manager Ron Coleman cited disappointing sales figures and insisted that at that time, the company were only selling around forty tapes a week, roughly equating to a value of about £2000. Coleman claimed that '[he] was told by various people, since proven wrong, that videocassettes were going to be the greatest explosion since colour television', but he was unequivocal as to reasons why he felt the sales were so disappointing: 'we are stymied by the Obscene Publications Act (OPA) which restricts the kind of tapes we can sell' (Wade 1980: 33), a view that was reiterated in the account of Tony Peters of the adult video label TCX. Peters expanded on Coleman's account and discussed the difficulties his company experienced working under the restrictions imposed by the Obscene Publications Act: 'We will not distribute anything that is not legal in this country, all our films are carefully vetted by a solicitor before we will put them on the market' (ibid.). When this is combined with Coleman's claims of being 'stymied by the Obscene Publications Act', and then contrasted against a database of adult film releases of the period (pre-cert.co.uk), what becomes clear is that *Television and Home Video*'s suggestion that 60–80 per cent of all videocassettes sold were adult in nature does not hold up to scrutiny. If it ever had any basis at all, it was either a distorted popular perception that had been inflated by the proportion of adult film companies advertising at that point. Or, more likely, these figures were not referring to official video releases but rather videos that were circulating illegally on the black market. Since it is impossible to know the numbers of videocassettes that were circulated in this way, it is impossible to know how this may have contributed to the economy of the industry. While it is not just likely but an absolute certainty that pornography played a pivotal role in the adoption of video, it is clear that the lion's share of these videos was circulated illegally via black-market channels and that video distributed in this way does not represent the official face of the industry in any capacity. Based upon the quantitative data that we do have from that period, it appears that officially distributed pornography played only a minimal role in the marketplace, and while they were among the first to adopt and adapt their businesses to incorporate video technology, as early as 1981 the role that these companies played in the market was beginning to wane.

With officially distributed pornography playing only a marginal role in the early adoption of video, it is vital to map the early market and attempt to understand what was selling and from what quarters of the industry those films were coming. In a hugely significant but critically neglected study from 1985 Finnish scholars Heikki Hellman and Martti Soramäki performed a cultural comparison of the British and American video markets, assessing the performance of different types of film, and crucially, considering whether the films were released into the market by an independent or a major distributor. The study considered the years 1982 and 1983 and drew its information from the sales charts of the period. It broadly categorised films based upon their content and defining genre, and proposed five main categories with more specific subcategories: (1) social and psychological drama; (2) suspense and violence (which included the five subcategories of thriller, crime stories and spy and agent films, adventure and fantasy, Westerns, horror and science fiction); (3) humour and light entertainment (which contained the five subcategories comedy and farce, cartoons, musicals and live concerts and music videos; (4) sex; and (5) others, which contained anything not easily categorised, such as exercise videos like *Jane Fonda's Workout* (1982). Though the categories are in many ways arbitrary, the way in which the video nasties were grouped was in a similarly arbitrary fashion with the Department of Public Prosecutions list designating films as video nasties that might otherwise have been categorised as thrillers or dramas, rather than horror films. With this in mind, I would argue that these categories although broad, are sufficient to provide a generalised overview of the marketplace at that time and provide a window into what was selling and where that product was coming from.

Significantly perhaps, given preconceptions, in the above study, pornography accounts for less than 1 per cent of the US rental market, with the category of suspense and violence dominating the charts at 36.4 per cent. This was closely followed by the category of drama, which represented 35.6 per cent of the market. However, what is perhaps most surprising – especially given the claims about the prevalence of pornography during this period – is that films that were sexual in nature accounted for only 4.1 per cent of the British rental market, though this was still a far greater representation than was seen in the United States (which they suggested accounted for only 0.8 per cent of American rentals and only 0.5 per cent of American sales). Officially released adult films distributed in Britain in 1983 equated to 5 per cent of the total films distributed in that year. When that figure is contrasted with Hellman and Soramäki's rental figures of 4.1 per cent, a figure begins to emerge in which almost 20 per cent of the adult films being distributed in Britain in 1983 were failing to find an audience. They do go on to suggest that although films that were sexual or pornographic in nature were visible in both video markets at that time, these films tended to be accessed via unofficial outlets, acknowledging the black-market economy that had grown to capitalise on video in the

UK. However, films circulated through the black-market economy did not represent the official face of the industry, and as such cannot and would not be represented in mass-market charts. Considering the claims of Ron Coleman and Tony Peters and the perception that the sector was being stymied by the Obscene Publications Act (OPA), it is little wonder that many distributors hoping to capitalise on distributing pornography did so outside of official distributive networks and outside of the law.

With official sales of adult films beginning to plummet as more and more distributors joined the market, it is important to know what genres were popular with the consumer at that point. Hellman and Soramäki suggest that at that time, videos arising from the category of suspense and violence accounted for almost half of the entire British video market, with the subcategories of horror and thriller accounting for 63.8 per cent of the entire category. It is important to note that within that total, the percentage of videos that belonged to the suspense and violence category that were distributed by the independent sector totalled 57.6 per cent. That is, 57.6 per cent of all videos that thematically dealt with suspense and violence (and the subcategories associated with that) were distributed by the independent sector. Barrie Gold, of the video wholesaler Gold and Sons, insists that across the industry, major distributors and independents alike, horror films consistently sold better than any other genre. The success of the genre no doubt contributed to its increased visibility, a visibility that was about cause problems (Gregory 2005).

The Independent Video Boom

From inauspicious beginnings, the video industry quickly took shape, and in 1981 the inaugural UK video awards were organised by *Video Business* magazine. A host of famous faces turned out to celebrate the success of the format. Diana Dors collected an award on behalf of Mike Mansfield for her appearance in the Adam and the Ants music video 'Prince Charming', Oliver Postgate received a highly commended award for the BBC video release *Beebtots* (1981): a compilation video that incorporated his characters *Noggin the Nog*, *The Clangers*, *Bagpuss* and *Ivor the Engine*, and Godley and Creme collected an award as directors of the Visage video 'Mind is a toy'. Industry representatives were out in force, from independent distributors such as Electric, VCL and Videospace to extensions of television and record labels such as BBC Video, Channel Four, Thames Video, Chrysalis Group, EMI, Polydor and Virgin. Even Electric, a company that specialised in pornography, received a highly commended award for their latest release *Electric Blue 7* (1981).

In September 1982, the Link House Group organised the first Video Software Show held at Heathrow's Penta Hotel, attracting over eighty companies to what was claimed to be Europe's biggest trade show for video. The aim of the show was to invigorate the video industry by providing a networking space for wholesalers, distributors and retailers, as well as offering seminars on issues that were affecting the industry. Though the threat that video nasties posed had already begun to reverberate throughout the press, and had recently culminated in VIPCO's prosecution at Willesden Magistrates Court only a month earlier, James Ferman of the British Board of Film Censors chose not to address these issues directly and instead presented a seminar on 'Pornography and the Law'. Alongside this, Videomedia's managing director Maureen Bartlett addressed the issues of piracy that were facing the industry in a talk entitled 'Wrecking the Pirates' (Author unknown 1982b). These presentations took place in the wake of VIPCO's prosecution. VIPCO were prosecuted on 31 August 1982 and the Software Show took place on 7 September, just seven days later. One might expect that the gravity of this would have informed Ferman's address, but instead, he emphasised pornography and in doing so failed to address what was becoming a critical concern for the industry. Nevertheless, the show proved to be a huge success and the following February, just five months later, the show returned to the Penta, this time with 120 companies taking part in the exhibition, taking over 100 rooms and spilling into the hotel's foyer in order to meet the demand from distributors for space. Video was booming.

By 1982 there were 1800 video shops registered in England, Scotland and Wales with more being established every day (Sony 1982). The video industry had grown so quickly that the retail sector was struggling to keep up with the demand, and what would be classified as 'Mom and Pop' stores in the US – small, independent, family-owned and operated shops – appeared overnight to meet this demand. Corner shops, petrol stations, ice cream vans, literally any space that could hold video, was quickly being converted into a video shop to capitalise on the boom. With the industrial heartland of Britain decimated as the coal mines, shipyards and steelworks were all systematically dismantled, video provided a valuable opportunity to create a new industry that was not only stable, but that was resolutely working class. The decision to make video recorders available via rental schemes through Radio Rentals and DER had democratised what might have otherwise might have been an elitist luxury product that was out of the reach of the ordinary everyday consumer. This affordability meant that the working class quickly adopted the platform as a cost-effective alternative to the cinema, and distributors, who were often working class themselves, began releasing films to appeal to this audience. On the surface at least, the economic prosperity brought about by video would seem to embody many of the promises of Thatcher's Conservative government. The individualism that inspired her oft-quoted sentiment that there was 'no such thing as society' can be found in the success and economic prosperity of the independent sector. After all, independent British distributors were buying independently produced films, selling them through independent wholesalers to independent retailers up and down the country. In a depressed period in British history video was a booming business that was controlled by the independent sector nationwide – it was an economic phenomenon.

There is a tendency within established histories to minimise the economic importance of the independent sector, to imagine them as opportunistic or fly-by-night companies, and to assume that their interest in video was only fleeting. However, and as already illustrated, the company VIPCO had seen pre-tax profits of £1.5 million in 1982, equating to almost £5 million when adjusted for inflation today. Similarly, in 1983, the wholesaler Gold & Sons Ltd boasted a pre-tax profit of £10 million, the equivalent of £34 million today (Author unknown 1983a: 64). These were not short-lived or transitory organisations but companies that were deeply invested in making video a sustainable and profitable business. More than that, given the amount of money that was changing hands here, the distributors were understandably keen to tackle the problem of censorship head-on. As early as September 1981 there were debates appearing in *Popular Video* magazine about whether or not films released on video should be subject to any form of censorship. It was an emotive issue with many arguing that video was the last bastion of free expression, in which parents could determine what was suitable and what was not suitable for their own children. Some distributors, such as Precision Video, addressed the issue themselves and began incorporating the classification that their films had been given by the BBFC upon cinematic release. As a label that had up until that point specialised in family-friendly entertainment, censorship was not a problem that Precision had really had to deal with. However, their autumn 1981 release schedule contained three films that were more adult in nature and in light of the recent debates surrounding censorship, Precision felt it prudent to begin incorporating classificatory certificates. Walter Woyda, Precision's managing director, said 'we felt it was important to give a guide to families and point out that three of them were given X certificates when they were released in the cinema', but, he cautioned, 'we can only give a guideline . . . then it's up to the parents to decide whether they want to take the cassette home and possibly watch it in front of their children' (Author unknown 1981: 18).

Many shared Woyda's belief and this was a strategy would prove to be popular, and something even Warner Home Video had been practising since it launched its twenty-four-title range toward the end of 1980.

> [T]he policy started in the United States. Our parent company show the US Censor's certificate on their packaging. Since we use the same artwork here, we decided to replace it with the British version. We contacted the British Film Institutes and were able to obtain copies of the British censorship classification for each film,

said Geoff Grimes, the general manager of Warner Home Video, concluding that 'it is absolutely essential that parents should be aware that a particular movie might not be suitable for children' (ibid.). The problem for many lay in the fact that the majority of the films released on video had never received a cinematic release in the United Kingdom, so there was no classificatory certificate to carry over. To address this, some companies began co-opting American certificates into their releases, and while this did give some indication as to the content of a film, the practice was often adopted by distributors that were hoping to demarcate their releases as being more adult in nature. Because of this, these applications tended to function as an indicator of excess rather than offering a valid and functional classificatory certificate, and, as Kate Egan has argued, mock-legal classificatory certificates were often used to 'imbue their product with an appearance of responsibility', while simultaneously functioning as a 'guarantee of a film's explicitness' (2007: 63).

Nevertheless, with many feeling that the interference of the British Board of Film Censors was unwarranted, publisher Nicholas Malamatinas developed the Universal Video Software Index. The purpose of the index was simple and would address many of the issues the industry was facing, not least the issues arising when a film had never been classified by the BBFC. Malamatinas devised thirty-eight categories into which every film released would be grouped. Parents who were concerned about the content of a film could consult the CIER Directory to check the suitability of the film for the audience at home. The directory could be purchased from your local video dealer for a price of £4.99 and would be updated every two months as a means of incorporating the newest releases, with those new inserts costing £1.50. The scheme relied on the distributors themselves to categorise their own product, and then their assessments would be checked by the editors of CIER Directory as a means of ensuring that the films were adhering to the parameters of the pre-defined categories. With the need to conform to a classificatory system not the urgent battle it would later become, the scheme did not prove successful, fading away almost as quickly as it had arrived.

By June of 1983, the British Videogram Association in conjunction with the BBFC had devised its own voluntary code; this was to be administered by the newly appointed Video Standards Council (presumably a precursor for the organisation of the same name that would not officially come into being until 1989). Although voluntary in name, the mechanisms of the scheme were such that if implemented, distributors, wholesalers and retailers would have had little choice other than to join (Author unknown 1983c). The process was simple: a distributor would submit their video to the Video Standards Council for certification and the council would then determine whether it was suitable for release. If the film was later deemed to be suitable for release, it would be classified using U, PG, 15 or 18 certificates (the same codes used for cinematic releases), and only then would it be made available to wholesalers and retailers. However, were the film deemed to be unsuitable for release and then a retailer was found to be stocking that item, all distributors with an affiliation to the British Videogram Association (which as we have already seen primarily consisted of the major distributors) would stop supplying that retailer with their product, effectively preventing them from accessing mainstream Hollywood fare. So, if a video rental shop were found to be stocking a videocassette that had not been classified, then the major distributors would close their accounts and would stop providing them with their product.

This is the proposal that was developed by the BBFC and the BVA and was clearly developed in conjunction with the BVA's membership, the major distributors. However, not only does this proposal assume that major distributors would not be on the wrong side of this legislation, it constructs a binary between them as the moral arbiters and representatives of the 'official' film industry. This arrangement crucially has the major studios working in tandem with the official bodies and casts the independents as little more than squatters in Hollywood's back yard. The proposal raises many questions and provides few answers. As one might expect, it was condemned by the independent industry, not least from the retail sector – the video dealers who felt that were being unfairly threatened by the proposal. The Video Trade Association, the body that represented the retail sector, had never been consulted about the terms of the code. Independent distributors were most likely not consulted either but clearly the major studios had been consulted and they were prepared to forego the numerous sales they would receive if it meant that they could reshape the British market in their own image. The independent sector opposed the 'voluntary' scheme, considering it censorship by any other name, but their resistance was futile and the following year the Video Recordings Act was introduced, removing many of the companies that were felt to be a problem. One can only assume that the Act was born out of the same discussions between the BBFC and the BVA as the voluntary code that privileged the major labels only this time there was the added weight of it being mandatory governmental legislation. Returning to Richard Maltby's supposition that 'Hollywood was, is, and always shall be a cinema censored by its markets and by the corporate powers that control those markets' (2012: 237), what this voluntary code and the Video Recordings Act that followed it represent are the corporate powers beginning to exert their control over the marketplace. Unable to suppress the technology, through the Betamax case and the MPAA throwing all the might of the film industry at Sony, the major studios simply took control of the industry in the United Kingdom by aligning themselves with the various industrial and institutional bodies that were designed govern video.

The Independent Video Bust

John Berra has argued that independent cinema carries with it a wide variety of meanings, expectations and associations (2009: 9). He suggests that it evokes images of an industry unencumbered by the constraints of Hollywood, of artistic integrity unchallenged by the demands of commercial markets and of a product that is inherently politicised in its opposition to the mainstream. The realities are, of course, infinitely more complex, much less romantic and far beyond the scope of this book. Suffice to say, rarely in these constructions does independence bring with it negative connotations. Yet, the campaign to 'Ban the Sadist Videos' did precisely that. It distorted public opinion to such a degree that the independent video industry was soon the vilified target of misplaced concern. The benefits to the major distributors were obvious, but perhaps the most surprising aspect of this history is the willingness of the Conservative government to target independent business to achieve this goal. The Conservative government had presented themselves as champions of a free-enterprise economy based upon free trade. In their General Election Manifesto of 1979 they had claimed they would prioritise industry, commerce and job creation. They emphasised the importance of small businesses to the country's economy, and they declared that they were opposed to what they described as 'socialist panacea-import controls', claiming that this 'would restrict consumer choice, raise prices and invite damaging retaliation against British goods overseas'. Yet they backed a bill that simultaneously devastated the independent video industry in the United

Kingdom and resulted in the restriction of consumer choice and the raising of prices. A government reneging on the promises of its electoral campaign is nothing new, but to deviate so far to score minor political points seems unnecessary and outrageous.

In all likelihood, and irrespective of governmental interference and institutional wrangling, the market would have always naturally found in favour of the major studios: they produced big-budget films with recognisable stars and they have dominated cinema for more than a hundred years. Certainly, other markets followed a similar trajectory as that seen in the United Kingdom without the assistance of an equivalent Video Recordings Act. In a pioneering study of the characteristics demonstrated in the development of the West German video market, Radewagen and Zielinski (1984) suggested that video must pass through three distinct phases before being successfully adopted and moving into full market diffusion. They observed that initially the introduction of video was characterised by early adopters producing software that was primarily educational in nature. From there, the second stage, which they referred to as the 'video boom', saw the market dominated by genre films, including Westerns, Easterns,[4] war films, horror films and pornography, before, finally, a third stage that saw the adoption of the technology by large multinational companies producing high-cost theatrical films aimed at a wider demographic. While the British video market does not map to model exactly, it is nevertheless a useful study when attempting to understand whether what happened in the United Kingdom was a foregone conclusion and something that can be seen in international video markets. While the first stage of Radewagen and Zielinski's model was not evident in any meaningful way in the British video market, the second and third stages offer a comparable trajectory to that demonstrated in the UK. The UK moved straight to the second stage, the 'video boom', with early adopters releasing genre films, particularly horror films. From here, the British video market follows the West German market and moves away from the 'video boom' and from a market defined by genre films and into the third stage, towards a market dominated by large multinational companies producing high-cost theatrical films aimed at a wider demographic. Critically, in the United Kingdom this change is facilitated and expedited by the Video Recordings Act, and what that Act does is provide a clean break between a period that was dominated by the independent sector and a period that was suddenly not. By 1997, the hesitation first felt by the major studios had waned sufficiently that 'all of the MPAA member-studios joined the DVD Forum', a multi-industry organisation to promote digital video discs (DVDs) (Benson-Allott 2013: 102).

Notes

1. The case became significant and set a legal precedent that continues to be cited in technological copyright cases today, protecting technological developers from lawsuits from the entertainment industry, irrespective of whether the technology has the capacity to be used in the infringement of copyright, providing that the technology has uses that are not related to copyright infringement. Pamela Samuelson suggests that 'the Sony decision is the most significant legacy of Justice Stevens in the field of intellectual property law and its significance is likely to continue in mediating disputes between copyright industries and creative information technology developers and users of information technology' (Samuelson 2006: 1831). Moreover, it has been used in such cases as the file-sharing programs KaZaA (2001) and Grokster (2005).
2. Benson-Allott argues that Cronenberg's Videodrome 'dramatizes the colonial pressures Canada's entertainment industries felt during the Format Wars' (2013: 84).
3. Taking their name from the first three letters of each of their first names, *Der*ek and *Ann*e – Derann (2014).
4. The term Eastern is not elaborated on in their chapter but is assumed to be films of East-Asian origin.

CHAPTER 4

Historicising the New Threat

While it is important to acknowledge that there are a number of challenging films included in the videos that became known as the video nasties, it is equally important to recognise that none of them is without historical precedent, and all draw upon the established traditions of cinematic horror. Nevertheless, much is made of the supposed new threat that these films posed, this despite the fact that many of the films included in Department of Public Prosecutions (DPP) list pre-date their British video release by more than ten years. Indeed, the earliest example, Herschell Gordon Lewis's *Blood Feast* (1963), received its original American theatrical debut a full twenty years before its problematic introduction to the UK. Despite this, many of the criticisms that were first levied at the video nasties began from the flawed proposition that these films were something new, an idea that does not hold up to scrutiny. Setting aside the fact that many of the films were already over a decade old when they were released on video – for example, *Blood Rites* (1968), *Love Camp 7* (1969), and *Night of the Bloody Apes* (1969) – thirty-one of the films included on the notorious DPP list had already received a British theatrical release prior to their introduction on video; that is, almost half of the list compiled by the DPP had already undergone the strict process of classification through the British Board of Film Censors in order to enable them to be released into the British marketplace in the years prior to their release on video. In spite of this, the *Daily Star* insisted that 'Nasties are far removed from traditional suspense or horror films' (Graham 1982); the *Daily Mail* claimed that 'These videos are not spine chillers in a tradition that stretches back to Conan Doyle or Edgar Allen Poe' (Author unknown 1983b). Even the Conservative MP Graham Bright pitched in, arguing that 'all too many people believe that a nasty is something like a hotted-up Hammer movie, it isn't it is something entirely different' (Petley 2011: 46).

Julian Petley has suggested that this idea that the films constituted a new threat is among the most serious of the misconceptions about the video nasties (2011: 45), misconceptions which have endured despite having no real basis in fact. There are two separate but interdependent factors that have contributed to the endurance of the idea that the video nasties represented a new threat. The first is the belief that Britain had no real established tradition of cinematic exploitation before the video nasties, and that because of this these films represented a seismic shift from the Gothic horror traditions of Hammer and Britain's glorious past. This is a perspective that clearly informs Graham Bright's concern (Petley 2011: 46), and it is a perspective that ignores, both the tradition of contemporary British horror that can be seen to begin in earnest in 1960 with Michael Powell's *Peeping Tom*, but it is also ignorant of the fact that on their original release many of the Hammer films were equally divisive and just as problematic. Perspectives like this tend to imagine the United Kingdom as a vacuum, failing to acknowledge the rich history of theatrical exhibition that routinely imported films that would now be broadly categorised as exploitation cinema. The second factor is the belief that that the marketing materials employed in the promotion of the video nasties represented something uniformly excessive, and it was this that constituted something new, threatening and different. This is a narrative that recycles the hyperbole of the tabloid headlines in their belief that the video nasties were representative of a 'new threat'. Indeed, so pervasive is this narrative that it can be found in academic accounts, journalistic accounts and accounts designed to appeal to fans and collectors alike. It forms one of the cornerstones of the established history of the video nasties and continues to inform how we understand the early video industry in the United Kingdom.

This perspective is most overtly articulated in Julian Petley's account in which he suggests that 'it was these various forms of advertising [. . .] that first aroused the moralists' wrath'. And that

> the video industry (or at least those sections of it eager for a quick profit at any price), was itself partly to blame for the moral panic soon to be whipped up by the National Viewers' and Listeners' Association (NVLA), the tabloid press, teachers, churchmen and others. (2011: 23)

This is one of the cornerstones in the history of the video nasties. It can be seen in journalist, author and film critic Kim Newman's suggestion that 'to a great degree, the whole video nasties scandal was whipped up by the advertising methods rather than the content of the films themselves', arguing that 'the video trade should take responsibility' since the advertising methods they used dared the audience, asking 'can you watch our latest gruesome horror?' (quoted in West 2010), and it can be seen in the distributor and cultural intermediaries Nigel Wingrove and Marc Morris's declaration that 'the early video sleeves are indeed an unbelievably over-the-top mixture of outrageous graphics and in-your-face visual shock tactics, guaranteed to offend' (liner notes 1998).

While this belief provides the foundation for the accepted history of the video nasties, the sum effect of these narratives is an oversimplification that is every bit as hyperbolic as any of the tabloid headlines that first instigated the moral panic, and this has perpetuated an image of the independent video industry that has reduced them to the level of pantomime villains in a moralistic play. This reduction is still visible and can be seen in Julian Upton's recent reassessment of the early video era, 'Electric Blues' (Upton 2016: 25). In an otherwise excellent article, Upton problematically divides the independent video industry of the period into two separate groups, the 'opportunistic independents' and the 'respectable independents', and in doing so perpetuates a binary common to most histories of the video nasties. He suggests that the opportunistic independents were small, growing businesses that were run by risk-taking entrepreneurs, arguing that they were resistant to unionisation and casually flaunted copyright law. He argues that these distributors were more concerned with producing an affordable product that would appeal to the less well-off and therefore open up the market, going on to suggest that these opportunistic independents were 'seemingly indiscriminate regarding content', and because of that, they appeared 'downmarket' and 'lower class' (ibid.). By way of comparison, the 'respectable independents' were well-resourced, often working under an established parent company. Upton argues that they were more measured and cautious in their approach and demonstrated a 'by the book' attitude that was not evident in the business practice of the opportunistic independents, insisting that they were 'concerned more with quality than affordability', were careful with content and would not release pornography. Because of these many reasons, they can be perceived as 'respectable', and therefore 'middle-class'. While much of Upton's article is concerned with mapping the early video industry, his decision to do so through inherited moralistic judgements about the perceived good or bad qualities of these distributors raises questions, not least because it perpetuates the class-based narratives that were so prevalent in the campaign against the video nasties in the first place. The notion that the 'respectable' independents often operated under a parent company suggests a process of media conglomeration, a strategy that was more likely to be employed by the affluent major studios and implies that smaller companies were inherently untrustworthy simply by virtue of their size. Upton's otherwise measured account illustrates how our understanding of the period continues to be shaped by the rhetoric of tabloid journalism that told us to be fearful of this industry of outsiders who were threatening the nation's enjoyment of 'legitimate' film.

This is not to dismiss these accounts; one of the main reasons that this version of history has survived for so long and gone largely unchallenged is because, to a large extent, aspects of these histories have merit. Certainly, distributor Mike Lee has talked openly about the profits he made from pirated films before establishing VIPCO and there was a period in the 1990s when he was rumoured to be living as tax exile abroad. However, where caution needs to be drawn here is through an oversimplifying of the narrative to such a degree that *all* smaller companies, at *all* periods of their incorporation, are depicted as inherently untrustworthy or illegitimate. If the tax avoidance practices of Google and Amazon in recent years have taught us anything, it is that the size of an organisation is not an accurate barometer of moral rectitude.

One of the most problematic aspects of these inherited histories is that these conclusions are typically drawn from the same reactionary headlines that revelled in reprinting the covers for the 'lurid video nasties'. Of course, when considered in isolation, some of the promotions used to advertise the video nasties were every bit as lurid and gratuitous as the newspapers deemed them to be. They revel in the sexy and salacious, they show, often in explicit detail, victims being dispatched and they celebrate all that is base and corrupt. But crucially, and an aspect that is often overlooked, is that this is only applicable to a small handful of the long list of video nasties, and none of these designs is without historical precedent or contemporaneous parallels. Promotions of this type are as much a part of the cinematic tradition of horror as the horror film itself. Horror film producers and distributors have long relied upon the excessive and the gratuitous as a means of promoting their latest horror and in order to challenge the claims made about the new threat that the video nasties posed we need to first begin by situating these promotional strategies within the marketplace that already existed in the UK for this type of promotion. To accomplish this, this chapter will continue by charting the evolution of the American market for exploitation cinema. As many of the video nasties either originate in the United States or owe a debt to America's long-established tradition in hyperbolic promotion, it is useful to foreground the evolution of this marketplace before considering how it differed from the marketplace in the United Kingdom. The purpose of this is to provide a more objective view of the types of films that were being released into both markets and to gain an insight into the way these films were sold. It then becomes possible to isolate cultural differences, specifically those employed in the promotional strategies used by the different distributors in each market, and examine the contribution these differences may have later made to the reception of the video nasties. To ensure that the films chosen were released into both markets contemporaneously, Hammer Films was selected as the company that represents Britain's most successful, if somewhat respectable (retrospectively at least), entryway into the global exploitation/horror market. While not necessarily playing to the marginal travelling cinemas of Depression-era America, or even necessarily to the romanticised grindhouse cinemas of New York's 42nd Street, the popularity of Hammer during this period provides an opportunity to assess how the same films were promoted in different territories. By examining how the films of Hammer were promoted in the UK and the US at the time of release, this section aims to determine whether there were any cultural differences evident in the approach adopted and what this can tell us about the different markets.

The American Market for Exploitation Cinema

Though they did not develop organically, the video nasties are perhaps best understood retrospectively as a unique subset of the exploitation film, albeit a governmentally imposed subset. Pam Cook defines the exploitation film as a commercial category and 'a market term for those films produced at minimum cost for maximum return which take up, "exploit" the success of other films – replaying the themes, star-stereotypes and genres of more lavish, up-market productions' (1976: 122). Thomas Doherty argues for a more layered definition suggesting 'three distinct and sometimes overlapping meanings' (2002: 2), arguing that in the first place, exploitation is foremost a promotional strategy used as a means of attracting an audience into the cinema. In this definition, the exploitation refers to the exploitation of the film itself by the advertising campaign, as a means of capitalising on any asset associated with the film, no matter how tenuous that might be. Doherty's second definition suggests that exploitation can be used to denote to a communicative strategy, where the term 'refers to the dialogue a movie establishes with its viewers' (2002: 5), and where, he argues, the 'exploitation' refers to the audience being exploited by the film. His third definition suggests that in later evolutions of the term's use (citing an article that appeared in *Variety* in 1946), the word has been used as 'a pejorative description for a special kind of motion picture' (2002: 6). He describes these as 'films with some timely or current controversial subject which can be exploited, capitalised on, in publicity and advertising', in which he includes 'the bizarre, the licentious, and the sensational' (2002: 7). Other definitions have tended to politicise the exploitation, emphasising perceptions around its perceived marginality and its opposition to an equally amorphous mainstream, most notably seen in Jeffrey Sconce's definition of 'paracinema', which, he argues, is 'less a distinct group of films than a particular reading protocol, a counter-aesthetic turned subcultural sensibility devoted to all manner of cultural detritus', going on to suggest that 'the explicit manifesto of paracinematic culture is to valorize all forms of cinematic "trash", whether such films have been either explicitly rejected or simply ignored by legitimate film culture' (Sconce 1995: 372).

Though all of these definitions are useful and have some influence over what we consider to be and how we understand exploitation cinema, for the purposes of this discussion I am primarily concerned with the promotional methods employed in the marketing of films that, either by design or otherwise, come to be labelled as exploitation. Even though it is often presumed that this kind of promotional strategy was perfected in American cinema of the 1950s, Eric Schaefer has argued that promotions of this type pre-date cinema, tracing a lineage from the exploitation cinema of the 1950s to the turn of the century carnival 'barkers', epitomised by the outlandish promotions of P. T. Barnum (1999: 122). Barnum is perhaps best known as the figure that popularised the circus sideshow in the US and famously exhibited physical deformity as entertainment, as well as producing a series of hoaxes designed to draw in the crowds. The phrase 'there's a sucker born every minute' is commonly attributed to him, although there is evidence to suggest that it was said by a competitor of Barnum's and was intended as a comment on Barnum's business practice (Brooks 1982), it is nevertheless a useful starting point when discussing this type of promotion, since hyperbolic deceptions are often central components in the advertising strategies used in the promotion of exploitation film.

In her exploration of American Film Cycles, Amanda Ann Klein observes that typically, 'advertising for exploitation films [. . .] promised an experience they did not necessarily deliver' (2012: 7), and what could be understood as hype and showmanship may have dishonest or devious connotations evoking hucksterism and ballyhoo; however, these promotions were rarely understood as deceptions, and Eric Schaefer has suggested that audience were complicit parties in that showmanship. Schaefer claims that not only would this hucksterism and ballyhoo have been understood as hype and showmanship, but that was integral to turn of the century promotions that relied upon what he describes as 'that noisy, vulgar spiel that drew audiences to circuses and sideshows', and that was a 'was a hyperbolic excess of words and images that sparked the imagination' (1999: 103). As motion pictures became more widespread, these early circuses and sideshows were replaced by cinemas. Beth Kattelman has noted that 'many of the earliest producers and distributors of exploitation films were, in fact, already working with stage shows prior to getting involved in motion pictures, so they just adapted already familiar stage ballyhoo techniques to the selling of films' (2011: 63). Often transgressive or titillating, the product developed reflecting the changing social mores: in the 1920s and 1930s it was the cautionary tale that drew the audiences, films like *Reefer Madness* (1936) and *The Wages of Sin* (1938), which capitalised on drug use and prostitution respectively, and which were both considered problematic under the Motion Picture Production Code.

In the 1940s it was the sex hygiene films that would inform and titillate in equal measure, with the most successful of these, *Mom and Dad* (1945), crisscrossing the country in true carny style. Reports note that the film was always introduced by eminent hygiene commentator Elliot Forbes, although 'Forbes' was simply a pseudonym for any number of actors travelling with the show, bringing with them an imprimatur of medical credibility and a hook to entice audiences. In the 1950s, the nudist film, a genre popular since the early 1930s, was revived. Expounding the benefits of a naturist lifestyle, *Garden of Eden* (1954) was a thinly veiled guise to show nudity on the screen, and the film's reception was not without its problems, with the producers forced to defend the merits of the film in court. This led to a landmark ruling by Judge Sam M. Driver that 'nudity per se [was] not obscene' (quoted in Schaefer 1999: 300), and Schaefer suggests that this was one of the most important factors that contributed to 'the ban on nudity in motion pictures and [. . .] to the breaking of the New York censor board' (ibid.).[1] Ironically, *Garden of Eden* was one of the first films to benefit from another legal precedent, Joseph Burstyn, Inc. v. Wilson, 343 U.S. 495 (1952), often referred to as the 'Miracle Decision'. Through the Miracle Decision, the Supreme Court had determined that film was an artistic medium, affording it the same First Amendment rights as any other form of creative expression, effectively applying freedom of speech protection to motion pictures. And it was this same ruling that prevented video nasties being targeted in the same way in the 1980s.

Over time, the hyperbolic cries of the 'carny barkers' gave way to hyperbolic posters, often displaying graphic representations with straplines that made extravagant claims that mimicked the rhetoric of the early showmen. Kevin Heffernan has commented that typically these independent films 'were publicized with an unusual emphasis on their topical or horrific content', and that 'these shrill come-ons were a direct consequence of the marginal or at least secondary role these films played in the exhibition marketplace' (2004: 64). During the 1950s, increased cultural anxieties over communism and the rise in radical leftism contributed to a wave of films that can be seen as either fuelling or responding to the 'Red Scare'. In horror and science fiction this allowed for films that were more nuanced in their approach, perhaps most famously with the political allegory *Invasion of the Body Snatchers* (1956). The film is most often read as a warning against communist invasion and brainwashing, and because of that, it is seen as an important film and was added to the United States National Film Registry by the Library of Congress as 'culturally, historically, or aesthetically significant' in 1993. However, *Invasion of the Body Snatchers* was not the first film to incorporate political messages into a science fiction plot, though many were more flamboyant in their approach. In 1955 Roger Corman directed *The Day the World Ended* (1955). Often credited as the first post-apocalyptic film, the film is prefaced with an introduction that reads: 'what you are about to see may never happen . . . but to this anxious age in which we live, it presents a fearsome warning . . . Our story starts with . . . THE END.' Rhetoric of this kind is significant in the evolution of horror and science-fiction film promotion and demonstrates the emphasis observed by Heffernan on their topical or horrific content. It is this type of promotion that can be seen in both the posters and the trailer for the video nasty *Blood Feast* (1963), in promotions that directly address the viewer. They suggest that the audience will 'recoil and shudder as you witness the slaughter and mutilation of nubile young girls – in a weird and horrendous ancient rite!' A line can be drawn from the carny barkers and theatre posters of early exploitation, through Corman and *Blood Feast* all the way to the rhetoric of *The Last House on the Left* (1972), with its poster tagline that urged its audiences 'to avoid fainting, keep repeating that it's only a movie'.

The British Marketplace for Exploitation Cinema

British exploitation film history has been widely explored over the last twenty years, including Leon Hunt's *British Low Culture: From Safari Suits to Sexploitation* (1998), to Chibnall and McFarlane's *The British 'B' Film* (2009) and more recently, I. Q. Hunter's *British Trash Cinema* (2013). However, the marketing of the exploitation film in the United Kingdom has received comparatively little attention, and while it is beyond the scope of this book to offer more than a cursory examination of the full history of marketing methods employed by UK based producers and distributors, it is nevertheless important to provide an overview of how the British marketplace relates to the American marketplace, mapping the differences and similarities between the territories and introducing key figures and companies operating in this market. Only then is it possible to interrogate the claims made about the video nasties and whether they presented a 'new threat'.

One of the most striking differences between the market in the UK and the market in the US is the starting point and subsequent trajectory. Where American cinema's fascination with transgressive cinema has a long and illustrious history going all the way back to Edison's early experiments with film, examinations of the British marketplace reveals very little sign of diversity until the 1950s and the release of the 1954 US nudist film mentioned above, *Garden of Eden*. The film was received with similar consternation from the British censor as it was in the United States, with the British Board of Film Censors initially refusing to grant a certificate to the film. However, since the BBFC's ruling could be overturned at local authority level, savvy distributor Nat Miller submitted the film to London County Council, who agreed with the American Judge Driver's pronouncement and determined that 'there was absolutely nothing obscene about it at all' (Sheridan 2011: 11). This ensured that the film did receive a release, and, galvanised by this success, Miller successfully petitioned 180 of the 230 local authorities around the UK, who then agreed to screen the American import. Shortly afterwards, the BBFC was forced to bend to public opinion and award the film a certificate. The success of this film encouraged British filmmakers who were keen to capitalise on the film's success by creating their own nudist films. Sheridan cites this as 'the roots of the British sex film' (2011: 10), with London's film district on Wardour Street busying itself capitalising on the newly liberated attitudes of the censor. Within a few years, the precedent set by the relaxation in attitudes to nudity allowed would provide a foundation for the production of a wide variety of films that incorporated nudity. What is especially notable about these beginnings and the subsequent trajectory of the British market, especially when considered alongside the American market, is that the British marketplace does not follow the same path, but ironically still sees the naturist film *Garden of Eden* released and becoming a catalyst for change. The tentative steps made in the US via the cautionary tale of *Reefer Madness*, through to the sex hygiene film of *Mom and Dad*, and then with the naturist film *Garden of Eden*, all of which had paved the way to relaxed legislation, while all present in the British marketplace, come in a different order and as a result of the *Garden of Eden*. The film was submitted in 1955 and although it was initially refused certification by the BBFC, by 1958 they were forced to bend to popular opinion and release the film. British producers began to recognise that this relaxation in regulation meant that they could begin capitalising on more exploitative fare, and they started to produce their own 'homegrown' naturist films. Those films quickly become a staple of the British exploitation genre, and by the early 1960s, British companies had moved into producing films that Sheridan observes, 'highlighted the ills of modern society [. . .] teenage pregnancies, juvenile delinquency [. . .] venereal disease [. . .][and] underage sex' (2011: 13), essentially producing the cautionary tale, as seen in the US with films like *Reefer Madness*, *Wages of Sin* or *Because of Eve* (1948). Just as with the US, these are films that at once warned of the dangers of these activities whilst simultaneously titillating audiences with the prospect of glimpsing the taboo. By the end of the 1960s, conservative Britain could even be seen to be embracing the sex film, albeit through the innuendo-laden, bawdy, postcard humour of the *Carry On* series. But in 1969, the BBFC received two films that would challenge what was deemed to be acceptable in a commercially released film. The first, *Women in Love* (1969), Ken Russell's still controversial adaptation of D. H. Lawrence's novel, has become emblematic of the censorship struggles in the United Kingdom; but it was the second, a little-known sex-education film called *Love Variations* (1970), that proved to be the most divisive for the board. *Love Variations* was produced by David Hamilton-Grant, a figure now forever associated with the video nasties moral panic (and a figure who will be explored in greater detail later). Pitched as a sex-education film, *Love Variations* was considered too problematic to allow a full national release, and John Trevelyan, the then secretary of the British Board of Film Censors, refused to award a certificate. However, both he and Lord Harlech, the president of the BBFC, expressed their 'joint approval of the manner and the integrity with which the film had been made' (quoted in Barber 2011: 25), suggesting that it was not exploitative in tone and that the film had loftier educational goals.

In a shrewd move, Hamilton-Grant requested an endorsement from the BBFC to this effect, and both Trevelyan and Harlech obliged, advising Hamilton-Grant to approach local authorities, in much the same way Nat Miller had previously done for his release of *Garden of Eden*. Trevelyan further supported Hamilton-Grant by suggesting to Harlech that the BBFC enter the film in their records as a rejected film, sparing Hamilton-Grant the costs associated with a formal submission, feeling that 'this small company has probably not got much money in hand and applications to Local Authorities will involve certain expenses' (ibid.). The film itself only ever received a limited exhibition with only London County Council agreeing to show the film at selected cinemas in the West End. While *Love Variations* was controversial, it is also considered Britain's first ever sex-education film and in this way has parallels with the early sex hygiene films like *Mom and Dad*. While the British market for exploitation does not mirror the American experience exactly, with the release of *Love Variations*, the British marketplace had passed through the same cycles of production, as the American marketplace, just in a very different order.

However, *Love Variations* is not just a significant film in terms of production trends. It is a significant film because it highlights the relationship these producers have to the independent video sector. The film was produced and distributed by Oppidan Film Productions, a company that had been formed by Hamilton-Grant and exploitation filmmaker Ray Selfe. Alongside Miracle Film Productions, New Realm, Eagle and Tigon, Oppidan became one of 'the most prominent sex film distributors of the seventies' (Sheridan 2011: 22), and Simon Sheridan describes Ray Selfe as 'the workhorse of the British film industry'. Selfe is remembered mainly for his role as a producer, developing titles such as *Under the Bed* (David Hamilton-Grant, 1977), *Four Dimensions of Greta* (Pete Walker, 1972) and *Sweet and Sexy* (Anthony Sloman, 1971). In relation to *Sweet and Sexy*, Selfe explained that:

> It was a co-operative film whereby most of the people involved would not get paid, not even the actors, in order to save money, after being shown the door by Tigon, we literally crossed over Wardour Street and fetched up at Miracle Film Distributors, who liked the idea straight away and accepted it. (Sheridan 2011: 73)

The significance of this here is not in Selfe's production methods (no doubt most producers showed similar determination), but of how these companies begin to map the exploitation industry in the UK in the late 1960s and early 1970s, and how this relates to the companies and films that became embroiled in the video nasties moral panic. In relatively few steps, it is possible to get from the American-influenced nudist film of the 1950s to key players and companies of the 1980s video nasty scandal. Though celebrated in the 1950s by John Trevelyan and Lord Harlech for his manner and integrity, David Hamilton-Grant is now best remembered for his role in the video nasties moral panic as the last person to be sent to prison in the UK for publishing 'an obscene article for publication for gain' (this will be explored in greater detail in the next chapter). Similarly, the company Miracle Film Distribution, the company to which Selfe and Hamilton-Grant sold *Sweet and Sexy* after being 'shown the door' at Tigon, plays a pivotal role in supplying many of the films that subsequently became video nasties.

Miracle Film Distribution had become successful offering what was euphemistically known as 'continentals' – films often of French or Italian origin that contained nudity and that would often play as second features. Though the company's stock and trade was what we might now broadly refer to as European exploitation cinema, in the process they also released some significant films to the British market, including the film that launched Brigitte Bardot's international career, *And God Created Woman* (1956), and *I am Curious (Yellow)* (1967), the film that helped define the Swedish film industry of 1960s. They also included significant films by auteur directors such as Bernardo Bertolucci, Rainer Werner Fassbinder, Federico Fellini, Jean-Luc Godard and Pier Paolo Pasolini. However, alongside these canonical European art films, they also released a number of important horror films including *The Bogey Man* (1980), *Cannibal* (1977), *The Toolbox Murders* (1978), *The Living Dead at Manchester Morgue* (1974), *Zombie Creeping Flesh* (1982) and *Zombie Flesh Eaters* (1979). These were all successful films for Miracle theatrically, but became notorious on their release to British home video market in the 1980s when they were categorised as video nasties. Miracle were of huge importance to the company VIPCO, to whom they licensed a number of films, including *Zombie Flesh Eaters*, *The Bogey Man*, *Island Of Mutations* (1979), *Psychic Killer* (1975), as well as the company's earliest releases, *Caged Women* (1976), *Hot Sex in Bangkok* (1975), *Bed Hostesses* (1976) and Ray Selfe's aforementioned *Sweet And Sexy* (1971). Companies like Miracle and Oppidan not only illustrate the tradition on which these early video distributors were drawing, they literally supplied the product.

The Cultural Specificity of Horror Film Promotion

While it is possible to trace the marketplace for exploitation film in the UK clearly, this does not adequately reveal the types of promotion strategies that were being used, or indeed, how those approaches compared to the strategies that were being employed in the advertising of the same films in different territories. The advertising of Hammer films provides a useful means of critically exploring how the strategies employed in the UK differed from those employed in the US.

The company's output prior to 1955 had been diverse. However, after this date, they quickly became defined by a series of high-profile horror and science fiction films that continued up until the late 1970s; this began with *The Four-Sided Triangle* (1953) before developing *The Quatermass Xperiment* (1955). *The Quatermass Xperiment* was adapted from the 1953 BBC television series *The Quatermass Experiment* and was Hammer's first foray into this kind of genre filmmaking. Though the company are often remembered fondly as the respectable face of British horror, in this early promotion, they were clearly very keen to capitalise on the sense that the film was for adults only. On the release of the film, they retitled it from *Experiment* to *Xperiment*, an adjustment that was made in order to emphasise that the film had been classified as an X, the X certificate denoting the BBFC's new compulsory adults only category. The film provided an opportunity for Hammer to capitalise on the illicit associations of the newly formed category with a bold white serif font, with the *X* of *Xperiment* given prominence through its exaggerated size and red colouring. The poster for *The Quatermass Xperiment* depicts an image, described by Marcus Hearn as 'the tragic astronaut' (2010: 20), Victor Carroon, infected with an alien virus and reaching out from the confines of the poster. However, the imagery plays only a secondary role to the title, *The Quatermass Xperiment*. The red of the *X* is given further contrast set as it is against the overall green hue of the poster, the contrast suggesting a bloody wound, ripped and slashed directly into the background. Although perhaps naïve by today's standards, the poster can be seen to represent exploitation in its purest form, capitalising on an association. Traditionally exploitation film marketing utilises an element that can be exploited in the promotion of the film, whether that be nudity or sex, violence or, as in the case of *The Quatermass Xperiment*, an idea. The illicit connotations brought about by the association with the newly introduced adults only X certificate was an idea that Hammer would return to, both in the Quatermass sequels and in *X the Unknown* from 1956.

Despite often supplying the BBFC with scripts for approval prior to shooting, Hammer was not immune to either censorship or derision from much of the press. The Gothic tradition for which Hammer is best known began in 1957 when the studio produced *The Curse of Frankenstein* (1957), a film that is significant not only because it indelibly associated Hammer with the uncanny, but also because of the vitriol it provoked in the press. Dilys Powell of *The Sunday Times* wrote, 'for years I have rushed to defend the cinema against the charge that it debases. In the case of the current series of horror films, I have changed my mind' (Meikle 1996: 43). Similarly, film critic Derek Hill commented that 'only a sick society could bear the hoardings, let alone the films' (Hutchings 2004: 84). Peter Hutchings has observed that at that time the films were 'seen as both the product of a broader cultural degradation and potential instigators of further degradation', and in that respect, despite their contemporaneous reappraisal, and as acceptable as *The Curse of Frankenstein* may appear today, the meanings and associations of the film have changed over time, and what once appeared lurid and exploitative may now appear quaint to a modern audience (ibid.). In this way, the initial reaction to Hammer's output was indicative of the same kind of response as that seen with the video nasties. However, considering these British promotions in isolation provides only a small part of the picture, and with the reaction to the video nasties usually likened to a cultural invasion, it is worthwhile considering how the promotions for the same films may have differed in an American context. The posters of Hammer provide an excellent opportunity to consider how the promotions for the company may have differed domestically and internationally, and a significant dissimilarity is evident.

With early examples from Hammer's back catalogue the imagery used within the posters remains largely consistent, with neither the American nor the British posters being overly gratuitous, and for films where an alternative artwork is used it is typically comparable in style and tone. The most significant difference lies in the taglines used in the different territories, with the posters for the British release typically referring to the narrative of the film it is promoting. An early example of this is the UK cinema poster *The Curse of Frankenstein* that says 'No-one who saw it lived to describe it', a tagline that can be seen to be referring both to the film itself and to the creature depicted in the film. The US poster, on the other hand, displays a self-referential and hyperbolic quality that is not present in the majority of the British posters for Hammer's releases during this period, an acknowledgement of the construction of the film within the marketing, suggesting that it 'will haunt you forever – please try not to faint'. Similarly, the UK marketing for *The Mummy* (1959) reads, 'Torn from the tomb to terrify the world!' whereas the US version reads 'Fear will freeze you when you face . . . The Mummy'. This acknowledgement of the part that the audience will play through their engagement with the film gives the taglines of the US marketing a hyperbolic quality that is not typically reflected in the UK releases. The claims of the effects that you will experience when viewing the film are part of the US ballyhoo tradition going back to P. T. Barnum, while in the UK, without that tradition of ballyhoo to draw upon, the taglines typically followed a more conservative line that was less direct and less hyperbolic. However, this is not to suggest that this approach was never adopted by UK promoters. In 1961, Hammer's British promotion for *Taste of Fear* (1961) claimed:

> This is positively the only photograph we are allowed to show you. Under no circumstances may we give away any of the startling secrets of this Great Screen Thriller. IT IS IMPERATIVE THAT YOU VIEW IT FROM START!
> – THE MANAGEMENT.

The campaign in both the UK and the US was (if not actually produced by) very reminiscent of the work of Saul Bass and the campaign appears to be an attempt by Hammer to piggyback on some of the success that Hitchcock was experiencing by borrowing an aesthetic common to his films. In the US, the poster 'was commended as the best of 1961 by the Motion Picture Association of America' (Hearn 2010: 75), though this acclaim did not translate into commercial success on either side of the Atlantic. The lack of success in the promotion of this film might explain why Hammer returned to a more traditional approach for their UK marketing, even in 1963, when an opportunity to blend the ballyhoo traditions of the American B-movie with the Gothic traditions of Hammer presented itself in the form of *The Old Dark House* (1963). The film was a co-production between William Castle and Hammer and was directed by Castle, famous for his B-movie cinema of the 1950s and 1960s. Castle is perhaps most remembered for his use of gimmicks, capitalising on promotional devices such as 'Emergo', where a skeleton was propelled across the auditorium towards the end of *The House on Haunted Hill* (1959); 'Percepto' in *The Tingler* (1959), in which Vincent Price broke the fourth wall, yelling 'Ladies and gentlemen, please do not panic. But scream! Scream for your lives! The tingler is loose in this theater!', triggering buzzers fitted to the seats of the theatre; 'Illusion-o' for *13 Ghosts* (1960), which allowed the brave to view, or the frightened to remove, ghosts by watching through the 'Ghost Viewer/Remover'; and *Homicidal* (1961), where he offered the audience a 'fright break' – an opportunity to leave if the experience was too shocking and they were too frightened. Though often understood as entirely reliant upon spectacle, Catherine Clepper has argued that the theatrics employed by Castle work to expand the 'narrative space to include the auditorium', destabilising 'the standard conception that the movie is *there* and we are *here*' (2016: 55, emphasis in original). But nevertheless, Castle's affinity for these gimmicks has meant that he has become synonymous with a particular kind of ballyhoo. However, for whatever reason, his partnership with Hammer was more restrained. There were no gimmicks used in the promotion, and even the posters showed restraint, tending towards a more traditional emphasis on narrative rather than focusing on spectacle or the affective response viewers might experience when watching the film. Though not conclusive, this discrepancy highlights an intriguing difference between the promotions used in the UK and the promotions used in the US during this period, and an aspect of the promotions of the video nasties that needs to be explored more fully. This emphasis of hyperbole and spectacle over narrative is, of course, common to American exploitation cinema, and while not totally absent from British promotions, it does provide a foundation from which to begin to scrutinise the promotions used in the marketing of the video nasties and a means by which to measure cultural differences. In the following chapter, I will explore the types of advertising used in the promotion of the video nasties and will align these approaches to traditional advertising practice, considering whether these promotions were vastly different from the promotions already seen in the marketplace and whether they display a reliance on sex, violence and ballyhoo.

Note

1. In many respects, these debates over nudity can be seen to mirror earlier controversies surrounding the bedroom or sex farces of playwright Avery Hopwood and his censorship battles on Broadway in the 1920s. Hopwood was famously embroiled in a high-profile court case that attempted to ban his play *The Demi-Virgin* (1921), and which earned the producer, Al Woods, a reputation for his involvement in the censorship struggles. Ronald H. Wainscott has argued that that for Woods the case was 'more a function of economics than artistic integrity' and that the publicity provided by the court case had made the play a huge financial success (1997: 90).

CHAPTER 5

Trailers, Taglines and Tactics: Selling Horror Films on Video and DVD

In 1983, Sam Raimi's inaugural independent feature film, *The Evil Dead* (1981), a film that was made for an estimated $375,000, was pitted against Steven Spielberg's big-budget, studio-backed action-adventure *The Raiders of the Lost Ark* (1981), a film with a budget of $18 million.[1] Both films were released on home video in the United Kingdom in 1983, and despite their vastly different budgets, they were sold side by side in the democratic space of the video rental shop, a level playing field in which packaging and posters would compete for the attention of the consumer and, irrespective of production budget, be afforded the same amount of space upon the walls and shelves. Promotional strategies varied, though most, including those of the major distributors, were not as sophisticated as one might expect, with few fully reflecting the established promotional strategies that had been developed from almost one hundred years of theatrical exhibition.

The majority of these early video promotions were mostly reliant on reproducing the film poster in-store and on the video packaging. This is particularly true within the independent video distribution sector, who were responsible for selling non-major studio films such as *The Evil Dead*. In this sector, even when a film had already been widely exhibited theatrically in other territories and an array of different promotional material was available to publicise it, independent distributors would invariably return to the default promotional strategy of the poster. The degree to which other forms of promotion, such as trailers, were used varied wildly: on occasions when trailers were circulated, they often took the historic form and literally trailed the main movie on the videocassette, rather than preceding it, meaning the original film had to be watched in order to access the new marketing material. Since distributors only ever promoted their own, often limited catalogues, the opportunities that these strategies provided were limited, with a small number of new films available to publicise. The success of the trailer as a viable form of promotion relied explicitly upon the distributors consistently releasing films that were successful, and if a film was successful, that ongoing circulation would ensure that the video renting public would see the trailer for their forthcoming releases. However, because most distributors carried broad catalogues that often included a range of genres that were designed to appeal to a broad demographic, this kind of promotion could often appear unfocused and was therefore unreliable.

To sidestep some of these issues, many independent distributors released entire videocassettes that showcased their latest releases by collating their trailers onto one focused trailer tape. The target for these cassettes was typically the retail sector rather than the consumer market. In this way, distributors could promote their latest releases to video rental shops up and down the country, with the retailers identifying and then buying in the specific videos they felt would appeal to their individual customer base. Because of the prohibitive cost of videocassettes at this time, these trailer tapes received limited circulation among consumers. By contrast, the more widely used promotional strategy of the film poster presented a cheap, visible and viable alternative to the trailer that was not reliant on the circulation and success of a previous release. By simply reproducing the artwork that was used as the front cover of the video sleeve, distributors had an inexpensive advertising campaign. These images would then be reproduced as magazine advertisements and as posters and pop-up displays. Posters of this kind would often be included as inducements for retailers to purchase the latest editions of magazines like *Video Business*, and again, significantly, this was a practice that was dominated by independent distributors, with the films of the major distributors not as visible in these enticements. The importance of the poster to this early home entertainment marketplace cannot be overstated. It was the central means by which distributors communicated their latest releases to the video renting public, and almost a decade before Blockbuster video entered the British market, independent British rental shops were comfortably stocking independent videos alongside the releases of the major Hollywood counterparts. However, this democracy would be short-lived and the relationship was far from harmonious. Throughout the 1980s, the independent sector was struggling beneath the surface, critically aware that the major distributors entering the market could spell disaster for them if they were unable to present themselves and their product as a competitive alternative. Interviewed in 1982, Des Dolan, the managing director of Go Video Ltd, suggested that

> the going is likely to get a lot tougher for independent video labels this year, now that the majors have got themselves together. 'The Indies' will have to respond very positively. Any independent which is not very aggressive in its marketing stance – and in the way it competes with the majors – won't be here next year. (Dolan 1982: online)

While Dolan's fatalistic words would prove prophetic, his aggressive marketing stance is best remembered as the defining characteristic of the video nasties.

A number of important historical accounts and analyses reinforce the sense that it was the advertising methods which were to blame for the moral panic that followed, and this has become an accepted tenet of that history. Martin Barker, Julian Petley, Kim Newman and Kate Egan have all credited these promotions with the dubious honour of being the catalyst for the moral panic. Kate Egan has argued that this promotional material was so effective that the distributors themselves 'had given moral campaigners and the press all of the rhetorical materials they needed to construct and power the rhetoric of their law and order campaign' (2007: 72). Egan's account is particularly interesting, as she seeks to address what she sees as an oversimplification in popular retellings of the video nasties, arguing that there has been an 'almost black and white retelling of a small, innocent video culture swallowed whole, and destroyed by the evil machinations of a censorious establishment' (2007: 47). Believing that this narrative needs to be complicated, Egan, as many have before her, selects the most extreme examples of the promotional material associated with the video nasties to support her thesis and then builds upon the rhetoric of the press campaign against the video nasties to reiterate the image of a sector comprised almost entirely of opportunistic and 'duplicitous' distributors (ibid.).

Egan's method of sampling has been the standard approach in the analysis of the video nasties, but this approach has also contributed to the perennial problem with most of the existing histories of this era. Popular histories, academic accounts and interventions from cultural commentators have all isolated the most extreme examples as a means of illustrating what a video nasty is, and then have gone on to use these examples as a way of explaining, if not justifying, the panicked reaction that followed. While it is not my wish to excuse the distributors of any wrongdoing, or to suggest that there are not extreme examples evident within the category of the video nasties, it is methodologically problematic to allow two or three examples of extreme approaches to promotion to stand in place of a full assessment of the material. As already acknowledged, when considered in isolation, some of these promotions are every bit as lurid and gratuitous as the newspapers claimed them to be. However, in assessing the relative extremism of these promotions, a full range of examples that were available and on display in video shops across the UK needs to be considered, not just the most extreme examples from that catalogue but the video nasties in their entirety, collectively, as a set. To realistically begin to measure any degree of difference from the marketplace that these distributors were operating in and the standing of these 'transgressive' or 'alternative' products against mainstream promotional practices and histories, the video nasty marketing needs to be understood in the context of the era in which the videos were produced and being distributed and the marketplace into which they were released. To undertake this analysis, I turn to and expand upon Janet Staiger's analysis of early advertising discourse in turn-of-the-century Hollywood cinema. Using this, I will look for commonalities across the set to consider how uniform the posters and promotional material were as a whole, before then considering whether those examples that were considered the *most* extreme share any consistencies with contemporaneous promotional cultures, both of the wider film industry but also from other media texts being produced at the time, such as publishing. The chapter then concludes with an assessment of other contributing factors to the broader perception of the category as a container for extreme and/or transgressive film.

An Analytical Model to Measure Promotion

Any analysis of promotional material is likely to contain an element of subjectivity on the part of the author; perhaps even more so when the dominant assessment of that imagery insists that it shares a collective aesthetic of excess, as is the case with the video nasties. This acceptance often makes it difficult to look past the hyperbole of the existing public discourse and other narratives that have consistently underlined the belief that the imagery was the catalyst for that moral panic. Nevertheless, to begin considering these promotions objectively outside of the media furore, it is first necessary to understand whether there is an aesthetic common to all of the video artwork that was being exhibited on video shelves around the country, concentrating specifically on the videocassette sleeves. Once this is done, consideration can be given to the outliers: those few examples that are consistently cited as the *most* problematic, and yet are commonly taken to stand for the whole collection of movies, and frequently named as archetypes of the excessive category.

To measure these commonalities, I have repurposed a model that was developed by Janet Staiger for use in the analysis of the advertising discourse surrounded early Hollywood cinema (1988). Using three examples, *Life of an American Fireman* (1903), *Uncle Tom's Cabin* (1903) and *The Great Train Robbery* (1903), Staiger highlights an emphasis on novelty, genre, brand names, realism, authenticity, spectacle, stars and creators, as well as the importance given to the emotional experience one might expect to experience when watching any given film. This work suggests that these were the common elements that were consistently foregrounded in the promotion of these early films (1988: 121) and highlights that reliance on the use of superlatives in advertising discourse can be traced back to the earliest days of cinema. While this reliance might not be the hyperbolic excess of the video nasties promotions, it is nevertheless a useful matrix to begin measuring the emphasis given over to any particular element, in the promotion of any given film. In order to adapt Staiger's matrix in a more meaningful way to examine the later films in the video nasties era, the criteria have been appended to incorporate two additional elements. Firstly, and in reference to the earlier examination of the promotions of Hammer, I employ a section to record whether the taglines employed make explicit reference to the narrative or not. Secondly, I have recorded whether the sleeve or poster uses illustration or photography centrally in its design. Photography and illustration are often assigned very different cultural values in the marketplace, and because of that, carry with them very different connotations. This could be a contributory factor in whether an image might be categorised as 'explicit'. With the addition of these two elements, the final matrix consists of nine categories through which it is possible to begin to measure the various attributes of these promotions.

To summarise, the matrix documents any emphasis given to novelty, genre, brand names, realism, authenticity, stars and creators, affect, photographic/illustration and narrative, and all are recorded as a means of determining the differences and consistencies inherent in these promotions. To outline how each of these characteristics has been defined, 'novelty' is used here only to describe something that could be considered more ballyhoo in nature, something that draws upon the traditions of P. T. Barnum or William Castle and can be seen to draw upon that tradition of hype and showmanship. 'Genre' is recorded if the artwork itself makes a specific reference to dominant or established genre characteristics, such as a use within taglines of 'the horror of', the terror of', etc. 'Brand names' refers to the use of company names, and into which all brand names, logos and symbols are all are recorded, whether recognisable as a successful company or not. Realism is noted when there is a specific reference to the apparent realism or realist aesthetic of the film. 'Authenticity' is recorded when the promotional language makes claims as to the authenticity or to the authentic nature of the film. 'Spectacle' is extended here to incorporate anything that might constitute the spectacle or the spectacular within the imagery, including warning logos and straplines. If a sense of emotive or physical response is described, then this is recorded under 'affect'.

'Stars and creators' are recorded if star figure, including actors, directors and producers, are referenced or named in the promotional materials, regardless of whether they are actually known 'famous' people or not. 'Affect' is drawn from Staiger's final criterion of the emotional experience of watching a film, though this is reconceptualised through Carol J. Clover's concept of 'body genres' (1987), films which Linda Williams has suggested 'privilege the sensational' (1991: 2). The latter two categories not taken directly from Staiger's model 'Photography/Illustration' and 'narrative' have been explained above. A table of the results of this analysis can be found in Appendix I.

One might assume that since Staiger's list prioritises criteria such as stars, creators and brand names, it would be mostly inapplicable to video nasties, a category of film that has been historically defined by its supposed difference to mainstream cinema. Indeed, without familiar studios producing the films or recognisable mainstream distribution labels releasing them, video distributors would seem to be limited in the approaches that they could adopt when marketing these films, particularly since most lacked bankable stars or named directors. In such cases, it would seem logical that distributors would be forced to rely heavily upon bombastic, hyperbolic claims regarding the affective qualities of their films. However, on examination, a much more complex picture emerges.

Of the seventy-two films that make up the Department of Public Prosecution's video nasties – that is, inclusive of the thirty-nine titles that were banned outright (see Appendix II) and the thirty-three that were dropped from prosecution but still liable for forfeiture (see Appendix III) – no fewer than thirty-seven make explicit reference to the stars of the film, while thirty-eight make reference to the creators. Perhaps more surprising than that is the fact that in spite of the absence of recognisable company names and logos, sixty out of the seventy-two sleeves include the branding of the company, company name or logo. While I will return to examine branding more thoroughly in the next chapter, it is worth noting at this stage that in traditional discussions of the video nasties these companies are always framed as transitory and opportunistic. Nevertheless, almost all of the companies had invested in brand identities that foregrounded their logos in packaging, posters and idents. This, if nothing else, suggests a model of sophistication not usually commented upon, and tactics that are undoubtedly an attempt to create brand awareness and recognition for their product and their company; certainly not the actions of transitory, opportunistic fly-by-night companies.

The analysis also suggests that two of Staiger's original criteria, authenticity and realism, play only a minimal role in the promotion of video nasties, with the only real example of this being the pseudo-documentary *Faces of Death* (1978). This film purported to be made up of actual footage of death and murder and the distributor capitalised on these ideas by categorising the film as 'true-life horror' in small text on the spine of the sleeve. Alongside this, references to horror as a genre and its application as a marketing device are also surprisingly few. But, given that all accounts of the video nasties reinforce the 'lurid' or 'shocking' qualities present in the promotion of the video nasties, what is perhaps most unexpected when surveying these materials is that the categories that would be most likely to represent such an aesthetic – namely, those of affect and of novelty – are only minimally represented. There are, for instance, only eleven video sleeves that employ affective straplines, with only two utilising novelty. It is also notable that while twenty-eight of the seventy-two sleeves incorporate photographic elements, only one of these – *The Driller Killer* – can be seen as deviating from typical approaches that one might associate with those of more mainstream productions. Moreover, the cultural differences demonstrated in the overview of Hammer's promotions and the emphasis on the affective response one might expect to experience are not evident in any meaningful way, with only six of the seventy-two films following an American model of explicitly detailing the expected affective response that one might experience when watching the film.

What is empirically overwhelmingly visible, when looking at the publicity materials for the video nasties as a set, is that spectacle is employed more than any other category in the matrix, though this is perhaps to be expected. In his 1986 article 'The Cinema of Attraction[s]: Early Film, Its Spectator and the Avant-Garde', Tom Gunning describes the reliance on spectacle over narrative in the films of Hollywood (1986: 63), describing 'the Hollywood advertising policy of enumerating the features of a film, each emblazoned with the command, "See!"', suggesting that this demonstrated 'the primal power of the attraction running underneath the armature of narrative regulation' (1986: 70). Eric Schaefer has linked this kind of promotion with the promotions of American B-movies of the 1950s and 1960s, and his study *Bold! Daring! Shocking! True!* (1994) highlighted that these types of films displayed a similar emphasis on spectacle, enumerating what viewers will see and feel and that they similarly draw attention away from any narrative elements to prioritise both the visual spectacle and the bodily affect one may expect to experience while watching the film. This is the most dominant marketing and promotion tradition that the video nasties publicity materials can be seen to be employing, and a clear line can be observed from the promotions of P. T. Barnum and an emphasis on the carnivalesque that build upon a tradition of hucksterism and ballyhoo. It is also crucial to note that in his 1986 article, Gunning suggests that cinema of the 1970s and 1980s 'reaffirmed its roots in stimulus and carnival rides, and in what might be called the Spielberg-Lucas-Coppola cinema of effects', suggesting a dominant desire across popular cinema to privilege spectacle over narrative (Strauven 2006: 387). While Gunning's article is primarily concerned with film production and exhibition before 1906, one conclusion we can draw is that for Gunning, even though they differ in their promotional strategy, a film like *Raiders of the Lost Ark* displays the same emphasis on spectacle as a film like *The Evil Dead*. While one might expect the horror film to function as a point of crossover anyway, a genre of film that has historically emphasised spectacle in both its content and in its promotion and that draws directly upon those traditions of ballyhoo to prioritise the affective qualities of its entertainment through the celebration of the spectacle, Gunning's observations hint at a similar emphasis in 'the cinema of effects', and suggest that there is very little that is fundamentally different between the promotion of these marginal cult offerings and big-budget box office successes. Because of their inherent similarity, a quantitative analysis can tell us only so much, so it is worth applying a qualitative analysis as a means of isolating particular issues prominent in these promotions.

Sex and Violence

This section moves on from the matrix's quantitative data to a more qualitative analysis of the findings, determined by the categories which lend themselves to a thematic exploration of the visual imagery used in the videocassette artwork. Typically, concern over the imagery used in the promotion of horror films falls into one of three categories: (1) sexual imagery, (2) violent imagery, or, and what is often deemed to be more problematic, (3) images of sexualised violence that combine both elements, often to provocative effect. As demonstrated (and challenged) throughout this book, it has been suggested that it was complaints about the lurid and gratuitous nature of the artwork used to promote these films that incurred the wrath of moralist campaigners and the right-leaning press alike, but little assessment has been made of the promotions of the video nasties in context and alongside other promotions of the period. Instead, most accounts typically isolate the most extreme examples, often *The Driller Killer*, *I Spit on Your Grave* or *SS Experiment Camp*, as a means of highlighting the most problematic attributes of the video nasties. Isolating these three extreme examples of promotion takes the full catalogue of promotions out of context and prevents the measurement of their perceived extremity against more mainstream promotions that were also in circulation over thirty years ago. Given the inconclusive results generated by the broad analysis of the sleeves as a whole, it is necessary to isolate specific examples of imagery that might be considered as problematic on the grounds that the images are excessively sexual or excessively violent in nature. However, rather than consider these in isolation (as others have done), this section draws parallels between these few examples and similar imagery found in the market at the same time, with the aim of determining the degree to which these promotions differed from standard industrial practice.

It is certainly true that a number of video nasties contain imagery that is sexualised in nature, most notably: *Beast in Heat* (1977), *Blood Feast* (1963), *The Cannibal Man* (1972), *I Miss You Hugs and Kisses* (1978), *I Spit on Your Grave* (1978), *Late Night Trains* (1975), *SS Experiment Camp* (1976), *The Toolbox Murders* (1978), *Mardi Gras Massacre* (1978), *Prisoner of the Cannibal God* (1978) and *Women Behind Bars* (1975). Nevertheless, the degree to which the artwork for these films can be seen as explicit is incredibly subjective. While each, to varying degrees, incorporates the naked or semi-naked figures of eroticised women as part of their design, it should be noted that all of the designs listed above, excluding *I Miss You Hugs and Kisses*, are illustrations rather than photographic representations, and that while *I Miss You Hugs and Kisses* is photographic and shows the protagonist Elke Sommer partially submerged in a swimming pool and in a wet t-shirt, it is far less explicit than the average pin-up included on page 3 of some of Britain's best-selling tabloid newspapers of the period. This is not to excuse the imagery, but simply to highlight that the degree to which these designs differed from established industrial practice visible elsewhere is debatable and therefore the ways in which these promotions might have contributed to the furore that followed is equally up for debate.

Most poster designs reflect the origin or the narrative of the film that they are promoting. For example, the artwork used to promote *Blood Feast* (1963) makes bold claims as to the content of the film, exclaiming 'nothing so appalling in the annals of horror'. Nevertheless, the general aesthetic used here reflects the period and the location in which it was produced and exhibited; namely, drive-in exploitation cinema of the 1960s. Similarly, the eroticised artwork for *Prisoner of the Cannibal God*, which depicts Ursula Andress tied to a stake, can clearly be seen to be drawing upon a long tradition of boys-own action adventures popularised in comic books such as *Sheena, Queen of the Jungle* from the 1940s onwards. This image is only marginally more sexualised in nature, showing the shape of her nipples through her wet top. Overall, while some of the films listed do depict sexualised imagery, most are not excessive by the standards of the time, though ironically may appear more excessive to a modern eye.

Despite appearing excessive in isolation, there is a continuity here with visual modes of promotion used to advertise popular fiction of the period. Book publishers such as Arrow Books and the New English Library both published a range of horror titles related to the occult and black magic, both rebranding these lines in the 1970s to include photographic imagery. These covers were dominated by the images of naked or semi-naked women and were released contemporaneously to the video nasties and did not spark the public outcry that the video nasties did. Significantly, for Arrow Books at least, this photographic rebrand seems to have been inspired by release of the films *To the Devil a Daughter* (1976) and *The Devil Rides Out* (1968) and was an attempt to capitalise on photographic imagery that more closely reflected to the look of the Hammer films that had been adapted from these books. The adoption of photography in this way appears to have been in an attempt to give this range of books the look and feel of a film, as well as to increase declining sales in the wake of the video boom (Humphreys 2015). But what is of particular importance here is that despite the use of highly sexualised photographic imagery, these pulp paperbacks were never targeted by the censors and moralists in the same way as the video nasties.

Of the seventy-two films in the video nasties list, the three whose promotional materials have been most frequently cited as problematic in regards to depictions of sex and sexual violence towards women are *SS Experiment Camp* (1976), *The Beast in Heat* (1977) and *I Spit on Your Grave* (1978). It is, therefore, worth addressing each of these films in some detail while attempting to contextualise the promotions for these films within a longer tradition of established industrial practice. It may not be entirely coincidental that the films that are often considered the most problematic among the video nasties are those that depict rape, something that is compounded by the figure of the Nazi and the setting of the concentration camp. With both subjects, there is an expectation that the material is approached with care and sensitivity, something which rarely happens in the world of exploitation film. *SS Experiment Camp* and *The Beast in Heat* are controversial films with controversial titles. While *SS Experiment Camp* follows the 'consensual' sexual experimentation on the female prisoners in a concentration camp, *The Beast in Heat* features a half-man, half-beast human hybrid that has been genetically engineered by Nazi scientists to deliver the systematic rape and torture of the male and female inmates of an internment camp. These are challenging films, and the promotional materials for each of them reflects this, though,

I would argue, not in an overly excessive way when considered alongside other cover images of the period that also employed sexualised and violent imagery in the promotion of media texts such as pulp novels.

Des Dolan, the managing director of Go Video Ltd, the distributor responsible for releasing *SS Experiment Camp*, admitted that he thought that some of the advertising could be perceived as excessive, but he also conceded that he needed to ensure that his product stood out from that of his competitors. Dolan has previously stated that 'the industry need[ed] some sort of guideline that video advertisers [could] follow' (Martin 2007: 14). The cover image for *SS Experiment Camp* famously featured the body of a naked woman being tortured and crucified upside down, while a superimposed image of her Nazi captor looked on. However, while the image became notorious, what received far less publicity was the fact that Dolan himself had exercised some degree of sensitivity in relation to the cover images that were used to promote *SS Experiment Camp*. In an act of self-censorship, Dolan had the image amended so that the female figure was only topless rather than using full frontal nudity that depicted female genitalia, again, mirroring some of the aesthetic choices of the page 3 content (ironically, the same publications that led the campaign against the video distributors). Of course, the major difference between these two kinds of imagery is that typically page 3 girls are not usually threatened in the way that the figure on the cover of *SS Experiment Camp* is, but some of this is tempered by the fact that this image was an illustration rather than a photograph, so it could be argued with some degree of certainty, that this image is far less explicit than its tabloid newspaper counterpart.

The imagery used to promote *The Beast in Heat* is similar in its approach to that of *SS Experiment Camp*. Here, a clearly distressed woman is depicted running away from the titular beast. Meanwhile, a swastika banner hangs, draped over the body of what can only be assumed to be the beast's most recent victim. There is no question that it is a problematic and challenging film, but this also needs to be contextualised as part of a long tradition of Nazi exploitation films, films that are collectively known as Nazisploitation. These films have a long tradition and have at least in part been inspired by the success of art-house films, such as Liliana Cavani's *The Night Porter* (1974), Pier Paolo Pasolini's *Salò, or the 120 Days of Sodom* (1975) and Tinto Brass's *Salon Kitty* (1976). At this time, powerful voices had been raised in defence of shocking, sexually explicit and violent by internationally acclaimed auteurs such as Pasolini. Even James Ferman, the secretary of the British Board of Film Classification, became an unlikely oppositional voice against the censorship of Pasolini's provocative and divisive *Salò* in 1975. After the Department of Public

Prosecutions (DPP) had seized *Salò* under Section 3 of the Obscene Publications Act (1959), overruling a decision the board had made some three years earlier to make it available un-certificated to private members clubs, Ferman defended the BBFC's original position and argued that the DPP had been wrongly advised, declaring:

> It seems to me that your advisors have misunderstood the law of obscenity in Britain and have allowed their own sense of outraged propriety to colour their view of the film's legality. The portrayal of evil in works of art is not the same thing as its endorsement. (Ferman 1979)

Whilst it is unlikely that Ferman would have ever launched a similar defence to include films like *SS Experiment Camp* and *The Beast in Heat*, there are resonances in his argument that need to be acknowledged here. Ferman's suggestion that 'the portrayal of evil in works of art is not the same thing as its endorsement' has significant ramifications for how these types of films might be judged, including how promotional material is considered. Granted, *The Beast in Heat* is not an equivalent of Pasolini's *Salò*, or for that matter Tinto Brass's *Salon Kitty*, but, nevertheless, while these films may appear objectionable and tasteless to some, that should not colour any assessment that tries to historicise promotional materials of this type. There are clear precedents for many of the promotional strategies being used for *SS Experiment Camp* and *The Beast in Heat*. For instance, American men's adventure magazines like *Man's Epic* were eroticising the image of the Nazi as early as 1963. These post-war pulp magazines, aimed squarely at an adult market, revelled in reworking the image of the Nazi into a sexually dominant figure that took great pleasure in torturing young women, and while I am not excusing this imagery, it is important to acknowledge that it is part of a long tradition that is evident across many media. Similar imagery was also used in 'Stalag fiction', a short-lived genre of Nazi exploitation that was popular in Israel and elsewhere in the 1950s and early 1960s. The degree to which magazines of this type would have been available in the UK is difficult to ascertain, so there possibly an element of cultural specificity that needs to be considered here, but what is for certain, is that these magazines were available by 1963 and remained in circulation until the late 1970s, repeatedly returning to the image of the Nazi as source of erotic depiction. What is also difficult to determine is the degree to which magazines of this type may have influenced film production. The earliest sexploitation film set in a Nazi camp is *Love Camp 7* (a film which also features on the video nasties banned film list), produced in America in 1969. This became a template for the modern Nazisploitation film and was possibly produced to capitalise on the success of magazines of this type.

While the artwork used to promote *I Spit on Your Grave* did not depict the image of a female being tortured by a Nazi officer, it would prove to be no less contentious. Ric Meyers calls the cover image and marketing campaign associated with the film 'a masterpiece of cunning ingenuity' (2011: 107) and describes the picture as a 'richly coloured photo of a bruised, scratched woman taken from the back', suggesting that you can 'just see how battered she was because all she was wearing was a flimsy, ripped one-piece undergarment of some nature – exposing her back and her rear as well as her arms and legs' (ibid.).[2] However, while Myers was keen to celebrate the artwork as a masterpiece, Andi Zeisler has argued that the emphasis on the 'image of the shapely rear of its heroine barely covered by her ripped, dirt smeared underwear' (2008: 72) is indicative of the problematic trend toward increasingly misogynistic depictions of women (2008: 72). However, while Zeisler clearly takes issue with the image, she significantly does not single out *I Spit on Your Grave* as an anomaly, but instead considers the imagery as one of the more visible examples of a broader problem and something that can be seen in a whole host of other promotional images used to advertise any number of mainstream Hollywood films. This is an approach that has been highlighted in the work of Marcia Belsky, who, frustrated by 'the still standard practise of fragmenting, fetishizing and dehumanizing the images of women we see in film, TV, book covers, and advertisements' (Belsky 2016: online), started the online project the 'Headless Women of Hollywood'. Belsky suggests that 'by decapitating the woman, or fragmenting her body into decontextualized sexual parts, the woman becomes an unquestionably passive object to the male gaze', going on to suggest that, 'the consistent fragmentation of women's bodies, with particular focus on the boobs, butt and lips, separates the sexualized female body parts from her wholeness' so that 'the viewer does not have to morally reconcile the woman who is being objectified with her complete humanness' (Pound 2016: online).

While this is undeniably an issue that can be seen across all kinds of promotion, the significance of Belsky's research project here is that it very clearly highlights that images of the kind used in *I Spit on Your Grave* are not limited to the exploitation film but are a common trope evident across popular culture. Laura Bates (2016) highlights a distinct subset of the 'Headless Women of Hollywood' trend observed by Belsky in which the female figure was fragmented by a view that was fixed through a character's legs (Belsky 2016: online). Here, Bates defines these posters as those 'which seek to entice the potential moviegoer by presenting them with a viewpoint from between a woman's naked or stocking-clad legs'. This trope has been used to promote films as diverse as Mike Leigh's *Naked* (1993), the Farrelly Brother's *Kingpin* (1996), and *Kingsman: The Secret Service* (2014). It is an approach that has been parodied in the Austin Powers sequel *Goldmember* (2002) and adapted to include men in the campaign for *3:10 to Yuma* (2007), but was perhaps used most famously in Roger Moore's fifth outing as 007 agent James Bond in *For Your Eyes Only* (1981). Surprisingly, there are several parallels between these two films despite their apparent differences. The narrative of both films focuses on women taking revenge; Jennifer Hills taking revenge for her gang rape, and Melina Havelock avenging the death of her parents. It is significantly the exact same trope that is presented on the poster for *I Spit on Your Grave* (2016). However, and despite the fact that *I Spit on Your Grave* and *For Your Eyes Only* were both released on video in the UK in the same year, the former seemed to attract as much condemnation for its cover as it did for its content. However, when they are considered side by side, to borrow the words of Zeisler, they both feature the 'image of the shapely rear of its heroine barely covered'. In both images, the women's bottoms and legs are tanned, shiny and eroticised. In both images, the women are seen holding a weapon in their right hand, a knife in *I Spit on Your Grave*, and a crossbow in *For Your Eyes Only*. The major difference between these two films is in the content of the films themselves. *For Your Eyes Only* features British agent James Bond attempting to recover a communications device from the Russians, while *I Spit on Your Grave* is a rape-revenge film that depicts an incredibly graphic depiction of a gang rape that has lost none of its power to shock in the thirty-plus years since it was released. However, there is nothing in the promotional materials for *I Spit on Your Grave* poster to indicate that she has been the victim of a rape. In fact, a viewer would need to have seen the film first in order to interpret the taglines and straplines used for both the poster and the video sleeve. Instead, the sleeve of *I Spit on Your Grave* prioritises the revenge component of the narrative by exclaiming that, 'this woman has just . . . cut, chopped, broken, and burned four men beyond recognition . . . but no jury in America would convict her', under which it reads 'an act of revenge'. These taglines only ever hint at the events that led to the enactment of this revenge, so as problematic as the sleeve might at first appear, not least for its potential to eroticise rape, it needs to be considered alongside other films that have adopted similar practices. On a purely promotional level, films such as *For Your Eyes Only* eroticise and fragment the female form in similar ways, so I would argue in this context and without having seen the film, on a semiotic level the promotion can only be seen to be as problematic as that seen in a number of mainstream promotions.

The Spectacle of Violence

There is an expectation of violence when approaching a category of film as controversial as the video nasties, a category that is defined by its perceived extremity and its supposed difference to mainstream entertainment. There is a similar expectation when approaching the marketing materials for these videos, especially since it is the promotional materials that were credited with causing the whole furore in the first place. As already demonstrated, the sexualised imagery used in these promotions is largely in line with other forms of promotion from the period and, in some cases, the video nasties even appear tame when compared with some of the more sexualised photographic pulp covers of Dennis Wheatley novels. This would suggest that it was violent imagery that was the root cause of any concern and the catalyst for the furore that followed; certainly, *The Driller Killer* is routinely presented as the most problematic example. However, on closer examination, this is only partially true. The violent imagery used to promote the video nasties contains components common to the promotion of the horror film, incorporating familiar elements like the victim in peril, often being terrorised by their assailants, or iconography like skulls and blood splatters. This is imagery and iconography that is typical of the horror film and is semiotically very similar to the imagery used in the promote a variety of mainstream horror films, books and comics. However, there are specific kinds of imagery that have historically been more problematic than others, for instance, it is well known that James Ferman had difficulties with the imagery and titles of films that emphasised power tools, among other things. It is possible that this was a hangover from the early days of video censorship, when several films that made reference to power tools in either their titles or cover designs were highlighted as problematic, and although the BBFC were not part of the selection process that identified the video nasties, this certainly seems to be an element common to the films selected by the DPP and the BBFC. The most famous instance of this was of course *The Texas Chainsaw Massacre*, which, while not a video nasty, was often linked to the list and as such was liable for forfeiture. Films such as *The Driller Killer* and *The Toolbox Murders* figured prominently in this regard. There were other films that were targeted whose imagery made less overt reference to power tools. Jess Franco's *Bloody Moon* (1981) featured the screaming face of a female victim on the sleeve, accompanied by the blurred image of the blade of a whirring circular saw. However, despite the imagery referencing power tools, the image is fragmented almost to the point of abstraction, so it seems unlikely that this was the cause of any concern.[3]

Perhaps the most iconic image of the video nasties moral panic and one that certainly gives credence to the view that the artwork was to blame for the ensuing panic is the video sleeve and poster for VIPCO's release of Abel Ferrara's *The Driller Killer*. Here, a man screams in agony as a drill is pushed into his forehead and the blood streams into his eyes. Above his face, the tagline exclaims in red block lettering that 'the blood runs in rivers, and the drill keeps tearing through flesh and bone', while the title *The Driller Killer* runs underneath punctuated by the graphic of a drill bit to form the letter 'I' in the words 'DRILLER' and 'KILLER'. In their comprehensive collection of pre-certificate era video sleeves, *The Art of the Nasty*, Nigel Wingrove and Marc Morris have speculated that *The Driller Killer* could be 'the most over-the-top video cover ever seen in the UK' (1998: 20). It is, without question, a bold and challenging image, and while there are many who are keen to credit the sleeve with the dubious honour of the most gratuitous and few who would attempt to argue for the artistic merits of such a design, it is important to acknowledge that despite the apparent extremity of the design, it is nevertheless still not without a precedent.

The trashy covers of pulp fiction horror paperbacks offer the most direct visual parallel to the seemingly excessive imagery of *The Driller Killer*, with the most immediate similarities to be found in the imagery of Herbert Van Thal's *Pan Book of Horror Stories* series. Van Thal's anthology series began in 1959 with an aesthetic not dissimilar to that of the 1950s American horror comics, such as EC comics, which most famously published *Tales from the Crypt*, *The Haunt of Fear* and *The Vault of Fear*. But by the late 1970s, this aesthetic had developed, possibly in response to the promotions of Arrow Books and the New English Library that were increasingly using photographs and aligning themselves with a cinematic aesthetic. The rebranding of Pan's series prioritised a central image of a human face typically contorted in a torturous pose, and while many featured images of the faces of dead people in various stages of decomposition (such as the cover for the first, tenth and twenty-eighth), others featured the decapitated heads of a figure: floating in a chamber pot and on a shelf, using the eye sockets, mouth and ears as a vase for flowers (the eighth and twenty-ninth respectively). However, it is the covers for the twenty-second and twenty-third volumes that are the most intriguing, both in terms of their similarity of the image used for the sleeve of *The Driller Killer*, but also in relation to the period in which they were released. Released in 1981 and 1982 respectively, the twenty-second and twenty-third editions of *The Pan Book of Horror Stories* are directly contemporaneous to *The Driller Killer*, which was released on video in the UK in February 1982.

The image on the cover of the twenty-second edition features the blistered face of a woman on fire, looking up, clearly in much distress as her face bubbles and burns, and the image used on the cover of the twenty-third edition of the anthology follows a similar narrative, featuring what appears to be a close-up of a burned and blackened face screaming as blood runs from their mouth and down their cheek. These sleeves are every bit as gory and violent as the artwork used for *The Driller Killer*, and they all emphasise the death and torture of their central figure. One of the factors that could be seen to differentiate the images used in the promotion of videos from the images used in the promotion of books are the hyperbolic taglines that we usually associate with the exploitation film. For instance, the taglines for the video nasty *The Driller Killer* exclaim that 'the blood runs in rivers, and the drill keeps tearing through flesh and bone', something that is clearly drawing on the kind of hype and showmanship of early exploitation promotion that is perhaps found less often in world of book jacket design. Interestingly, there are also parallels between the imagery of *The Driller Killer* and the Pan books to be observed in mainstream film distribution: George Roy Hill's *Slaughterhouse Five* (1972) was adapted from the Kurt Vonnegut's novel, owned by Universal and released by CIC, offers the most striking parallel, featuring the bloodied face of a victim in close up on the video sleeve from 1985.

Ballyhoo

It is perhaps appropriate, given the notoriety of David Hamilton Grant, that it is his company World of Video 2000 that can most easily be aligned with the hyperbolic exploitation tactics of the early ballyhoo showmen. Even before his prosecution for the release of *Nightmares in a Damaged Brain*, Grant landed himself in hot water when he took a little-known sci-fi horror called *Night Fright* (1967) and repackaged and retitled the film in an attempt to exploit the furore of the video nasties moral panic and the global success of Spielberg's science-fiction fantasy *E. T. the Extra-Terrestrial* (1983). With *E. T. The Extra-Terrestrial* yet to be released on home video, in a moment of inspiration, Grant reworked John Henry Alvin's iconic artwork for the film so that the child's outstretched finger was tip-to-tip not with the finger of a benevolent alien, but with the outstretched claw of a hostile alien. The parody was enough to alert Universal International Pictures who quickly countered with a legal action that forced Grant to withdraw the film and to subsequently retitle it *The Extra-Terrestrial Nasty* and amend the artwork in the process to something that was less recognisably derivative of the Universal

Pictures' original design. Undeterred, World of Video 2000 moved on, orchestrating a fantastically carnivalesque campaign to promote *Nightmares in a Damaged Brain*. In a strategy evocative of the sideshow ballyhoo of Barnum, the company appeared at the Manchester software show in May 1982 and invited attendees to 'guess the weight of the human brain'. The company had brought with them a human brain in a specimen jar, and while the brain was prosthetic, the stunt proved enough to generate a considerable amount of publicity for the company.

While Grant would become notorious on the back of *Nightmares in a Damaged Brain*, the stunt itself was the brainchild of Larry Utall, an American record company executive with twenty-eight years industry experience working with acts like Blondie, David Cassidy, Gary Glitter and the Bay City Rollers. Utall had partnered with World of Video on a UK distribution deal, and it had been his idea to retitle *Nightmares in a Damaged Brain* from its original title of *Nightmares*, in a bid to avoid any confusion with an Australian film of the same name. The film was released just as the video nasties moral panic was erupting and, with a title as controversial as *Nightmares in a Damaged Brain*, the British press leapt on it. Rather than discourage the attention and defuse any building concern, Utall and World of Video 2000 decided to capitalise on the controversy in the hope of maximising revenue. When he was interviewed in August 1982, Utall conceded that while it might have been tasteless publicity stunt that had led to the film being seized by the police, it had also increased sales to 4000 cassettes at that point, with the expectation that this would climb to 5000 by the end of the year (Hayward 1982: 36). Of course, and as already detailed, the celebrations would be short-lived, since on 3 February 1984 Grant was imprisoned for distributing *Nightmares in a Damaged Brain*, releasing a version of the film that was fractionally longer than the BBFC certificated version that Grant had released through his company Oppidan. He was sentenced to eighteen months in prison and would become the last person in the UK to serve a custodial sentence for being in possession of over 200 copies of an obscene article for publication for gain.

The degree to which the 'guess the weight of the human brain' publicity stunt contributed to that verdict is impossible to measure, but the campaign received mainstream press attention that no doubt contributed considerably to the notoriety of the film, and because of that, to the notoriety of Grant himself. Before Hamilton-Grant was prosecuted, Utall suggested that it was this 'tasteless exercise . . . that caused *Nightmares in a Damaged Brain* to be seized by the local constabulary, but paradoxically it helped shift videos' (Hayward 1982: 36). Famously, in Grant's defence, QC and human rights lawyer Geoffrey Robertson engaged Derek Malcolm, the film critic for *The Guardian*, as an expert witness in the case. In Malcolm's testimony, he argued that the film, while not a classic, was well executed, to which the presiding judge replied that the German invasion of Poland had been well executed (Gregory 2005), illustrating perfectly just how preposterous the campaign against the video nasties had become. While World of Video 2000 was unique in this kind of carnivalesque approach to their promotion, Palace Video demonstrated a similar reliance on ballyhoo in their promotions for *The Evil Dead*, though relying on novelty over the carnivalesque. The company had released the film both theatrically and on home video on the same day, and their video campaign included a competition to win a year's supply of red meat. Despite the similarity of this campaign to the 'guess the weight of the human brain' competition, and its relative bad taste, a prosecution against Palace and *The Evil Dead* was unsuccessful, leading Palace to re-release the film with a banner proclaiming 'not guilty' across the sleeve (Figures 5.1, 5.2).

With relatively few distributors adopting the stunts and novelty evident in the earlier theatrical and cinematic promotions, the taglines and straplines offer the most visible acknowledgement of the tradition of which these films were part. The promotional materials for the Herschell Gordon Lewis film *Blood Feast* offers the most obvious link to this past, simply repurposing the artwork from the 1963 American campaign.

Figure 5.1 *The Evil Dead*'s promotional competition to win a year's supply of red meat.

Figure 5.2 Video sleeve for the second release of *The Evil Dead* following Palace's successful defence of the film in court.

However, it is a reworking of the tagline for another Gordon Lewis film which provides the basis for the promotions used in *The Last House on the Left* (1972). In 1965, Gordon Lewis, the 'godfather of gore', released *Color Me Blood Red*. The film was promoted with the affective tagline 'you must keep reminding yourself, it's just a movie, it's just a movie'. Although this tagline had first been used the year before to promote William Castle's *Strait-Jacket* (1964), it became inexorably linked with *Last House on the Left* when it was released in 1972. The cinematic promotions reworked the tagline into a phrase that advised the audience 'to avoid fainting, keep repeating: It's only a movie, only a movie, only a movie' and, on the American theatrical release poster, this phrase was accompanied by images that asked 'can a movie go too far?', displaying a tongue-in-cheek attitude with a warning declaring that the film was 'not recommended for anyone over 30'.

For the British video campaign, any hint of that humour was removed, with the poster and front of the sleeve starkly presented without the embellishment of photographs or illustrations. The image is purely typographic presented over a plain black background. The upper third of the image is taken up by the title *The Last House on the Left* in bold red capital letters, while underneath the familiar tagline 'to avoid fainting keep repeating it's only a movie . . . only a movie . . . only a movie . . . only a movie . . . only a movie . . . only a movie . . . only a movie' is reprinted. To the left of that is a warning that insists that the film is 'not recommended for persons under 18', and underneath that, again in red capital letters, is a disclaimer that suggests that 'due to the specific nature of the horrific and violent scenes in this film the front cover is not illustrated to avoid offence'. I would argue that this creates a sense of intrigue and raises questions about how horrific 'too horrific' may be; however, in *Blood Money* (2011), his exploration of the first teen slasher cycle, Richard Nowell argues that monochromatic horror film posters that either used colour sparingly or not at all, are indicative of a trend to reposition the horror film as a prestige genre (2011: 100). Here, however, the minimalistic monochromatic design is used explicitly as a mechanism of extremity to differentiate it from more traditional horror fare. In the UK particularly, the effect of the plain black background mirrored the effect of licensed adult stores that, since 1981, had been forbidden from displaying their products in their shop windows under the Indecent Displays Act. Here it functions counter to Nowell's belief, with the decision to adopt a monochromatic colour scheme and not illustrate the cover at all perhaps the most hyperbolic of all of the strategies adopted in the promotion of the video nasties. As a strategy, arguably it keeps the viewer out; only hinting at what might be so horrific behind the blacked-out minimal design of the poster, which simultaneously challenges the viewer, telling them that they will be scared, so much so they will need to reassure themselves that 'It's only a movie, it's only a movie, it's only a movie'. The minimalistic design is akin to putting the video in a brown paper bag so as to protect delicate sensibilities from offence.

Not only is this one of the most hyperbolic strategies, but I would argue that it is these promotions that have the most in common with their exploitation antecedents, borrowing the ballyhoo and hype of 42nd Street, New York. While the links here are implicit, the legacy of the grindhouse on the video nasties is significant. Graham Humphreys, the creator of *The Evil Dead* artwork, has suggested that he was inspired by the music of the American psychobilly band The Cramps when he was designing the poster. Tracing this back, The Cramps themselves borrowed the retro styling of the grindhouse, something which is evident in their image and in their lyrical content, consistently drawing on horror and sci-fi B-movie iconography. When Humphreys used this as an inspiration, he knowingly drew upon the iconography of American exploitation and infused his design with this aesthetic, and in doing so, demonstrates neatly the dialogue that exists between the markets of American exploitation cinema and the video nasties. However, while these parallels are demonstrative of this dialogue, it still only accounts for a fraction of the promotions, and even those that do incorporate those ideas tend to do so conservatively. Though many are still keen to attribute the furore of the moral panic to the designs and marketing methods, these promotions were by no means the only examples of challenging imagery in a wider marketplace. The parallels seen in the pulp fiction and comic book market of the same period raise interesting questions about why the artwork for the video nasties is remembered as a hyperbolic flurry of excess, while these other forms of promotion went unchallenged. As demonstrated throughout this chapter, despite it being possible to convincingly map some the advertising strategies used in the promotion of the video nasties to the exaggerated hyperbole of American exploitation, there remains very little evidence that any of this could, or even should, be held responsible for the moral panic that followed, at least not in any meaningful way. In the absence of any conclusive evidence, it is necessary to consider any other element that may have contributed to the popular perception of the video nasties and either directly or indirectly acted as a promotional tool that may have contributed to a broader cultural awareness and a greater understanding of these films and what they represented.

Publicity as Paratextual Marketing Campaign

Despite the credit usually given to the power of the promotional materials for the films themselves, the single most important factor in the widespread understanding of what a video nasty was then, and remains still, the campaign that was mounted by the tabloid press of the period against the films and their distributors. However, it is problematic to take these reports at face value, and rather than accept these as objective accounts that reported responsibly on the concern that was being felt around the video nasties, I conclude this chapter by reconceptualising the campaign as what it ultimately became, an indirect extension of, and supplement to, the direct marketing strategies developed by the distributors. It then becomes possible to align the rhetoric of the campaign with the rhetoric of American exploitation cinema of the 1930s and 1940s, which in turn allows a clearer picture to emerge of the role that the tabloid press played in the construction of the 'new threat' that the video nasties posed. This simple shift in thinking reveals that the campaign itself was more visibly reliant of the rhetoric and hyperbole of exploitation cinema than any of the interventions by the distributors themselves, and suggests that this contributed to a national understanding of what a video nasty was and in doing so established a lasting recognition of the category as one of excess.

In his archival volume *American Film Taglines*, Robert Cettl suggests that exploitation cinema is reliant on sensationalism within both the content of films and also, more specifically, the taglines used to promote these films. Cettl argues that the emphasis on 'emotion and indulgence', as well as 'aberration and extremism', situates the rhetoric of the genre closer to that of the headline-grabbing style of tabloid journalism (2014) than perhaps conventional cinematic promotions. Cettl's observation provides an interesting perspective on the history of the video nasties. Indeed, in the absence of any substantive evidence to support the popular narrative that attributes the moral panic and the effects of censorship to the supposedly gratuitous and lurid packaging used by the distributors, it is necessary to reconsider the campaign to 'Ban the Sadist Videos' as what it has retrospectively become – the largest and most pervasive marketing campaign ever afforded to a disparate number of unconnected independent films. Cettl's observations provide an interesting lens through which it is possible to reconceptualise the rhetoric of tabloid journalism as the rhetoric of exploitation and, in doing so, assess the role that hyperbole of this kind played in the popular perception of the video nasties.

In his work on tabloid journalism, Martin Conboy has argued that

> it is in the language of different types of newspapers, not in their layout, that the distinction between tabloids and the serious press lies; that is, between the neutral language of aiming to be considered as serious newspapers of record and the 'emotionally charged' language of the popular tabloids. (2005: 14)

Similarly, it is in the emotionally charged language of the popular tabloids as they reported on the video nasties that the most significant parallels can be found to the rhetoric of exploitation. Conboy suggests that tabloid newspapers have demonstrated a preoccupation with documenting both 'sensation' and 'human interest stories', and it is here that the familiar emphasis on 'emotion and indulgence' and 'aberration and extremism' observed by Cettl can be seen (2014). You do not need to look far to find parallels between the world of exploitation cinema to the rhetoric of the tabloid journalism and the coverage of the video nasties moral panic; however, these 'emotionally charged' stories can perhaps most easily be aligned with the Public Service exploitation films of the 1930s and 1940s. These are the films that presented titillation as a cautionary tale, and through the films already discussed – *Reefer Madness* (1936), *The Wages of Sin* (1938) and the sex hygiene film *Mom and Dad* (1945) – purported to take an explicitly moral line as a justification for depicting challenging material. The promotions for these films reveal the same emphasis given over to both 'sensation' and 'human interest stories' as that displayed in the tabloid press, and in stories that similarly claimed to be a warning of the potential perils of the video nasties. While this emphasis was not as visible in the promotional posters for these early exploitation films, many of which were lacking in sophistication, and failed to offer a sustained narrative in quite the same way as lengthy press campaign might, the trailers can be seen to offer intriguing parallels.

The trailer for *Reefer Madness* is particularly revealing in this regard, principally for its reliance on a familiar narrative. The trailer begins with an emphasis on innocence, showing high school boys and girls innocently dancing at the local soda fountain, unaware of the dangers of marijuana. What follows is a depiction of the ease and availability of the drug (here shown growing in their neighbour's yard), before the characters are seen to succumb to a downward spiral of addiction, entering a world of 'debauchery, violence, murder, suicide'. The trailer is hyperbolic and excessive in both its delivery and approach, employing scare tactics as it moves through four key stages to communicate a narrative of concern before finally revelling in a frenzy created in the aftermath of addiction. By isolating these four stages, it becomes possible to measure the degree to which the video nasties campaign can be seen to utilise similar elements in its construction and begin to gauge how far the press campaign against the video nasties can be seen to correspond to the marketing tactics employed in the promotion of American exploitation cinema of the 1930s and 1940s. The four stages evident in the narrative of *Reefer Madness* are (1) innocence, (2) home, (3) addiction, and (4) the attribution of addiction to social decline. Obviously, the narrative of *Reefer Madness* is primarily one of drug addiction, and while the video nasties are not, that does not prevent the same familiar emphasis on addiction in the narrative constructed by the tabloid press.

The first stage foregrounds the sense of innocence at the start of the trailer for *Reefer Madness*, where the boys and girls are seen dancing at the soda fountain. This is underlined by the narrator, who refers to their innocence twice in the first ten seconds of the trailer. In the second stage, this innocence is threatened, not by a distant and far off threat but from somewhere closer to home. Here, a drug user is shown hiding in a wardrobe before the narrator announces that we 'will see the ease with which this vicious plant can be grown in [our] neighbour's yard'. Proximity is critical to the narrative here, with a fundamental aspect of the narrative being the emphasis given to communicating that this drug is a threat to you (the viewer), to your home, and your whole way of life. By the third stage of the narrative, the story has turned to one of addiction, with the narrator summarising the downward spiral of drug addiction before, in the fourth and final stage, the effect of the drug is linked to innumerable social problems, from debauchery and violence to murder and suicide. The narrative is exaggerated for effect and borrows the language of the popular tabloids, revelling in 'sensation' while providing an 'emotionally charged' 'human interest story'.

As already illustrated by Conboy, there is a measurable difference 'in the language of different types of newspapers [. . .]'; 'between the neutral language of those aiming to be considered as serious newspapers of record and the 'emotionally charged' language of the popular tabloids' (2005: 14). While the popular tabloids could rarely be accused of employing this 'neutral language' in regards their coverage of the video nasties, the overall rhetoric can nevertheless be seen to begin fairly innocuously before escalating over time, gradually becoming more and more exaggerated and amplified as the campaign developed. As with *Reefer Madness*, the narrative of the campaign begins with a threat to innocence and a threat to the home. Here, it was the ideas of child protection that would prove to be fundamental in the success of the campaign against the video nasties.

Beginning in May 1982 with 'How High Street horror is invading the home' (Chippendale 1982) and 'This poison being peddled as home entertainment' (Dawe 1982), the newspapers were initially concerned with the threat that these films posed to the home and society more generally. The figure of the vulnerable child, while present, played only a peripheral role in the campaign at this point. However, children and the protection of childhood would subsequently become an integral part of the rhetoric that was mobilised around the video nasties. Headlines that can be seen as comparatively unemotional in their approach, such as 'Children in video peril' (Dover 1982) and 'Children turned on by TV horror' (Merrin 1983), quickly escalated into headlines declaring 'we must protect our children NOW' (James 1983, emphasis in original), and culminated in the *Daily Mail*'s hugely problematic headline 'The rape of our children's minds' (Author unknown 1983b). These headlines about child protection became amplified and augmented by headlines that likened the effect of horror videos to the effect of drugs, and that recast the distributors as drug dealers, who were seen as profiteering from the addiction of children. Headlines like 'Hooking of the Video Junkies' (Neighbour 1983) or 'Outlawing the Sadism-pushers' (Author unknown 1982c) became commonplace, and it is from here that the narrative can be seen to enter the fourth and final stage of the model, where much like marijuana in *Reefer Madness*, the video nasties are believed to be the sole cause for all manner of social problems and become a catch-all explanation for any deviance or aberrant behaviour. On 28 June 1983, the *Daily Mail*'s front page read 'Fury over the video rapist' (Miles 1983a), the article telling the terrible story of two women that had been attacked by eighteen-year-old Martin Austin. Austin is described here as a 'habitual glue-sniffer' and as 'emotionally immature' with a 'low IQ'. However, irrespective of all of this, the attack was attributed to what was described as 'an unremitting diet of horror videos' (Miles 1983a: 1). A similar article that appeared on the front page of the *Daily Mail* on 13 July 1983, entitled 'A video nasty killer' (White 1983: 1), suggested that video nasties were the 'trigger that finally turned a young psychopath into a killer' when a young man with pre-existing mental-health problems murdered his best friend. In 'Sadism for six-year-olds', Dr Clifford Hill of the Parliamentary Group Video Enquiry suggested that 'we may be priming a timebomb which will explode in the midst of our society' (Miles 1983c: 1). Meanwhile, the *Daily Mirror* attributed a horrific sexual assault of a horse with bottles and sticks to '"video nasties" or a new moon' (Jackson 1984: 5). As inconceivable as it is that any of these crimes could be attributed to people watching horror films, this trajectory of the narrative correlates with the last stage of the model as demonstrated in *Reefer*

Madness where, after a loss of innocence and a threat to the home, society is lost through a downward spiral of addiction that triggers rape, murder and deviance.

Aside from a handful of hardened fans, who may have seen all of the video nasties, there are fewer still who could even name all of the films contained within the Department of Public Prosecution's lists, certainly beyond the more extreme and controversial examples. However, ask most people what a video nasty is and they will be able to tell you. They will understand the category as shorthand for excess, as a container for extreme cinema; but it is important to acknowledge that in most cases this understanding comes not from the films themselves but from the rhetoric of the press campaign that sought to 'ban the sadist videos'. Indeed, so pervasive is the rhetoric that the underlying message resonates even now more than thirty years after the films were removed from the shelves. It is simultaneously a critique of the films and the industry that produced them, and it has worked to instil a broader collective cultural understanding of what a video nasty is. This understanding has contributed to the formation of a kind of banned brand, in which the idea of a disreputable industry of video dealers has a commercial value in the contemporary marketplace. However, over time, the branding of the industry has evolved and as the home entertainment industry has grown, and formats have become obsolete, what constitutes a video nasty has evolved, as have ideas of authenticity that surround it. In the next chapter I will begin to examine the evolution of the industry, from the pre-certification period to the introduction of DVD, considering how the advent of digital platforms provided an opportunity to reappraise these films.

Notes

1. Figures from IMDb.
2. In her recent memoir, *Inside Out* (2019), Demi Moore has revealed that she is the woman on the cover of *I Spit on Your Grave*.
3. When this image is compared to other promotional material it appears no more shocking or contentious that the covers of the American comic book *Horror Stories*, incorporating similar elements, to similar effect. One issue of *Horror Stories* is particularly evocative of the *Bloody Moon* imagery. However, rather than simply focus on the victim's face the image presents the full body of a partially naked female victim being overpowered by two male assailants who are poised to dismember her with a giant industrial circular saw.

CHAPTER 6

Branding and Authenticity

Throughout the previous chapters, I have demonstrated that there was little to differentiate the promotional strategies of the independent video distributors from the strategies employed in the other sectors during the same period. Most of the promotions for these films bear all of the usual hallmarks of mainstream promotional strategies seen elsewhere in other quarters of the industry. Aside from a couple of excessive examples, the evidence does not support the idea that these promotions were different enough so as to have garnered the attention that followed. However, the similarities between the rhetoric of the tabloid press and the rhetoric of traditional exploitation cinema do reveal an interesting parallel that begins to shift some of the emphasis away from the distributors themselves and towards the coverage of the campaign. Contemporary understandings of the category of the video nasties are largely retrospective constructions that combine the reductionist rhetoric of the press campaigns with the subsequent sustained attempts to capitalise on the notoriety of the films, and because of this the definitions and meanings associated with the term have become compounded over time.

The current understanding of the video nasties can be seen to have formed over two distinct periods; the first period runs from 1982 to 1990, from the time when the first reports began appearing in the press, up until the moment that the films began to be re-released to the sell-through video market. Throughout this period, the video nasties are defined by their legal status and are constructed as a social pariah. This has a commercial value, but opportunities to capitalise on the video nasties themselves are limited. The second period runs from around 1990 to the present day and follows the formation of the sell-through market, the introduction of DVD and Blu-ray, and the move away from physical media altogether, toward media streaming services. Here, through the gradual legalisation of the films, the video nasties become a commercially viable and valuable commodity, and the expectations of these different formats began to reshape the market. As I will argue, while the idea of what a video nasty is was formed in the first period, it is in the second period that the idea becomes a cohesive brand, and it is here that the term begins to take on generic characteristics, even taking on more 'gentrified' and 'artistic' associations. I will explore these genrification and gentrification processes in more detail in later chapters, but in this chapter I now examine how the branding of the distributors associated with the video nasties changed over time and how ideas of their 'authenticity' have been negotiated and augmented by the expectations of digital formats, and the subsequent value that this authentic status comes to hold for the companies and the films themselves. This is important because in many cases, the branding of these distributors contradicts the assumptions of the sector and is often comparable to that of more mainstream distributors.

Branding of Video Companies in the Early 1980s: Logos, Idents and 8-bit Aesthetics

Despite the popular perception of the independent distributor in the early video era as a specialist in sex and horror, the majority of these video companies were not specialists at all. Rather, they were generalists, seeking to appeal to as broad a demographic as possible by carrying a diverse range of titles. It was not uncommon for a distributor's catalogue to include films designed to appeal to children or families (see Walker 2017), or the relatively new format of music videos, a range of mainstream genre staples like sports videos, action and adventure titles, as well as horror and softcore adult/erotica titles. In fact, aside from a handful of notable exceptions,[1] the concept of the specialist video label that was genre-specific and designed to appeal to, or that caters solely for, a particular market quarter was something that would not really emerge until the late 1980s when the sell-through markets were more fully established. In their study of early video markets, Heikki Hellman and Martti Soramäki suggest that often, 'large companies provide mass products for a mass audience or a wide range of products for different groups of customers, whereas a smaller firm may concentrate on a limited choice or few successful brands targeted for a specific customer segment' (1994: 30). However, while Hellman and Soramäki were keen to make a distinction between the practices based upon the size of these companies, Michael E. Porter suggests that generic strategies, such as 'differentiation'; creating uniquely desirable products and services, and 'Focus', offering a specialised service in a niche market, are not necessarily determined by the scale of the organisation (1980). As such, it appears, at least in the early years of the pre-certification video market in the United Kingdom, there were clear attempts by most companies, across the board and irrespective of size, to appeal to as broad a demographic as possible, though this is something that would change as the sell-through market for video became more established and the marketplace moved towards speciality labels.

American marketing consultant Phillip Kotler suggests that a brand consists of 'a name, term, sign, symbol or design or, alternatively, a combination of these which is intended to identify the goods and services of one seller or group of sellers and to differentiate them from those of competitors' (1991: 443). These individual elements are known as 'brand identities' and are collectively understood as 'the brand'. This is the result of the brand image, which is formed via brand associations by the consumer. The 'brand identities' employed by these early independents were not dissimilar to the 'brand identities' of any mainstream film, television or video company of the period; rather than utilise branding that emphasised particular genre tropes or genre-specific icons that might have limited their appeal, branding in the independent sector remained broad and designed to appeal to the masses. The emphasis is therefore on creating brand awareness so that any given brand can be distinguished from another, recognised for having particular traits, qualities and associations, but in order for that to happen, the brand needs to be understood, and the intended meanings need to be communicated to the consumer. This requires that the individual elements or brand identities remain consistent and work together to reinforce the central message of that brand. Unfortunately, these early video brands were often inconsistent, though that did not mean that they were not invested in creating a brand. Most attempted to instil a sense of quality in their branding practices and to create the sense of a trustworthy brand or the understanding that the product was the product of an official legitimate company. While this was accomplished in many different ways, it often relied on the reproduction of established icons or symbols. Thematically, for instance, many distributors, such as Go Video, VCL and VIPCO chose to incorporate illustrations of a map of the world or a globe into their promotions, obviously, to create the illusion of a global brand. While this is a minor point, it does suggest that these companies were, at least on some level, utilising coherent strategic communication and considering what and how they were communicating via their brand identity, rather than lazy chancers with little thought beyond the immediate shock value of their individual products. However, while the majority of these early companies were branded, in as much as they had a logo, name, term, sign, symbol or design, this was often the sum of their engagement and it could be argued that the simple incorporation of one of these elements does not necessarily constitute a brand.

Alongside attempts to create the illusion of a global presence, an 8-bit computer-generated neon aesthetic can be routinely observed across the idents of many of these early companies, such as Brent Walker, Cinehollywood and Inter Light Video, often employed in addition to the more traditional typographic emblems and symbols, such as monograms and logos. Many of the logos and idents reflect the fact that this was not only the dawn of home video but also of home computing and the home media revolution. Consequently, there is a visible sense of many distribution companies attempting to position themselves as future-facing with technology at their core. So, for instance, a common motif used by companies such as the Video Independent Productions Ltd (VIP) incorporates the horizontal line resolution of a television screen. This is mirrored in the logos and idents for Probe Video, RPTA Video and even the more established Rank Company, all of whom incorporate these lines into their branding. Moreover, the italicised logo of InterVision illustrates what appears to be an audio/visual waveform, and companies like Neon utilised the effect of neon tubing in their designs – all attempts to convey a definite sense of modernity and contemporary design that was further reiterated in the pulses and clicks of early synthesised soundtracks that score the idents.

While many companies chose to emphasise the modernity of the product, there were others that attempted to historicise video by emphasising video's rich lineage, usually by reinforcing the sense that this new technology was simply the latest iteration in a long line of established audio-visual technologies. For example, there are references to the nickelodeon movie theatres of the early twentieth century, to film reels (see the examination of VIPCO's visual identity later) and to celluloid film strips. There are even fanfares reminiscent of those used by 20th Century Fox throughout the studio era and beyond. This semiotic desire to capitalise on the associations with icons and motifs of established cinematic culture is particularly evident in the branding for the independent distributor Iver Film Services (henceforth IFS). Although perhaps latterly remembered in the UK as the distributor responsible for the controversial *The Texas Chainsaw Massacre* (1974) and the far less notorious video nasties *Night of the Bloody Apes* (1969) and *Night of the Demon* (1980), IFS was nevertheless quite reserved in its promotions. The company clearly strove to create the sense of an established 'film' company by capitalising on the fact that its offices were on the site of Pinewood Studios, enabling the company to bill themselves as 'The Professionals at Pinewood'. IFS sought to legitimise its brand even further by the incorporation of a golden statuette not dissimilar to the Academy of Motion Picture Arts and Sciences' OSCAR®, thereby incorporating the brand associations of the Academy into their own, and, therefore, imbuing their own products with a similar sense of quality. In a recent rebrand of the identity for the Academy, California-based design studio 180LA suggested that the OSCAR® itself had become a symbol of aspiration and excellence. The Oscars' brand associations suggested not only that the Academy was a leader in the film industry but also had a proud heritage associated with the conferment of cinematic excellence (Armin 2013: online). These are the very qualities that no doubt appealed to IFS when they sought to emulate them in their own promotions. At its most basic level, the OSCAR® image is that of an award. Consequently, in its association with the Academy's award, IFS implied that their catalogue was composed entirely of award-winning films and, in doing so, attempted to introduce a sense of legitimacy, quality and importance to its brand. While it may seem naïve to expect that an established icon like the OSCAR® could simply be mapped onto a different source and that its original meanings could be transferred to a different product, there is still a degree of sophistication in the recognition that the OSCAR® carried with it particular qualities or brand associations that could potentially be exploited by others; there does, however, seem to have been a lack of critical awareness that such an approach might equally be considered as an act of plagiarism, being not only a disingenuous practice but also an illegitimate one.

Given the desire to appeal to as broad a market as possible, the company that outwardly appeared to be the most marginal and genre-specific was, ironically, the company that had the most mainstream commercial success and that arguably had the most cultural impact: Palace Video (later Palace Pictures). Originally conceived by Nik Powell and Stephen Woolley, Palace was established as an imprint to release canonical art cinema, and they quickly developed an extensive range of videos in their home entertainment catalogue. Woolley has subsequently argued (see Gregory 2005) that the audience for video in the early days was not very sophisticated and that the company achieved only minimal success releasing films like *Aguirre, Wrath of God* (1972), *Mephisto* (1981) and *Fitzcarraldo* (1982), and that ultimately, this led the company to capitalise on the popularity of cult and horror films by investing in films like *The Evil Dead* (1982), *Plan 9 from Outer Space* (1958) and *Basket Case* (1981). It is this latter group of films that seems to have influenced Palace's early branding, as they developed an animated ident for their videos which features the silhouette of a spooky mountainside castle on a dark and stormy night. As lightning crashes around the castle, the silhouette is illuminated and neon lights edge the perimeter of the various towers and turrets, with the uppermost of those spelling out the name Palace Video Presents. This animated ident is without question the most accomplished, developed and extravagant of all of the early independent distributors. There is a definite sense of sophistication to the animation, imagery and graphics. Moreover, it is cine-literate; evocative of any number of classic Universal Pictures horror movies set in an old dark castle. This was used from 1981 until 1985 before the company rebranded itself in 1985.

However, and conversely, the branding also sent mixed messages about the product being sold and the affinity of the brand. There is relatively little here to suggest the company's more aspirational qualities and broader association with art cinema. For instance, Palace are perhaps latterly most known for their partnership with Channel 4 and with leading Irish art-house film director Neil Jordan, producing his films *The Company of Wolves* (1984), *Mona Lisa* (1986), *The Crying Game* (1992) (the latter nominated for the Academy Award for Best Picture) and *Interview with the Vampire* (1994). While the Palace ident does convey something of the aesthetic of low budget B-movies, an area for which they became associated, it does nothing to communicate the quality and importance of the company, in the way that the OSCAR icon did for IFS, and in that regard, does not really fully reflect the trajectory of the company as it progressed through the 1980s.

Branding Video Companies in the 1990s: A Comparative Analysis of Redemption, Tartan and VIPCO

Where the early distributors were generalists who tried to appeal to a broad demographic, the rise of sell-through market for video in the 1990s created specialist distributors that instead focused on specific markets, and that tended only to carry particular kinds of film. Horror film distribution in the UK during this period was dominated by three companies; Redemption Video, Tartan Video and VIPCO. Each was very different, although to varying degrees all carried video nasties as part of their catalogues. This section will consider the branding used by these three companies to promote video nasties, examining how this may have contributed to a collective understanding of the films and their post-1990s reworking into a distinct generic category in their own right, as well as being defined as a list of banned individual films.

Redemption Video was conceived as a specialist cult label in the early 1990s and although they only released one video nasty in their original series, *Killer Nun* (1979), they released numerous films that were peripherally related to the video nasties from directors such as Jess Franco, Jean Rollin, Dario Argento, Mario Bava, Bruno Mattei, Lucio Fulci, as well as releasing horror classics such as *Nosferatu* (1922), *Vampyr* (1932), *The Phantom Carriage* (1921), *M* (1931) and *The Cabinet of Dr. Caligari* (1920). The company was formed in the wake of Managing Director Nigel Wingrove's own censorship struggles with the BBFC over an eighteen-minute short film that he had written and directed entitled *Visions of Ecstasy* (1989). The film depicted Saint Teresa of Ávila, a sixteenth-century Spanish nun caressing the crucified body of Jesus Christ and culminated in a simulated sex scene. It was the last film to be refused a certificate by the BBFC on the grounds of blasphemy and the refusal led to a legal battle lasting seven years. The case took Wingrove to the European Court of Human Rights (Wingrove v. United Kingdom 1996), with Wingrove losing his home in the process. Wingrove claimed that the ban infringed his right to freedom of expression, but the court dismissed this claim on the grounds that his right did not supersede the criminal law of blasphemy in the UK. Despite receiving notable support from high profile figures, Wingrove was ultimately unsuccessful in his case. Had James Ferman left *Visions of Ecstasy* alone or had the Video Appeals Committee overruled his decision, Wingrove claims that it is unlikely that Redemption Films would have ever happened, with even the name 'Redemption Films' a conscious nod to the allegations of blasphemy in the BBFC's ban. Wingrove made it his mission to release what the company referred to as 'transgressive cult cinema' (as described on their website); however, given the contentious nature of its product and Wingrove's own personal investment in these censorship battles, Redemption could have capitalised on these struggles more visibly, perhaps making more of an asset out of the company's anti-censorship stance and its refusal to conform. Significantly, they chose not to brand themselves with this type of imagery and associations, opting for a more restrained strategy. There is often the expectation that exploitation be loud, crass and hyperbolic in its promotions. However, Redemption's branding remained subtle and invoking of abstract and artistic imagery in its approach, offering something more akin to middlebrow erotica, that stood in stark contrast to the video nasties' more common associations with pornography. This shift in aesthetic is therefore demonstrative of the shift in meaning that was beginning to take place, from a category of film associated with pornography, and therefore censorship, to a category of film associated with erotica, and therefore art. Employing only the limited colour palette of black, white and red, its design was built around Wingrove's own photography, which often featured his then partner Eileen Daly as a model. Wingrove had spent his early career as an art director and designer, and this imagery was an extension of this earlier design portfolio, which had featured work for fetish magazine *Skin Two*. The end result was a stylish and minimalistic brand design that prioritised graphic design, clear typography and stark black and white photography that incorporated this fetishistic imagery to great effect (Figure 6.1).

Figure 6.1 A selection of artwork used for Redemption's video releases.

While the imagery clearly appealed to Wingrove's own design sensibility, the final aesthetic was, more importantly, the result of an attempt to find a solution to an industrial problem. Redemption had a diverse catalogue that extended from early classics, such as *The Phantom Carriage* (1921), through to Jess Franco's sexploitation *Vampyros Lesbos* (1971) and Tinto Brass's Nazisploitation *Salon Kitty* (1976). These films not only originated from different periods and territories, but they had all been historically promoted in vastly contrasting ways, and with varying degrees of success. Redemption's remit was to emphasise high quality in its business model; they sourced the best quality negative of each film to ensure a good quality reproduction and they ensured that there was a consistency to the way each individual product was packaged based around the company's central identity rather than that of a singular film. Because the range of films was so diverse, it was not always possible to source original promotional materials or images of comparable high quality, making it difficult to maintain coherence across the full range of the entire catalogue. This problem led Wingrove to develop the company's signature style, producing a series of images that were often unrelated to the film being promoted but that nevertheless created a brand identity across the catalogue that defined (and continues to define) Redemption's output. Wingrove's decision to brand the company in this way created a striking visual vocabulary that defined the company's product. It established a sense of a cohesive and considered brand identity, which, because of the use of black and white art photography as the central medium reinforced the overall sense of quality that the company was striving for. In doing so, this aligned Redemption (and therefore the films in its catalogue) with an aesthetic commonly associated with distributors of world cinema and foreign-language film such as Artificial Eye. This in turn imbued the product with a value that moved away from their exploitation cinema origins and helped to reposition the films as important canonical works (something I will return to in more detail in the following chapter).

In Richard Stanley's somewhat premature 'Obituary for the Great British Horror Film', the author is quite dismissive of the output of Redemption Video (2002: 192). He argues that the company had simply taken 'films which had fallen into the public domain and . . . routinely tarted [them] up with saucy S&M-oriented covers', before going on to suggest that, 'being good little capitalists [Redemption Films] were just out to make a fast buck by recycling cheap product and flogging off creaky old warhorses that had already been playing the National Film Theatre and late-night television for decades' (2002: 192). However, with this polemic perspective, Stanley underplays the value that Redemption brought, often through the simple process of repackaging, re-classifying and re-releasing cult European horror films. Indeed, many of these, in spite of Stanley's claims, had never received a video release before. In *Sight and Sound* magazine, Richard Falcon argued that the process of re-releasing a film could provide 'an opportunity to reappraise' forgotten or marginal films, often applying an increased value to individual films, when positioned as part of a broader collection (1996). Redemption Films certainly illustrates this process (quoted in Egan 2007).

The restraint observed in Redemption's design extended to all aspects of the company's marketing strategy, and while the sleeves often featured eroticised fetishistic imagery, they were not usually gratuitous. Far from the 'carny-barkers' of old, Redemption's branding suggested a more nuanced approach that was far removed from the more hyperbolic ploys traditionally associated with exploitation cinema. In a retrospective history, the company's website suggests that,

> Redemption was a genuine ground-breaking film label which brought the works of Jess Franco, Jean Rollin, Dario Argento, Mario Bava, Bruno Mattei, Lucio Fulci, as well as numerous other films that had previously been banned as video nasties or that were just not available, to a wide mainstream audience. Redemption's highly distinctive black, white and red packaging became instantly recognizable on the shelves of retailers and Redemption's insistence on releasing films in their correct ratios, in their original language and, UK censors permitting, uncut, rapidly established Redemption's reputation among horror fans. Since its founding the Redemption label has gone through a variety of changes and challenges including having had more films banned by the BBFC than any other distributor (*Bare Behind Bars*, *The Sadist of Notre Dame*, *Sadomania*, *Love Camp 7*), launched in the United States, and generally striven to maintain its reputation and commitment to cutting edge and transgressive cult cinema.

If the prevailing sense of the marketing and promotion that surround the video nasties is one of hyperbole and extremity, Redemption definitely offered something that was subtler and more restrained, and that, despite incorporating erotic and fetishistic photography, helped to generate a sense of quality around the company and re-position the individual releases as being of similarly high quality or value. This is evident from the online description above, where company rhetoric foregrounds the concept of auteurs of exploitation above any mention of censorship or the notoriety of the video nasties. The emphasis on quality and authenticity is again reiterated in Redemption's insistence on releasing films in their correct ratios, in their original language and, 'UK censors permitting, uncut' (Salvation-films.com), which further demonstrates a shift in the perceived value of the cult film. Films that had traditionally been dismissed as having very little intrinsic value in the previous decade now had a chance to be repositioned and repackaged as 'arty', 'valuable' and 'high end'. Redemption's construction of itself as a company that was respectful of the films, recognising them as important canonical titles, is also revealing of a distinction between it and other companies such as VIPCO, a company that became the target of much criticism over the lack of attention to detail in the overall quality of its releases.

In Ken Gelder's introduction to lowbrow low-budget horror, he conflates Redemption's 'archival search for original, uncut, uncensored prints' with what he describes as 'the fannish interest in low-budget horror' (2000: 312). This dismissal seems to suggest that, for Gelder at least, Redemption's attempts to source and restore the best available print of any given film was tied to the fandom of company members rather than being indicative of any shifting sensibility in the marketplace that made it an industrial requirement. However, it could be argued that Redemption's continued efforts to source the best quality versions of these prints were indicative of Wingrove's recognition that his company needed to respond to the transformation in the marketplace that had occurred since the early days of video. This was no longer the early 1980s, and for Redemption to function effectively in this new marketplace it needed to capitalise on the growing sense of value that was increasingly being attributed to the cult film. It is perhaps telling that there is often no reference on the packaging to the fact that many of the films had previously been banned or censored, or even that they appeared uncut. The emphasis here is upon the quality of the presentation and the ways in which Redemption have constructed a sense of value around both its products and its company brand. It is possible that this could have appeared incongruous, given the overarching emphasis given to the overall quality of the brand, but it is important to acknowledge that this strategy seems to prevent the company capitalising on something that was so central in the promotional materials of many other companies, most notably VIPCO.

By way of contrast, VIPCO can be seen to engage in a bombastic flurry of hyperbolic promotion for its products, so it is probably not coincidental that they are the company that is most closely associated with video nasties. Established in 1979, they were one of the first UK-based video distributors, releasing a variety of different films into the marketplace. They are, however, retrospectively remembered as the notorious distributor that released more video nasties than any other, including *Andy Warhol's Frankenstein* (1973) *The Bogey Man* (1980), *The Driller Killer* (1979), *The Slayer* (1982) and *Zombie Flesh Eaters* (1979), alongside *Shogun Assassin*

(1980), *Nightbeast* (1982) and *The Nesting* (1981), films that were part of the Department of Public Prosecutions supplementary list of 'Section 3 video nasties'.[2]

The established narrative of the early video industry suggests that opportunistic distributors, having capitalised on the early 'video boom', then took the decision not to certificate their films when the industry became regulated. This is commonly believed to be due to a lack of financial resources and the belief that any potential for profit from their back catalogues had already been exhausted. This does seem feasible, especially given that the fee to certificate a film at that time was around £4.00 per minute of footage. For a distributor like VIPCO with a back catalogue of sixty-eight films and an average film length of ninety minutes, it would cost almost £25,000 to keep the company's back catalogue in circulation. Not surprisingly then, VIPCO, like many others, chose to step away from distribution. However, the common perception is that many of the companies were unable to shoulder the burden of these costs, when, in the case of VIPCO at least, this patently was not true. In fact, Michael Lee, VIPCO's managing director, took a costly detour to America to dip his toe into film production, financing and producing the film that would ultimately become *Spookies* (1986). The budget for the film was originally estimated at $250,000 but soon escalated to $300,000, with some estimates putting production costs as high as $500,000 (Evry 2014). When Lee returned to the UK, and in the absence of his own distribution company, he released *Spookies* through Stephen Woolley's Palace Premiere label. He began releasing films through the label Showchannel, before the wholesaler, Gold and Sons Limited, recognising the value that the old VIPCO brand might have in the modern marketplace, convinced him to sign an exclusive distribution deal.

Magazines such as *The Darkside – The Magazine of the Macabre and Fantastic* and *Video World* heralded the return of VIPCO in the early 1990s, with Allan Bryce playing an important role in repositioning the company in the new market, proclaiming the company as a 'legend' and a pioneer of the exploitation market (Bryce 1992). Under the banner of VIPCO's Cult Classics, the company initially released *The Deadly Spawn* (1983), *The Groove Tube* (1974), *The Bogey Man* (1980), *Spookies* (1986), *Zombie Flesh Eaters* (1979), *Shogun Assassin* (1980), *The Slayer* (1982), *King Frat* (1979), *Death Trap* (1976) and *Psychic Killer* (1975). These films were all from the company's own back catalogue and were films for which the company had presumably retained the distribution rights, although rumours persist that VIPCO often released films for which it did not hold the rights. To these titles the company added numerous other video nasties or related controversial horror films: films like *The Beyond* (1981), *City of the Living Dead* (1980), *The House by the Cemetery* (1981), *Night of the Bloody Apes* (1969), *Night of the Demon* (1980), *Cannibal Holocaust* (1980), *Cannibal Ferox* (1981). These were films that had not previously been distributed by VIPCO, but by releasing them in the 1990s, the company was able to align itself more explicitly with the video nasties.

Both the strategy and target market were clear and focused. The company was now overtly one which specialised in the re-release of canonical cult film. Where VIPCO's early branding was slight and somewhat inconsistent, the new branding created in the 1990s was focused, targeted, consistent and deliberately oppositional, setting out to appeal to the cult film market. Previously, VIPCO's branding had generally incorporated the company logo, a capsule-like shape that housed the stylised spools of a videocassette, inside which sit the letters V I P C and O. Occasionally, a rainbow band of colour was incorporated on the bottom right corner of some the video sleeves, but this only appeared intermittently. By the 1990s, when the company began specialising in cult and horror films, the branding was consistent and in keeping with the product that they were increasingly aligning themselves with. They maintained their original logo but this now acted as a marker of provenance and a celebration of video, something that would become increasingly important in the DVD market. All inconsistencies from the earlier branding disappeared, the rainbow stripe and global ident of their earlier iteration were all gone, replaced by a company identity that celebrated the illicit nature of the films, incorporating logos that screamed 'previously banned', and a more appropriate ident that incorporated clips from their films over a bloody red overlay.

Over the next few years, the company rewrote its own history, particularly through the imprints of VIPCO's 'Cult Classics', 'Vault of Horror' and 'Screamtime' collections, explicitly creating clear associations with the video nasties. Promotional flyers warned fans to 'buy them now before they ban them again!', suggesting, 'Yes VIPCO fans they want to throttle our label yet again, make sure you get your collection up to date – while you can!' Of course, by this point, there was no actual threat of the films being banned again. Rather, this constituted an explicit attempt to capitalise on the notoriety of the cultural cachet of the video nasties. Similarly, another flyer exploited the Orwellian parallels of the Video Recordings Act by exclaiming that 'in 1984 Big Brother wouldn't let you watch them! Now it's your decision!' In an interview for the *Darkside Magazine*, Michael Lee is referred to as 'a canny entrepreneur who spotted a gap in the market and filled it with zombie gut-crunchers and cannibal capers' (Slater 2002: 6), and this becomes a central theme in interviews with Mike Lee or about VIPCO. This helps to reinforce a proprietorial sensibility that became more and more important as the company developed. This is perhaps most evident in the name of their imprint, 'VIPCO's Vault of Horror'. The name is hugely significant, not only because it implies ownership over the video nasties, but also because it suggests that it was VIPCO that released all of these films originally, and in that regard was simply re-releasing films from its own vault.

Fundamental to this perception were promotional campaigns that sought to reinforce the illicit quality of the video nasties, an idea that can be traced back to the earlier incarnation of the company. Indeed, VIPCO can be seen to be one of the few companies that knowingly and visibly capitalised on the lack of legislation governing video prior to 1984. For instance, VIPCO knowingly released an uncut version of Lucio Fulci's *Zombie Flesh Eaters* in November 1981, less than a year after the film's original release on video by VIPCO in December 1980. In this case, the video cover remained unchanged, other than the application of a small red and white sticker on the front of the sleeve that read 'strong uncut version'. Lee later recalled the stunt:

> After selling thousands of copies, ten months later I decided that I wanted to put the cuts back in. Therefore, VIPCO released the 'Strong Uncut Version', put the price up, and sales rocketed like you've never seen before! Every cassette flew out the door and we couldn't keep up with demand. And every time we printed a batch of video sleeves – at a time we would print 5000–10,000 – a month later I would have to reorder more. (Slater 2002: 6)

These figures are difficult to verify, but it is clear that this strategy worked well for the company as it is something that they would go onto repeat many times. However, still constrained by the BBFC and unable to release strong uncut versions into the UK market, VIPCO released versions of a number of films bearing the 'strong uncut version' label to the European market. In the UK, VIPCO introduced the emblem of 'previously banned' as a way of emphasising the illicit quality of the films they were releasing. This stands in stark contrast to the approach adopted by Redemption; where Redemption highlighted the importance of the films in their catalogue, VIPCO actively traded on the illicit origins of the films and defined itself explicitly in those terms.

With the company still subject to the demands of the BBFC when certificating their films, their reliance on hyperbolic claims about the films would eventually lead to criticisms from fans feeling that VIPCO were beginning to misrepresent the nature of their releases. On the company's re-release of *Zombie Flesh Eaters* as part of the re-launch for the Cult Classics range, the company came under scrutiny when they, along with Allan Bryce of the *Darkside Magazine*, suggested that the release was the uncut version that had previously been banned under the Obscene Publications Act. The sleeve read:

> ADVISORY NOTICE
> 'Zombie Flesh Eaters' has been listed as a banned video and been unavailable since 1984. This is the original cinema version and has NOT been cut by the British Board of Film Classification for home video use. It is now passed as suitable for persons over the age of eighteen. However, some may still consider the content as unsuitable viewing material, and find certain scenes to be disturbing or offensive.
> IF IN DOUBT, DO NOT VIEW. VIPCO Ltd.

VIPCO was, however, somewhat economical with the truth of its advisory notice. *Zombie Flesh Eaters* was, of course, a previously banned video and had been unavailable in the UK since 1984. This was indeed the original cinema version – the version that had been certificated by the BBFC in January 1980 and widely exhibited theatrically. However, to receive the theatrical rating of an 'X' certificate, the BBFC had required cuts of one minute and forty-six seconds, and it was *this* theatrical version that VIPCO had released. This version had originally played in cinemas and after the initial cuts had required no further censorship by the BBFC for home entertainment release. This was also the original version that VIPCO had released on video before it had released the 'Strong Uncut Version' in 1981. Consequently, the company came under fire from fans, as did the *Darkside Magazine*, when it reiterated the claims of this being the uncut, unexpurgated version.

VIPCO's deception is all the more surprising when it is considered within the governing framework of the Video Packaging Review Committee (VPRC). Founded in 1987, the VPRC is a voluntary scheme of regulation designed to monitor the packaging used to promote video and, subsequently, DVD and Blu-ray. VIPCO was a member of the VPRC and thus governed by its general guidelines, which related to a various criteria, namely: legality (i.e., that the package conforms to the law and does not encourage illegal activity); decency (that packaging that was likely to cause serious or widespread offence was unlikely to be approved); honesty (that packaging must not exploit the credulity, lack of knowledge or inexperience of consumers, e.g., by leading the consumer to expect a product which is very different to the one being offered); truthfulness (that packaging must not mislead through inaccuracy, ambiguity, exaggeration, omission or otherwise); safety (that packaging must not condone or encourage unsafe practices); antisocial behaviour (that packaging must not condone or provoke violence or antisocial behaviour). Additionally, VPRC guidelines include areas to avoid, or at least treat with care: namely, sexual violence and threats of sexual violence, juxtaposition of nudity and violence, strong and realistic threats to defenceless victims, torture, excessive gore, details of strong violence, excessive blood (especially real), contemporary weapons, glamorisation of real, contemporary weapons, overt sexual activity (including clear suggestion of genital/anal sex, vulgar nudity, strong sexual references, text that promises brutality, torture, sexual violence or humiliation). These categories obviously present potentially huge problems for a company such as VIPCO, a company trading in films that were previously banned, that are contentious and are likely to dwell upon images of sex or violence. The ramifications of these restrictions on the packaging for a distributor releasing video nasties are clearly considerable.

Kate Egan has highlighted how the guidelines on the truthfulness of the packaging are almost contradictory in their message. They clearly state that 'claims made on packaging must be accurate and unambiguous' while adding a disclaimer that, 'certain licence is extended to copy where it is clear that the facts are being intentionally distorted by humour and exaggeration' (2007: 209). Egan has suggested that this disclaimer when applied to the promotion materials of the original video nasties positions them as 'blunt instruments, which, rather than being seen as a moral outrage or threat by the BBFC, the VPRC or the media, may now, in a contemporary British context, seem nothing more than harmless "exaggeration" or "humour"' (2007: 211). Although VIPCO's advisory notice was not highlighted as a particular issue by the VPRC, it does nevertheless represent a significant turning point in audience expectation regarding the representation of the video nasties in the marketplace. For instance, it could be argued with some degree of certainty that the VPRC's legislation governing 'exaggeration' and 'humour' has potentially limiting effects on the possibilities afforded to promotors that draw on the traditions of exploitation cinema. This is a market that was built upon exaggeration and humour and to restrict that is to misunderstand much of the promotional strategy of the exploitation film market.

However, it is significant that it was not the ruling of the committee that began to change the market so much as it was the response to tactics like this by the fans and the criticisms that began to appear over the inaccuracy of the description used for *Zombie Flesh Eaters*. VIPCO attracted further criticism over its practice of releasing unrelated films as sequels to successful releases. This was most apparent in the case of *Zombie Flesh Eaters 3*, a film which had previously circulated as the unrelated film *After*

Death (1989). This was a practice common in Italy, where many of these films originated. Indeed, the original *Zombie Flesh Eaters* was itself created as an Italian sequel to George Romero's *Zombies: Dawn of the Dead* (1978). In Italy, this practice would have been understood as *filone*, which, as Mikel Koven explains, literally translates as 'vein'. Koven places the word in the context of the phrases 'sullo stesso filone' (in the tradition of) or 'seguire il filone' (to follow in the tradition of), adding that the nearest English equivalent would be 'in the vein of' (2006: 5). However, and irrespective of how these films may have been understood in their native Italy, when they were promoted as unofficial sequels to unrelated films in the UK, they were not well received, evidenced by numerous reviews that describe them as 'a shameless cash-in', or in the case of *Zombie Flesh Eaters 3*, warn that 'they are now renaming even worse 80s Italian Zombie movies as unofficial sequels to the unofficial sequel. Don't be fooled by the title of this movie' (The Soft Machine Operator, 2002).

It is important to recognise something here that VIPCO did not. By the time they were releasing *Zombie Flesh Eaters 3* (1988), these films and their directors had become important, and this importance brought with it certain expectations about the way that these films could and should be presented. It is here that the hyperbole and hucksterism that typified earlier forms of exploitation, the video nasties included, becomes muddied. The ballyhoo, hype and showmanship that was integral to turn-of-the-century promotions was giving way to a more refined and deferential attitude toward the films. This gulf between the company and the fans became more pronounced on the introduction of DVD, with the format bringing with it the expectation that films should be digitally remastered, that they would include supplementary material, and that the distributors would care about the films as much as the fans. VIPCO's packaging boldly claimed that films had been digitally remastered, but this only led to further damage to the company's reputation when it was revealed that not only were many of their transfers in the incorrect aspect ratio, but that they were also displaying damage consistent with that of magnetic tape, suggesting that the DVDs had simply been copied from old VHS master tapes.

This period marks a significant turning point for the company but also for the presentation of the video nasties more generally, and this is something that can be seen across the market for cult and marginal cinema. The introduction of DVD had begun to reshape the marketplace, and the format had helped to influence audience expectation about the presentation of the product, with the platform providing an opportunity to repackage these films for a new generation of cineastes. Significantly, in the same period, mainstream commercial cinema was experiencing the re-appraisal of exploitation cinema through the work of Quentin Tarantino. His use of *Shogun Assassin* in the conclusion to *Kill Bill: Vol 2* (2004) allowed VIPCO to re-release the film again in a version exclusively for HMV. VIPCO had released the film originally in their pre-certification period, and then as part of their Cult Classics range in cut release for the British market and a 'Strong Uncut Version' for the international market. They released it again as part of the same imprint, this time as a widescreen presentation, and then they released it again in their Vaults of Horror imprint. However, in 2004 they released the film yet again, this time to capitalise on the success of *Kill Bill*. In the conclusion to *Kill Bill: Vol 2* the bride, played by Uma Thurman, can be seen watching *Shogun Assassin* with her child in bed before 'sleepy time', and before she confronts the eponymous Bill. VIPCO borrowed the distinctive red and yellow aesthetic of *Kill Bill*, and in case anyone was unsure, used the strapline 'the sleepy time film from *Kill Bill 2*'. According to Barrie Gold, this was the most successful release that VIPCO ever put out, and it was with a film that they had already released at least six times at that point. However, while the aesthetic was slicker and more polished, this piggy-backing on the success of another film reaches back to the exploitation tactics of old. The designed sensibility of Redemption marks the beginning of a shift and signals the beginning of a broader reappraisal that culminates with prestige releases of Arrow Video, and that is indebted to the expectations of the format. In the concluding section, I will look at the transition that the introduction of DVD afforded and will examine how this changed the marketplace for the video nasties.

Digital Nasties: Changing Meanings, Associations and Aesthetics

DVD was introduced to the UK market in the middle of 1998 with the first full year figures released by the BVA in early 2000. The uptake had been meteoric with sales reaching 4.1 million units in 1999, equating to an extraordinary growth of 5,000 per cent. David King, from the BVA's DVD Committee, attributed the monumental uptake in DVD to an increased awareness of the technology but also to the eagerly awaited release of *The Matrix* (1999) on DVD. This film was significant not only for its impressive sales figures (selling over 200,000 units in December alone) but because it was one of the first DVDs in the UK to fully embrace the possibilities afforded by the new platform by incorporating a range of innovative extras (Pearse 1999). However, while the addition of these supplementary features was unusual at this point, it would soon become the expectation, an expectation that would not be limited to new releases. For savvy distributors, this allowed them to reposition themselves and their product in the marketplace. As Robert Alan Brookey has observed, the inclusion of 'additional material on the DVD can be used as a very strategic marketing device . . . fram[ing] the film historically . . . as an important piece of . . . cinema' (2007: 199). It can function as a means of incentivising consumers to replace their existing collections and purchase films which they already own; the emphasis was placed upon the presentation of the product. The expectation was that the film was digitally re-mastered, presented in its original aspect ratio, with an importance placed on peripheral materials such as documentaries and directors' commentaries. These quickly became critical factors in the strategic campaign to persuade consumers to accept DVD.

For the video nasty, the transition from video to DVD was marked by the same expectations, transitioning films that had previously been understood as cinematic 'trash', and refashioning them into canonical cult cinema. But in the process, they would have to conform to all of the expectations governing the quality of any mainstream cinematic product. The original releases of the video nasties had been marked by scarcity, driven by the limited availability in the wake of censorship. This had contributed to the formation of communities of collectors, intent on finding all of the banned films. However, the apparent ubiquity of the DVD would seem to negate this impulse to collect, with distributors required to create an artificial sense that these films were sought after, as Barbara Klinger suggests:

> Forgotten, out-of-print, cult, exploitation, non-commercial, wide-screen, foreign, and other types of offerings that fall outside of the exhibition mainstream help to constitute the uncommon, sought-after media object, suggesting that the collector's trade has found a way to construct the categories of authenticity and rarity for mass-produced film artefacts. (2006: 67)

This would account for the adoption of versions that, especially in the case of the video nasties, might at first appear inauthentic. After all, this is a set of films that were defined explicitly by the medium of delivery – video – and a value that is reliant upon the scarcity of these original video versions. So the notion of video nasties on DVD might initially seem to be anachronistic. However, this is a contradiction that can only be resolved through an expanded notion of what constitutes the 'authentic object'. Unable to replicate the authenticity of the original videos, the parameters of what constitutes the authentic object must reconstructed, and in the case of DVD, this came to be based upon the capabilities, specificities and expectations of the medium itself. Arguably, the problematic releases of

VIPCO, complete with damage present on the original master tapes, represent the most authentic recreation of the original experience of video. It is a precise facsimile of the original cassette. However, what the shift to DVD reveals is the remediation that took place between the formats.

Raiford Guins observes similar remediation in the releases of Italian horror on DVD in the United States and frames this discussion in strictly binary terms. He argues that these films had historically been understood explicitly in terms of their dominant mode of distribution, home video, and suggests that the format of video itself had only served to reinforce the sense of a product that was deemed to be of low cultural value. He attributes this to a variety of factors including a lack of attention to detail paid to the packaging, poor translations used in the dubbing tracks, and crucially, an overall emphasis on extreme or gratuitous content in both fan discourse and promotional strategies. Because of this, Guins observes a binary between video and DVD, suggesting that video can be understood as a 'gore-object', whereas with DVD, he suggests, 'another set of discursive practices can be observed, which result in an elevation in the perceived value of the 'gore-object' into an 'art-object' (2005). This idea that the introduction of DVD functioned as a reparative process with specificities of the format itself emphasising the restorative capabilities of the medium is compelling. So too is Guins's suggestion that companies drew on a shift in fan discourse and repositioned a whole host of films as masterpieces of the genre by utilising an aesthetic usually reserved for 'worthy' directors. He observes:

> Whereas previously director's names may not have appeared at all, or received only marginal treatment on releases, titles on Anchor Bay and Image Entertainment correct this oversight. Directors like Bava and Argento are hailed as 'auteurs' and 'masters' of their respected works (which have also shifted from 'splatter' to 'horror,' a shift in semantics as well as a shift in value). (2005: 26)

Where earlier incarnations of Italian horror had been marked by their emphasis on 'gore' or 'splatter', DVD repaired and refashioned not only the product but also the vocabulary used to describe that product.

While Guins's study is explicitly in relation to the American marketplace and considers the refashioning of the *Giallo* on DVD, his distinction can be seen to have resonances with the British experience. Similar rhetoric can be seen around the video nasties, with a similar shift in semantics and therefore a similar shift in value. As useful as Guins's framework is as a starting point for discussing the British marketplace, it is also revealing of a significant discrepancy between the placement of products in the UK and US.[3] Although the reappraisals in the UK are similar to those observed by Guins in the US and seem to be driven by a similar expectation about the presentation of film on DVD, it is not the strict binary that Guins observes in the US market. This is most easily problematised through the presentation of the companies Redemption and VIPCO, companies that, as already established, had a very distinctive aesthetics and that both specialised in the release of canonical European and American horror on VHS, and later on DVD. Redemption's approach in particular challenges some of the distinctions observed by Guins in the US and suggests that such a clear demarcation is not as usefully applied to the British marketplace. While Guins is keen to make a distinction between the presentation of Italian horror on video and DVD, in the UK at least there is enough evidence to suggest that this reappraisal began in the early 1990s, long before the introduction of DVD, in the sell-through video market, most obviously seen in the marketing and branding strategies of Redemption, although it can also be seen in the reaction to some of the more deceptive practices employed in VIPCOs promotions.

As already demonstrated, VIPCOs approach had most in common with the traditional approaches of cinematic exploitation. It was typically hyperbolic, it was often humorous, and employed the language of exploitation cinema. In contrast, Redemption's approach can seem to be far more restrained. On a purely aesthetic level, the most obvious difference between the two companies lies in Redemption's characteristic black and white artistic aesthetic. The photograph, while commonplace in most promotions, is not an aesthetic that is typically associated with exploitation cinema, due no doubt to the perception that any depiction of the fantastic or horrific requires illustration to elevate through hyperbole while (as is often the case with horror and horrific imagery) simultaneously tempering the stark realities that a photograph might offer. There is also, however, a lingering sense of the photograph as an accurate representation of the 'real', a sense of captured immediacy that contributes to a collective sense that the image is not only not a construction, but that it is authentic. This same sensibility, by contrast, demarcates the illustration as an interpretation, mediated through the artist's hand. Exploitation cinema's affinity with illustration lies perhaps in its ability to depict spectacle without excessive cost or, indeed, excess. An ability to titillate and horrify in equal measure, often through suggestion, allowing it to remain less disturbing than a photograph. Even at its most explicit, a drawing remains a drawing.

Here, it is perhaps worth bearing in mind André Bazin's suggestion that both photography and cinema are objective representations and that photography satisfies our obsession with realism. He argues that 'no matter how skilful the painter, his work was always in fee to an inescapable subjectivity. The fact that a human hand intervened cast a shadow of doubt over the image' (1960: 5). It is this sense of an inescapable objective reality to the photographic image that informs Tom Gunning's work, employing the term 'truth-claim' to interrogate the nature of the 'reality' that is being represented (2004: 39). Yet, and as Susan Sontag argues, 'although there is a sense in which the camera does indeed capture reality, not just interpret it, photographs are as much an interpretation of the world as paintings and drawings are' (1977: 4). Despite the challenges to Bazin's claims, there nevertheless remains a pervasive sense of the photograph as an accurate presentation of reality, and something that is evident in VHS, DVD, and Blu-ray distribution of the cult film.

This sense of the authenticity of the photograph has been reinforced by almost four decades of film distributors continuing to align their product with a particular aesthetic, reinforcing a division that is most easily understood as reliance on either spectacle or narrative as a promotional tool. As already established, horror and genre films more generally have displayed a reliance on the use of spectacle in their promotions, primarily through illustrations that would highlight exciting film sequences and combine these with hyperbolic taglines to create effective campaigns. Conversely, distributors specialising in canonical or world cinema, films that would have typically been exhibited in art-house or specialist cinemas and seen as inherently valuable and worthy cinematic contributions, relied upon the narrative elements of their films and, as such, prioritised the photograph over the illustration to promote them.

This is first visible in the UK with the distribution company Tartan, a company that became successful by specialising in releasing canonical world cinema, such as the films of Bergman, Truffaut, Eisenstein and Godard. Tartan's releases were typically packaged in their signature minimalist white sleeves, which prioritised a single image on the cover. This image usually occupied less than half of the available space with the remainder given over to other graphical elements or simply to negative space. The still on the cover was usually a single frame taken from the film itself rather than a publicity still. These were often portraits and therefore emphasised the human, emotive aspects of the potentially character-driven narrative of any given film, thus avoiding an emphasis on the spectacle. Because of this, the overall feel was one of restraint. There is an understated quality to these releases that, by design, avoids exaggeration or embellishment in favour of simplicity. These are the opposite of the promotions seen with something like *I Spit on Your Grave*.

This same minimalism can also be observed in the releases of Artificial Eye, which again, released world cinema to a British marketplace, often in conjunction with the British Film Institute. These releases typically prioritise an orderly aesthetic consisting of the following components: distributor branding; film still; film title; film director; film review; film certificate; and, finally, the format of release. And while not specialising in the exploitation film, this is a practice of artistic elevation that begins on video and continues to DVD. These elements are common across various titles, typical of all releases regardless of their intended positioning in the marketplace. This places and reinforces the importance of each of the component parts or constitutive elements, which in turn contributes to the overall sense of these being an important product. Here, the photographic image remains central in the creation of a sense of value and, crucially, constructs an overall aesthetic that is reliant on narrative rather than spectacle.

This distinction remains largely consistent, with genre films typically prioritising spectacle through illustration and world cinema films usually prioritising narrative via photographic imagery. This was certainly the case until Redemption Video took the decision to brand the company through the use of photography. This not only complicates the idea that illustration is the domain of genre and that photography is the domain of world cinema, but it also collapses Raiford Guins's binary of VHS being the 'gore object' and DVD being the 'art-object'. This clearly demonstrates that the values traditionally associated with the horror film – and therefore horror film distribution – were beginning to be redefined in the 1990s.

Nathan Carroll suggests that reappraisals on DVD move beyond the simple restoration of the film print to a point in which 'the term operates through artificially restoring movie audiences' memories' (2005: 18). This, he claims, exposes an ontological crisis between the 'restoration rhetoric of digitization' and the 'sense of resurrecting the most authentic experience possible' (2005: 18). Carroll suggests that, in this regard, DVD involves a process of 'rearchiving the distribution of film memories under the predominant filing system' and, while the 'restoration rhetoric of digitization' observed by Carroll can be seen to reinforce Guins's claims that DVD ushered in a binarised market for exploitation (i.e., that of the 'gore-object' and 'art-object'), this binary begins to collapse when applied to the UK, and the distinct approaches of Redemption Video and VIPCO.

What is perhaps most important here is that even though this is the first period in which the distributors were capitalising on the video nasties as a bankable brand, they were doing so in conventional ways, creating consistent brand iconography and attempting to build brand associations. The inconsistencies of the early releases were gone and the new marketing strategies reimagined the films as part of a set and branded them accordingly, both as video nasties and as films in the catalogue of a particular distributor. However, distinctions were beginning to be made about the quality and care of the releases and the films were beginning to be reappraised, this in part because of the possibilities afforded by digital platforms. In the next chapter, I will continue to track the transition of the video nasties through the marketplace considering how the finite list of films became extended, taking on generic associations and how continued reappraisals have contributed to an altered sense of value within the product.

Notes

1. While this practice was not unknown it was fairly uncommon. Videomedia carried the imprint Vampix that released twenty-two horror films, while companies like Electric or Cal Vista specialised almost exclusively in adult titles.
2. These, while not prosecuted for obscenity, were still liable for seizure and destruction under a 'less obscene' charge. Like most independent distributors, VIPCO disappeared in the wake of the Video Recordings Act in 1984.
3. David Church argues that even in the US, the 'one-way flow of value' observed by Guins 'is an oversimplification of the video marketplace, especially since DVD is no longer considered a prestigious "new" technology' (2015: 15).

CHAPTER 7

'Previously Banned': Building a Commercial Category

Writing in 2007, Kate Egan observed that 'over time and in different contexts', the term 'video nasties' had been used to refer 'to a set of film titles, a specific set of video versions, a set of historical events and a personal consumption experience' (2007: 5). Here, Egan illustrates the inherent pluralism and mutability of the term, and while prior academic attention around the video nasties has largely prioritised the historical event, emphasising the moral panic, media effects, and censorship debates more generally, Egan's work shifts the conversation forward significantly by beginning to explore this history from a number of original and wide-ranging cultural perspectives, considering how the cultures of collecting and the personal consumptive practices that have grown out of the video nasties moment have altered what we mean by the term. Egan argues that 'in all these examples [. . .] the term "video nasty" remains constant, but what it refers to changes – focus is placed on different aspects of the videos, new objects, ideas and associations become attached or are detached from the category' (2007: 6), and these ideas begin to shape how we understand the category. Building on Egan's work, in this chapter I will explore how a general acceptance of what the term video nasty signifies has facilitated the phrase taking on generic implications, evolving beyond simple journalistic rhetoric and media moral panic into a commercially viable distributive category; a pseudo-genre into which films not historically thought of as being video nasties can be included and excluded as part of a discursive evolution and economic strategy. To accomplish this, this chapter will begin by situating the video nasties within a broader discussion of the horror genre, examining how the category relates to other notable subgenres and considering how debates surrounding genre formation more generally might contribute to our understanding of the video nasties as a genre in its own right. It will examine how the term has evolved discursively from a finite list of films into a broader functional industrial category and will consider the political implications and what is at stake when we choose to use word genre to describe a category of film as politically loaded as the video nasties.

Questions of Genre

Film genre is most simply defined as a film type: a category into which we can group films that share common tropes or attributes. How we determine those common attributes can be the subject of much debate, and for genre to function effectively and as it is intended it requires a degree of what Andrew Tudor has called a 'common cultural consensus' (1973: 139), in which a tacit agreement on what individual genres are collectively believed to consist of can be observed. Achieving this consensus can be complicated even further by the fact that not all genres are created or defined according to the same criteria. For instance, the Western, the war film, or the sci-fi film are genres that have traditionally been defined by their locale, and although other elements may be central to the narrative, more often than not it is the location that influences the designation above most other narrative considerations. Contrast this with what Linda Williams (drawing on the work of Carol J. Clover) has categorised as 'body genres': pornography, melodrama and horror, which become genres of film defined less by their location but rather by their ability to elicit an intense physical reaction – sexual arousal, tears and fear respectively (1991: 2). As if these very different conceptions of genre formation are not complicated enough, they can be complicated further when analyses move beyond stylistic, thematic or affective considerations to consider the role that the film industry itself plays in genre formation. Barry Keith Grant suggests that genre – but more specifically 'genre movies' – can be considered as an industrial category, 'commercial feature films which, through repetition and variation, tell familiar stories with familiar characters in familiar situations' (1986: ix). He suggests that in this way, genre has been instrumental in 'establishing the popular sense of cinema as a cultural and economic institution, particularly in the United States, where Hollywood studios early on adopted an industrial model based on mass production' (ibid.). Grant's perspective is mirrored in Franco Moretti's cartography of generic dispersion, 'Planet Hollywood', in which he argues that the taxonomy is not a scholastic construction, but rather it is 'a product of the film industry itself', designed to make 'it easier to recognize the film, and to buy the ticket' (2001: online).

Etymology aside, increasingly what might once have been understood as fixed textual categories drawn from rigid structuralist methodologies are now more likely to be understood as a series of complex discursive negotiations taking place between the audience and the industry. The earlier perception of genre as static and fixed categories has evolved to now acknowledge the evolution and formation of new categories as distinct sets or sub-sets of other genres; from Lars Von Trier's Digressionism (Romney 2014), to the non-representational films of the absolute film movement of the 1920s (Elder 2007), to the aesthetics of the neo-noir, or the hyperbole of the mockbuster (Calboli 2014). The development of these additional categories demonstrates a negotiation indicative of what Rick Altman has called 'the questions of permanence and coherence' that emphasise 'generic fixity', and a shift toward more a nuanced debate indicative of a 'user-oriented approach' to genre formation (1998: 2). It is through this 'user-oriented approach' to genre formation that I wish to examine the evolution of the video nasties, considering how, where and by whom the terminology has been used, as a means of reviewing how imposed cultural category has evolved to take on generic connotations.

In a discussion of the changeable boundaries of the horror genre, Brigid Cherry argues that we should not think of horror as one genre, but instead suggests that it is perhaps better considered 'as a collection of related, but often very different, categories' (2009: 3). Initially, she divides these categories up conceptually (drawing on the works of Steve Neale (2000) and Rick Altman), suggesting that subgenres, cycles and styles must all be considered as subcategories around which horror is used as 'an umbrella term encompassing several different sub-categories, all united by their capacity to horrify' (2009: 4). Cherry offers a selection of the subgenres available, and, in a list which – by her own admission – is not exhaustive, she still includes an entry for the video nasties which she groups with 'exploitation cinema' and 'explicitly violent films'. Cherry defines this subgenre as 'films focussed on extreme or taboo subjects, including violence and torture, as well as other controversial subject matter such as Nazi death camps, rape and other sexual assaults on women' (2009: 6). As examples, she cites the video nasties *I Spit on Your Grave* (1978), and *Last House on the Left* (1972) alongside other films which, while not typically thought of as belonging to or associated with the video nasties, share commonalities in their focus on the extreme or the taboo. Here, Cherry includes *Henry: Portrait of a Serial Killer* (1986), *Man Bites Dog* (1992), *Hostel* (2005), *Saw* (2004), *Audition* (1999), *Ichi the Killer* (2001), *The Devil's Rejects* (2005) and *Irréversible* (2002); all are listed as examples of a pluralistic sub-category (specifically named as Exploitation Cinema, Video Nasties and other forms of explicitly violent films) that sits alongside more traditional and established subgenres such as the Gothic, supernatural, occult and ghost films, psychological horror, monster movies, slashers, or the more extreme delineation of body horror, splatter and gore films (including postmodern zombies). Cherry's decision to include the video nasties as a subgenre in their own right is significant for two reasons: firstly, because the grouping of the video nasties with other forms of extreme exploitation cinema demonstrates the ways in which the term has evolved beyond its origins as a finite category, illustrating that for many, it is no longer limited to the films contained on a prescriptive list drawn up over thirty years ago; and secondly, that crucially, this evolution has been made possible by the terminology passing into everyday language as a synonym for 'extremity'.

In his essay on the evolution of the horror genre, David J. Russell suggests that 'despite the easy recognition and popularity of modern horror movies with audiences and critics, the exact boundaries of their collective definition as a genre have become increasingly difficult to discern' (1998: 233). Reflecting this in the broader public sphere, in 2010, Horroronscreen.com attempted to map the generic landscape, and suggested that all subgenres are derived from four main horror branches; 'Killers', 'Monsters', 'Paranormal' and 'Psychological horror' (Admin 2013: online). Into this 'Zombies', is presented as a sub-set of the 'Monsters' category, and 'Gore and Disturbing' is presented as a genre in its own right, with the suggestion that these categories 'are so popular that they can be considered as *proper* genres' [my emphasis] (2010). The website details a variety of subgenres including one named 'Small Creatures', which the creators of Horroronscreen.com suggest is another subgenre of the 'Monsters' category and into which films like *Critters* (1986) and *Gremlins* (1984) should be placed. Similarly, 'Torture' becomes a sub-set of 'Gore and Disturbing', into which films like *Hostel* (2005) or *Saw* (2004) are placed. Films are carefully grouped on Horroronscreen.com based upon shared formal, thematic and structural features. Significantly, the list does not follow Williams's concept of body horror, suggesting instead that body horrors are those films which centre 'on the human body, but instead usually involve body transformation, deformation and/or destruction', including *An American Werewolf in London* (1981), *The Fly* (1986), *Society* (1989) and *Cabin Fever* (2002) as notable examples. Alongside this, teen horror is dismissed as not distinctive enough to constitute a genre in its own right, with the suggestion that a film like *Fright Night* (1985) be considered a vampire film first and foremost.

What is perhaps most significant is the website's dismissal of productive or distributive categories, and because of that, its exclusion of otherwise well-recognised subgenres. There is no place for Asian horror with the suggestion that there should not 'be a genre for each country/continent'. There is also no place for found-footage horror, which is described as 'not really a genre, but a way of shooting', and instead, the emphasis on genre identification here is through shared textual commonalities. Horrorscreen.com's approach does not acknowledge either the formation of *newly* created sub-sets that arise from specific productive or distributive contexts. For instance, in recent years a number of new categories have entered the popular lexicon; most notably, the French Extremity, J-Horror and torture porn. The 'New French Extremity' was a term coined by *Artforum* critic James Quandt to describe a series of transgressive films created by French directors in the early part of the twenty-first century (2004), while J-Horror (an abbreviation of Japanese Horror) was primarily created by the distribution strategy of the British distribution company Tartan Palisades and its series Tartan Asia Extreme in the early 1990s and 2000s. 'Torture porn', meanwhile, originated as a reductive term coined by journalist David Edelstein in New York Magazine to describe movies that he suggested were so 'viciously nihilistic that the only point seems to be to force you to suspend moral judgments altogether' (2006). Although not explicitly describing the type of narrative or necessarily communicating very much beyond an expectation of either a cultural stereotype or the affective 'type' of film, these categories can nevertheless be seen to function discursively as subgenres under the broader umbrella of horror. For Horroronscreen.com, genre remains a category that communicates shared formal, thematic and structural features; however, this fails to acknowledge the fluidity and debates that persist around genre and genre formation, something which is evident in the video nasties.

The way in which video nasties have come to be perceived as a subgenre in their own right was, as Kate Egan observes, less to do with 'shared formal, thematic and/or structural features' than it was a specific set of 'historical and political circumstances' (2007: 3). Drawing on the work of Rick Altman, Egan challenges scholars to move beyond the limited view of the video nasties and to reconsider the category as a user-oriented discursively constructed genre instead. Here, Egan suggests that what emerged was 'a situation where a mishmash of films with different production contexts, and released chronologically in their native countries, are all released, at once, in a historical vacuum on the British video market' (2007: 51). However, this idea was met with some resistance, most notably from Julian Petley, who preferred that the term be used to refer to a cultural category rather than an explicit genre. Petley argued that it was only the more lurid of these which came to be tagged by the press and the moral entrepreneurs as 'video nasties' and felt that this was 'hardly a basis for treating this as constituting a genre' (2007). For Petley, the video nasties remain a resolutely political – not generic – category; a category of film that was governmentally imposed and that continued to function as a stark reminder of the censorship that the category ushered in. Petley contextualises his argument within the contemporary climate, citing BBFC figures for 2007, and writing that during that period the BBFC 'cut 206 of the 950 videos which were passed at 18', equating to 21.68 per cent of the total number submitted for classification. From this, he quite rightly argues that the Video Recordings Act 'continues to exert a malign and oppressive infuence on British film culture' (Petley 2007: 331). While Egan's book attempts to document the changing meanings of the video nasties, Petley's review demonstrates what is at risk should we forget how the category was originally formed; however, in the twelve years since Petley's review it has become increasingly difficult to ignore the evolutionary processes that have taken place, and increasingly important to recognise that for different groups of people and in different contexts, not only can these two definitions exist side by side, but that both *do* exist, and to acknowledge one does not necessarily invalidate the other.

While not as burdened with political baggage as the video nasties, the genre of the 'melodrama' has been the subject of similar debate, with Rick Altman's examination of the application of the label revealing similar dualism. Altman's definition was written in response to a polemical article by Steve Neale, in which Neale had argued for a fixed meaning and a collective acceptance that the current use of the term 'melodrama' did not accurately reflect the original uses of the category, and that film scholars had been incorrectly labelling romantic dramas and weepies as melodrama. Neale argued that the films originally categorised as constituting a melodrama by film scholars in the 1970s and 1980s had more in common with what Hollywood critics, journalists and publicists understood and designated as action and suspense-based genres in the 1930s, 1940s and 1950s, and that this was therefore how the term should be considered and employed. In response, however, Altman argued that the features Neale had highlighted were merely temporary designations and that since genres grow and evolve, it is not only possible but also crucial for alternative meanings to co-exist without one disavowing the other through a process Altman called 'genrification' (1998: 54).

Genrification, according to Altman, occurs over time and, in the right contexts, when the categories used to describe cycles of film (invariably using adjectives) mutate into fixed textual categories (i.e., nouns). Altman argued that this could (and, indeed, would) give rise to the formation of new genres. As examples of this, he cited comedy, melodrama and epic, since these are genres that have all evolved, all having their roots in descriptive terms for the 'type' of content/experience audiences might expect to receive but eventually becoming fixed/named categories that denote other narrative and stylistic features. A similar evolution can be observed in the application of the term video nasty. This was originally invoked as an adjective, a descriptive journalistic term applied by moralists and the most censorious elements of the British media that was used specifically to denote a series of unrelated films that were deemed to be too excessive for public consumption. However, over time and in specific contexts, the designation has evolved to incorporate expanded meanings that, as we have seen with Cherry's application, can include all forms of taboo and extreme film. This builds upon Egan's suggestion of a finite genre and expands the category, which, as I will discuss, moves the video nasties further away from their origins and is largely a result of attempts to capitalise on the video nasties as a coherent brand.

When discussing the applicability of genre to the video nasties, it is worth acknowledging that its deployment as a functional category can be separated out into two distinct areas, both of which are defined by the legal status of the films themselves and the manner in which these films have been made available, and that this can be reduced to a distinction between circulation and distribution. In *Spreadable Media: Creating Value and Meaning in a Networked Culture* (2013), Henry Jenkins, Sam Ford and Joshua Green suggest that although media conglomerates may often cite 'circulation' figures, 'such circulation is concerned with making audience members into receptacles for mass-produced and mass-distributed content' (2013: 1). Here, the term circulation refers explicitly to the movement of media content that 'is largely – or totally – controlled by the commercial interests producing and selling it', and this leads Jenkins et al. to conclude that this approach is indicative of a model of *distribution* rather than *circulation*. Instead, they argue that circulation should be considered to be a more complicated endeavour, and effectively the result of participatory culture which reconfigures the consumer as an active agent in the process, that is fundamental in the 'shaping, sharing, reframing, and remixing media content in ways which might not have been previously imagined' (2013: 1). Although this distinction in this context is largely the result of the interactive opportunities provided through technological advances like Web 2.0, it is with the idea of media being shaped, shared, reframed and remixed through the institutions of production, distribution, exhibition and consumption that resonate with the way in which participatory cultures have continued to shape the collective understanding of what constitutes a video nasty.

In their original form on video, be that on VHS, Betamax or V2000, the video nasties were only ever officially available for a short time. By the time the campaign had reached its peak retailers and wholesalers were fearful about what films they could legally stock and Kim Newman bravely took the decision to publish what had up until that point been a private police document – the list of films that were being categorised as video nasties in the *Monthly Film Bulletin* (1984: 353–4). By then, it was no longer possible for distributors to safely and legally profit on the back of the genre, so the official distribution channels disappeared. But this did not mean that the market disappeared; the moral panic had ensured that there was a demand for these films so the market moved underground and the films circulated illegally for many years. Henry Jenkins has argued elsewhere that 'fandom generates its own genres, developing alternate institutions of production, distribution, exhibition, and consumption' (1992: 270), and in many ways the video nasties epitomise a genre that has evolved from the fandoms that surround it. These fandoms took the video nasties and repurposed a journalistic headline and reworked it into a functional commercial category. Initially, this was through home-produced fanzines, but these fanzines grew into glossy publications from publishing houses like FAB Press. Once attitudes around these films had relaxed sufficiently to allow the films to be released officially in the British marketplace again, then a second period of official distribution began, initially on video, and then on DVD and Blu-ray. Within these different periods, the meaning of the video nasties is not static. It changes, undergoing augmentations that see the category shift from a discursively constructed genre into an industrially adopted commercial genre.

Video Nasties as a Discursively Constructed Genre

To effectively discuss how the institutions of 'production, distribution, exhibition, and consumption' highlighted by Jenkins may have contributed to an increased sense of the video nasties as a distinct genre in and of itself, it is first necessary to consider how these institutions may differ across the differing contexts of circulation and distribution. Only then is it possible to assess the role that these institutions may have played in extending and reinforcing the notion of the video nasties as a genre. Almost any horror fan who is old enough to have lived through the 1980s and 1990s in Great Britain will have some recollection of the video nasties. They will likely have a story related to their own engagement with a particular film, whether that relates to their own affective responses to that specific film, or often about how they first accessed these films. By the time I was old enough to be fully aware of the video nasties, the films were already conspicuous in their absence and had already begun to take on a mythic quality. If you wanted to see them all, then their legal status demanded commitment and persistence in circumventing the law to be able to find and access them through illegitimate means and subcultural communities.

Traditionally, histories of the video nasties have been primarily concerned with issues of censorship, and as such, they often concluded with the introduction and implementation of the Video Recordings Act (VRA) in 1985. However, while the introduction of the VRA may have stalled the official distribution channels of the video nasties, it did very little to prevent the continued circulation of these films through complex illegal underground networks. In 1992, ten years after the video nasties were first mentioned in the tabloid press, Trading Standards officers conducted nine raids across Liverpool, Leicester, Cardiff, Redruth, Solihull, Kettering and Rochester (Connett 1992: 6). The officers had posed as video dealers in order to infiltrate a lucrative black market dealing in illegal videocassettes, passing everything they had learned to Interpol in a vast international operation. Liverpool's chief trading standards officer, Peter Mawdsley, suggested that 'an underground network of dealers was involved' and that their intelligence had revealed that the industry operated mainly through correspondence and a sophisticated network in which these videos could change hands for up to £100. Trading Standards were convinced that the revelations about the ring would lead to the prosecution of a seedy underbelly profiteering from the sale of real snuff films, but in reality, the films that the Trading Standards officers confiscated were already known to the Home Office, having found notoriety as video nasties almost a decade earlier.

What Trading Standards had actually uncovered was the domestic end of a sophisticated network that had been developed largely to facilitate in the circulation of the video nasties. In the absence of official channels, horror fans had developed strategies and networks through which these films would circulate, often importing the films illegitimately, duplicating them illegally, swapping them through classified advertisements and passing them from person to person at film fairs. Accounts of engagement in these networks are commonplace and can be found on web forums such as the Pre-cert Forum (http://www.pre-cert.co.uk), in documentaries such as *The Video Nasties: The Definitive Guide*, and in academic work on the fan cultures that surround the video nasties, such as Egan's *Trash or Treasure* (2007).

However, while the narrative of activities within these networks is well documented, what are less well considered are the ways in which these underground networks may have contributed to an expanded notion of genre around the video nasties. In her work on cult cinema mail-order catalogues, Joan Hawkins observes that in that context, the traditional notions of what might constitute genre were often dispensed with in favour of listings that prioritised the affective response that audiences might be expected to experience from their engagement with the films (2000: 4). As examples of this, she cites instances where films that would conventionally be understood as European art cinema – such as Jean Luc Godard's *Weekend* (1968) or *Alphaville* (1965) or Pier Paolo Pasolini's *Salò* (1975) – are sandwiched between the video nasty *The Werewolf and the Yeti* (1975) or *Cannibal Holocaust* director Rugerro Deodato's *The Washing Machine* (1993). Hawkins argues that the descriptions used to define these examples of art cinema often relied on a kind of rhetoric that 'film historians would take great pains to avoid' (2000: 4). Citing Pasolini's *Salò* as a notable example of this, she records that the film is presented in the *Encyclopaedia of European Cinema* as one that links 'fascism and sadism, sexual violence [*sic*] and oppression', while the fanzine listing 'simply notes that the "film left people gagging"' (2000: 4). Drawing on definitions around body genres, Hawkins illustrates that 'the operative criterion here is *affect*: the ability of a film to thrill, frighten, gross-out, arouse, or otherwise directly engage the spectator's body' (2000: 4), observing that this is given priority over any other textual considerations. She cites examples of German Expressionist cinema such as *Nosferatu* (1922), of New York's avant-garde such as *Andy Warhol's Frankenstein* (1973), along with pre-code era oddities such as Tod Browning's *Freaks* (1932) and experimental surrealist classics such as Luis Buñuel's *Un Chien Andalou* (1929), as well as notable examples in the European auteur cinema tradition such as Polanski's *Repulsion* (1965), all of which rub shoulders in catalogues more broadly devoted to horror. In so doing, Hawkins's work suggests a democratisation of genre and a levelling of cultural hierarchies to such a degree that notable examples of art cinema mix indiscriminately with work arising from what might historically have been considered as low cinematic genres, each film being reclassified according to its affective capability.

While not discussing the video nasties directly, Hawkins's notion of an affective category is fundamental in the understanding of how early formations of the video nasties evolved and transformed the category into a functional genre. In their first incarnation, the video nasties are a finite set of films that were deemed to be of low cultural value and that were grouped together based upon the furore that surrounded them and a perceived collective aesthetic of excess. The fact that these films were banned and removed from the shelves only served to reinforce these ideas, with the added demarcation of 'nasty' only further emphasising a sense of the affective response one might expect to experience if one were to engage with these films directly. Over time, the category grew organically, evolving to incorporate films that would not have traditionally been classified as video nasties but were seen to be similarly transgressive, horrific or affective. Fanzines like *Flesh and Blood*, *Eyeball*, *Headcheese and Chainsaws* and *Samhain* were all instrumental here, performing a curatorial role that grouped films together on their ability to shock and/or offend and revealed the video nasties to be the most visible face of a longer tradition of cinematic exploitation (Figure 7.1).

However, even the finite set of films is not as stable as it might at first appear. Earlier iterations of the DPP's list famously included films like *The Exorcist* (1973) or *The Texas Chainsaw Massacre* (1974), while lesser known and far less notorious films like *Cataclysm* (1980) or *Mausoleum* (1983) made their way on and off the lists at various times. The lack of clarity about what might constitute a video nasty reached ludicrous levels when raids in the early 1980s confiscated *The Best Little Whorehouse in Texas* (1982), a major-studio comedy with major stars that was based upon a big Broadway musical, and *The Big Red One* (1980), Samuel Fuller's celebrated epic Second World War drama based on his own experiences during the war. While *The Best Little Whorehouse in Texas* could hardly be considered a video nasty, the fact that it was seized in raids gives it more right to carry the moniker than many other films currently considered as 'legitimate' parts of that body of texts. However, the fact that the film is comedy destabilises any likelihood of finding a shared formal, thematic and/or structural feature within the films.

Moreover, in recent years, a third list of supplementary titles has surfaced with what has become known as 'Section 3' titles; eighty-two films that the DPP believed could be prosecuted under the lesser charge of Section 3 of the Obscene Publication Act (see Appendix IV). In practice, this meant that a magistrate could order the confiscation and destruction of a film if it was deemed unlikely that it would achieve a conviction at the High Court. While purists might not accept the additional eighty-two titles as legitimate video nasties, increasingly, there are many collectors who are choosing to incorporate these films into a broader list of films that have been seized by the police or banned by the BBFC but not typically classed as video nasties. Here, films such as *Maniac* (1980), *Mother's Day* (1980), *The New York Ripper* (1982), *Straw Dogs* (1971),

Figure 7.1 Vincent Damien (V. D.) O'Nasty, *Viz*.

Basket Case (1982), *Blood for Dracula* (1974), *City of the Living Dead* (1980), *Macabre* (1980), *Madman* (1981), *Night of the Seagulls* (1975) and *Terror Express* (1980), even other withdrawn or controversial films such as Kubrick's *A Clockwork Orange* (1971), *The Exorcist* (1973) and

Scum (1979), have all become collectibles, often as a result of their association with video nasties.

While there are some who would argue for terminological precision, what these various additions suggest is that the term video nasty is permeable and is not as prescriptively defined as was once thought. Moreover, its function simply as a synonym for any film that presented extreme filmic violence is visible as early as 1991, as evidenced in *Viz* magazine's comic strip about cineaste serial killer Vincent Damien – (V. D.) – O'Nasty from that year (Figure 7.2) (Donald 1991). V. D. O'Nasty's habit of watching and mimicking 'gratuitously violent videos' makes reference to three films: *The Texas Chainsaw Massacre* (1974), *Alien* (1979) and *Psycho II* (1983). As already discussed, *The Texas Chainsaw Massacre* overlapped with the video nasties list as a Section 3 'nasty' and effectively as the poster child for the whole campaign; however, the latter two, while certainly of the right era, would never have been considered video nasties.

What this demonstrates is that even in the early 1990s, the complication of the distinct label of video nasty had begun, and from this point on it became increasingly difficult to discern the borders of the category and determine which films should be deemed as appropriate to qualify for inclusion. Another issue that compounds the definitive nature of the category is the fact that there was a second video nasties scare – again in the early 1990s – which followed in the wake of the murder of the Liverpool toddler James Bulger by two pre-teen children who, the press reported, had had access to 'extreme horror films' like *Child's Play 3* (1991). It culminated in a campaign spearheaded by *The Sun* that cried 'for the sake of all our kids ... burn your video nasty' (Author unknown 1993: 1). While this panic took place a decade later, completists could theoretically append to the original list the additional titles that were targeted during this second wave press campaign of moral panic, theoretically leading to the potential inclusion of films such as *Child's Play 3*, *Dolly Dearest* (1991) and *Pet Semetary* (1989) that were all presented as examples of problematic horror in the tabloids. However, perhaps more important than trying to isolate which specific films might warrant inclusion in an expanded notion of the video nasties is the question of why other films might warrant inclusion in the first place.

The various video nasty lists group together films based on their perception as transgressive films; it is this that marks them out as *extreme* examples of a genre that is already defined by its ability to horrify (per Brigid Cherry's list). Implicit in this demarcation as 'extreme' is a suggestion of difference from a more palatable and socially acceptable mainstream – even in terms of horror cinema. This is something that can be

Figure 7.2 *Headcheese and Chainsaws* Fanzine.

seen frequently throughout the original video nasties campaign, where the video nasties are othered against the output of the more socially acceptable face of horror. Graham Bright argued that 'All too many people believe that a nasty is something like a hotted-up Hammer movie. It isn't, it is something entirely different' (*The Times*, 2 November 1983; Petley 2011: 46). These judgements served to reinforce a sense of the video nasties as inherently oppositional objects. It is not uncommon for films that fall outside of the mainstream to be celebrated as inherently political texts anyway, if for no other reason than for their believed distance from the institutions and industry of mainstream film production. These perspectives often imagine cult fandoms (which can, and often do, construct identities around horror texts of all kinds, including the 'nasties') as somehow separate from, and outside of, mainstream consumer practice. In *Fan Cultures* (2002), Matt Hills observes that there is 'an expressed hostility within cult fandoms towards commercialisation and commodification' and that this has created a tendency to theorise fan practices as 'somehow anti-consumerist' (2002: 28). This idea of cult consumption as being inherently oppositional undoubtedly has its origins in the dominant perception of the films themselves as inherently oppositional, and of an industry that pitches an amorphous imagined marginal industry against an equally amorphous imagined mainstream. This, in turn, reinforces a sense of the cult object as separate from and resistant to commercialisation and commodification. At a purely thematic level, Mark Jancovich, Antonio Lázaro Reboll, Julian Stringer and Andy Willis have challenged an inherently oppositional reading of the cult movie, suggesting that while 'some fans clearly revere specific films as works of true artistic and political independence, in which the distinction from the mainstream is directly associated with political and/or cultural non-conformity, other fans view the films they celebrate with a patronising affection or even downright contempt' (2003: 2). Nevertheless, the notion of resistance continues to play a fundamental role in the construction of cult fandoms, especially those informed by censorship debates, which as Hills has argued elsewhere, is often the engine that drives horror fandom, with fans opposing the very forces that help create their subcultural capital (2005: 98). However, this does not remove these practices from conventional consumption, with Hills's work problematising the construction of a fan identity that is explicitly at odds with more traditional consumer identities, instead of arguing that this resistance is representative of a dualism between both identities that cannot be resolved.

Issues such as these are only compounded further when we apply these ideas about the cult film directly to the video nasties. Because of their legal status, there is a temptation to imagine the video nasties as somehow existing outside of the traditional understandings of commercialisation and commodification. Because of their legal status and the ways in which they have circulated, there is a temptation to imagine the video nasties as somehow existing outside of the traditional understandings of commercialisation and commodification, and therefore to imagine that they are therefore indicative of anti-consumerist practice. Here, the video nasties are not only discursively constructed as being *thematically* different from the mainstream, in line with Jancovich et al.'s observations on the cult film, but they are also discursively constructed as being *economically* different from the mainstream, somehow existing outside of mainstream practices of consumption. The inability to access these films via official channels for many years has undoubtedly contributed to a sense that the video nasties are inherently anti-consumerist *cult texts*, but it is important to acknowledge that many cult film fandoms construct themselves as marginal or authentic, be this in their resistance to popular tastes or in their perceived difference from mass-produced commodities and mainstream commercial products. This is a dialectic that seeks to construct value based upon the perceived difference from, and relationship to, the mainstream, and in the case of the video nasties, as with cult film more generally, as constructed objects that have become 'celebrated as symbols of political and/or cultural non-conformity' because of their extremity, marginality and legal status (Jancovich et al. 2003: 2). However, and as I will demonstrate, the development of the video nasties as a functional genre has been significantly aided by the contemporary industry and by the processes of commodification that continue to surround the category.

An Industrially Reinforced Genre

Rick Altman has suggested that 'most generic labels carry sufficient prestige that they are retained for the designation of newly formed genres' (1998: 34), an assertion that is supported by the endurance and adoption of the label 'video nasties' as a generic term in the broader public sphere. The most obvious example of this is the listing in the Oxford English Dictionary that defines the video nasty as a colloquial term used to denote 'an explicitly horrific or pornographic video film', demonstrating neatly how the category has moved from journalistic or legislative rhetoric and into a generic category. Use of the term in this way reinforces the notional sense of extremity that has become indelibly associated with the category and illustrates how this is often at the expense of any specific historical or socio-political context. If this is reflective of Tudor's 'common cultural consensus', then, and as already demonstrated, the popular understanding of what a video nasty consists of has evolved, transforming the finite list into an expansive all-purpose category of excess or extremity. Because of the haphazard way in which the video nasties list was formed there was always some debate about whether controversial films like *The Exorcist* and *The Texas Chainsaw Massacre* should be included in any final list of the video nasties. However, while these anomalies are well-rehearsed aspects of the debate surrounding the video nasties, where the borders of the category really begin to shift are in the books from the late 1990s that detail the history of the video nasties and that present them as simply the most visible face of a long tradition of exploitation film. While much of this has been an organic process that has taken place over a number of years within the pages of fanzines and in the communities of collectors invested in extreme cinema, it would be a mistake to imagine an industry free from commodification since much of the expansion of the category has come from the curatorial role performed by boutique DVD labels and specialist publishers.

This growth can be most clearly seen in the coffee table books that have documented the video nasties moral panic. In 1998, Nigel Wingrove and Marc Morris published *The Art of the Nasty* and Allan Bryce published *The Original Video Nasties: From Absurd to Zombie Flesh Eaters*, books that collated the covers of the video nasties alongside an entertaining and informative history. In 2000, David Kerekes and David Slater published *See No Evil: Banned Films and Video Controversy*, a book that considers the video nasties alongside other contentious films and as a part of a long history of film censorship in the UK. In 2001, Bryce produced a sequel to *The Original Video Nasties: From Absurd to Zombie Flesh Eaters*, entitled *The Video Nasties 2: Strike Up the Banned: A Pictorial Guide to the Movies that Bite!*, collating what are described as 'equally outrageous releases that somehow missed being dredged up in DPP raids' (2001: 6). The book presents these additions as if they should have been banned, but for some reason had avoided prosecution – and in this way, shifts the role of gatekeeper from government institution to cult fan. In 2005, Francis Brewster, Harvey Fenton and Marc Morris adopted a similar approach when they published *Shock! Horror!: Astounding Artwork from the Video Nasty Era*, again expanding the category. In 2007, *Darkside Magazine* published John Martin's *Seduction of the Gullible*, a significantly revised version of a book that Martin had written in 1993. This new version followed a similar trajectory to *Shock! Horror!*, expanding the category while detailing the specifics of the press campaign against the video nasties, and providing an overview of the second video nasties scare in the 1990s. Finally, in 2009, Marc Morris and Nigel Wingrove published a second edition of *The Art of the Nasty*, which similarly expands the category to a type. These books take great care to reproduce the sleeves of the videocassettes and to detail the original films included in the video nasties list, but the majority of them also append the original list, presenting the video nasties together with an array of other films that are deemed to be significant. *The Art of the Nasty*, for instance, creatively groups these later additions under the headings 'the ones that got away' (2009: 45), 'nice and sleazy does it' (2009: 57), and 'the good, the bad and the vomit-inducing' (2009: 95), and in that way presents them as simply the most visible face of a much longer tradition. Of course, these films do belong to a longer tradition of exploitation cinema, but the books have also all contributed significantly to the cultures of collecting that exist around video and the video nasties in the UK. Cassettes are frequently listed on eBay as belonging to the films of *The Art of the Nasty*, or individual films may be given provenance and prestige if they originate in the collection of Marc Morris or Harvey Fenton.

In this way, these books can be seen to follow the discursive construction of cult film observed by Joan Hawkins in relation to paracinema catalogues. However, while they perform a similar curatorial function to these early magazines, it is equally important to acknowledge that there are economic drivers at work here, with a financial motivation to extend the category coming from distributors and publishers alike. As a finite group of films, there are limited opportunities to capitalise upon the video nasties, and once the early books had reproduced the covers of the video nasties, there were few places left to go. However, by appending the category their distributors and publishers moved away from simply performing a curatorial role to a conscious and deliberate market strategy that elevates other titles not previously associated with the list.

The effect of this approach is the expansion of the category beyond the limits of the thirty-nine official video nasties; the thirty-three 'dropped' titles; or indeed, the eighty-two Section 3 titles, to incorporate other films that are considered as important or canonical, framing products as belonging to the 'age' or 'era' of the video nasty or as arising from other notable, but largely industrially constructed subgenres, such as Eurohorror or the *Giallo*. Indeed, Eurohorror presents a useful parallel through which to discuss the evolution of the video nasty through the industrial application of the category. Peter Hutchings suggested that in spite of the obvious existence of European horror, the category did not exist as a meaningful category prior to the 1980s and the era of video (2012: 18). Significantly, Hutchings attributes its success and adoption as a category with specific meanings in no small part to the wealth and success of European horror films released on video during this period, many of which similarly contributed to the concept of the video nasties. Hutchings acknowledges that upon their first release, these films were not separated as a distinct European subgenre but were marketed simply as horror, observing that over time what 'emerges [. . .] is a compelling sense of a European horror cinema defined through marginality and resistance, defined precisely through its extreme difference from more readily available entertainments' (ibid.). He goes on to suggest that increasingly it would seem that 'the identity of Eurohorror resides precisely in its visible difference from what is perceived as the American commercial mainstream' or, more specifically, 'the more a film looks American, the less value it has as an example of Eurohorror'[1] (2012: 15). This construction of difference, which is fundamental to the positioning of Eurohorror, is accomplished through what Hutchings has termed 'the romance of marginality and the gravitational pull exerted by the idea of some kind of dramatic form of cultural transgression' (2012: 22), words which evoke and involve criteria that are familiar as the defining features of the video nasty. While the category of Eurohorror can be seen to mirror many of the criteria of the video nasty in its emphasis on transgression and marginality, I would suggest that the designation of a film as Eurohorror simultaneously allows for a valorisation that is not based solely upon an ability to excite or to horrify but rather reconstructs a sense that these films are important, canonical works in their own right.

While Hutchings's work prioritises textual film analysis, it is important also to acknowledge the role that the object and a valorisation of paratextual marketing materials play in these generic constructions. Raiford Guins has argued that previous understandings of European horror on video were based upon the presentation of the product, which frequently demonstrated a lack of attention to detail paid to the packaging, a lack of quality in the translations used for the dubbing tracks, combined with an overall emphasis on extreme or gratuitous content visible in both fan discourse and promotional strategies (2005: 17). Guins argues that this has reinforced a sense of video, in this context, as having a low cultural value, or what he calls the 'gore-object' (ibid.). Conversely, he suggests that with the introduction of DVD 'another set of discursive practices can be observed, which results in an elevation in the perceived value of the "gore-object," transforming its value into that of an "art-object"' (ibid.). For Guins, the introduction of DVD was a reparative process, and he suggests that in a format that emphasised the restorative capabilities of the medium, companies drew on a shift in fan discourse and repositioned a raft of films as masterpieces of the genre, utilising rhetoric previously reserved for directors considered to be part of the auteur tradition.

What becomes increasingly evident, then, are the ways in which the process of re-categorising films for consumption can alter the perception of value inherent in the product. In this way, genrification can be seen as having a 'gentrifying' effect, one that re-classifies, re-values and re-positions a product based upon different sets of generic criteria. While I will explore these processes of gentrification more fully in the next chapter, it is important at this stage to acknowledge that the processes of genrification and gentrification can be seen to be reliant upon each other and that they are concepts that often overlap significantly. While Eurohorror can increasingly be seen as a sub-category or genre in its own right, re-appraised and re-valued through a process of gentrification, this process is not always observed, and often inconsistencies can be seen in the market strategies adopted for films arising from the exact same traditions. For example, the subgenre of the *Giallo* film and, in particular, the promotional strategies employed by a company like Shameless Screen Entertainment, arguably the most visible distributor of the subgenre in the United Kingdom, can be used to illustrate the inconsistent market strategies that surround the video nasties.

Ostensibly a branch of Eurohorror, the *Giallo* is an Italian subgenre that incorporates elements typical of the crime, horror and thriller genres. Literally translating as 'yellow', the genre takes its name from distinctive yellow covers used by the Italian publishing house *Il Giallo Mondadori* (Mondadori Yellow (books)) that were used to package early Italian translations of crime novels from British and American writers such as Agatha Christie, Edgar Wallace and Raymond Chandler. Over time in Italy, *Giallo* came to be used as a synonym for the thriller and the category was extended to incorporate film in the 1960s. While the *Giallo* continues to be understood in this way in its native Italy, applied to domestic and foreign films alike, in the United Kingdom and the United States, Giallo is far more likely to be used explicitly to describe films of Italian origin that contain graphic and stylised sexual violence. Because of the scope of application in the Italian definition, many of the video nasties would have been understood as Giallo in their native Italy. However, in the UK, films such as *The House on the Edge of the Park* (1980), *Late Night Trains* (1975) and *Killer Nun* (1979), which all could be variously positioned as Giallo (Italian thrillers with graphic sex and violence), were primarily understood as video nasties, but might just as readily be classified as examples of Eurohorror (that is, as films of European origin that are significantly different from the American mainstream) or, in the case of these three films, as official video nasties (i.e., as films banned under the Obscene Publications Act between 1982 and 1984). The multiple ways in which we can categorise these films demonstrates the fluidity of these terms and highlights how the application of genre is not necessarily limited to identifying iconography present in the film text but can often have more to do with how they are positioned in the marketplace through the marketing strategies of individual companies.

Shameless Screen Entertainment is a company with a very clear marketing strategy that trades explicitly upon the associations and connotations of both the Eurohorror and the video nasties subgenres, but that aligns itself explicitly with the *Giallo* tradition. This can be most clearly seen in the company's branding, which is inspired by the yellow pulp fiction promotions of those early *Il Giallo Mondadori* paperbacks. However, this can also be seen to be drawing upon Astra Video's pre-certificate release of the controversial video nasty *I Spit on Your Grave* (1978). The acidic yellow of the company's branding provides a vibrant background for the straplines that boast of 'the sickest movie ever made!' (Lucio Fulci's *New York Ripper*, 1982), 'where whores meet saws!' (Sergio Martino's *Torso*, 1973) and 'at last the slut is uncut!' (Giulio Berruti's *Killer Nun*). This exploitation hyperbole is usually married to images of sex and violence on the rear of the sleeve. Taking *Flavia the Heretic* (1974) as an example, the rear of the sleeve includes nine stills from the film. Of those nine, six feature eroticised images of nuns either fully or partially nude. Of the remaining three, one features a nun being impaled by a spear, while another features a decapitated head on a spike. This is fairly typical of the promotional strategies of Shameless, and the company's use of stills that overtly promise films that deal in sex and violence.

However, while there is a sense of the distributor revelling in an aesthetic that is largely appropriated from earlier ideas about how exploitation marketing should function, there is an incongruity to some of the presentation. Alongside the hyperbolic straplines and images of sex and violence is a section that carefully details the technical specifications of the release. This includes the original year of release, the aspect ratio of the film, the running time, and whether the film has been cut by the BBFC; in cases where the film has been cut, then the release details by how much. Moreover, this is located below a section that details the film's personnel and which presents not only all of the cast and crew and their roles but also earlier significant credits, even providing historical portraits for their releases. Added to this, the company's website is quick to clarify that behind what they call 'the banter of [their] sales pitch, [. . .] is serious intent' and that they are 'determined not only to source the best possible materials' . . . 'but also the closest possible version to the director's original – and/or the director's preferred – vision of his film'. This will often detail the sources that the film was mastered from and will include supplementary materials like alternative language tracks, subtitle options, audio commentaries and other paratextual materials. This explanation almost functions as an apology or at the very least a disclaimer that the company understands that its chosen aesthetic might send mixed messages about the value of its product; it is invested in both the idea of exploitation cinema and the importance of exploitation cinema.

These approaches are illustrative of a contradiction that is not easily resolved. Shameless has taken a great deal of care to position itself in the marketplace as a distributor aligned with a particular product and a particular genre, namely, the *Giallo*. As a part of this, it has adopted a hyperbolic approach synonymous with exploitation marketing; borrowing from the carnival barker of the golden age of exploitation, the 42nd Street poster, or even the tabloid headline in the case of the video nasty. This presents the company's product as cheap, shoddy and/or extreme while reinforcing a sense of the films as being of low cultural value. Yet, in spite of all of these gaudy 'come-ons' and the carnivalesque lure of the titillation of this type of promotion, what at first appears anachronistic, on closer inspection would seem to be a superficially affected aesthetic, which re-appropriates elements of the golden age of exploitation in a package that is positioned as having significantly more value. In other words, underneath the shrill exterior is a secondary layer that emphasises a sense of the importance of each of these films and endeavours to position them as important through their sub-cultural pedigree (by detailing earlier significant credits for the cast and crew), through the technical specificities of that release or through the mission statement of the company that clarifies their intent. All of which suggests that the lurid promotional devices are not to be taken at face value.

While I will examine the reappraisal and repositioning of these films in greater detail in the next chapter, it is important to acknowledge here that the creation of a value in the products of Shameless follows the traditional notions of value that might be expected to be seen in the marketing and promotional campaigns of mainstream Hollywood film, demonstrating an emphasis on pedigree or awards, or on restoration and supplementary materials. The significant difference here lies in the marketing appeals that rework the notional cheap, shoddy and/or extreme aesthetic into something that can be more broadly understood as genre tropes. This involves a re-positioning and re-valuing these films through the technical specifications of the product and the inclusion of supplementary materials, despite simultaneously reinforcing a sense that the films have no value by drawing on an established idea of exploitation. Steve Neale has argued that 'genres do not consist only of films: they consist also, and equally, of specific systems of expectation and hypothesis that spectators bring with them to the cinema, and which interact with the films themselves'

(1990: 46). In this way, films arising from these alternative European traditions can be seen to carry with them specific systems of expectation, systems that, in this case, capitalise on a sense that these films are of low cultural value. As Eurohorror, as *Giallo*, as cult films, as exploitation and as video nasties they appear to be unified in an aesthetic that prioritises the inherently cheap and extreme, the titillating and the horrifying, and that belongs to a genre that has become recognised for being explicitly horrific or pornographic in nature. In many respects, this repositioning follows the elevation in the perceived value of the 'gore-object' observed by Raiford Guins (as discussed in the previous chapter), through which 'another set of discursive practices can be observed'. However, here, the overall emphasis remains one of excess. In the next chapter, I will explore how ideas of value have begun to reshape the market for the video nasties, destabilising traditional aesthetic notions associated with exploitation cinema, and will examine the gentrification processes that are taking place.

Note

1. Hutchings's essay is primarily concerned what does and does not become labelled as Eurohorror, often in spite of what are obvious European credentials. He cites *Resident Evil* (2002) as a film that perhaps should be considered as European: an American-British-French-German co-production, filmed mainly in Europe, by a cast and crew that contained numerous Europeans and is based upon a Japanese computer game – but is critically understood as American horror, and more specifically, a mainstream American horror.

CHAPTER 8

The Art of Exploitation

As much as the process of genrification discussed in the previous chapter has worked to extend the category of the video nasties by applying and reinforcing a collective genre identity to these films, the grouping, re-classification and re-release of these films on DVD and Blu-ray has created an opportunity to reappraise them in the contemporary media landscape. This reappraisal has not been based solely upon earlier conceptions of the video nasties, which constructed them as extreme, taboo or challenging, but has instead been complicated by the idiosyncrasies and expectations of the DVD and Blu-ray digital formats. These expectations have led to a process that can best be understood as (sub)cultural gentrification, in which films previously believed to be of low cultural value have been repositioned as important canonical works. With this, the aesthetics and language used to describe these films have changed radically, borrowing ideas more commonly associated with the 'quality' film, mobilising the figure of the auteur director, the canonical film, and the idea of collecting and distribution as 'curation' and 'archiving'.

Distributors have played a pivotal role in this and through processes of curation they have transformed a product that would have historically existed at the margins of popular cinema into a commercially profitable canonical asset. With this transformation, there has been a visible change in both the aesthetics and in the language used to describe these films, shifting from ideas of excess to something that more closely resembles the promotion of the important canonical films of art-house cinema. Historically, these kinds of film were understood to exist at opposite ends of the cinematic spectrum: at one end worthy canonical art cinema – films believed to have a significant artistic merit and therefore prized as culturally valuable – and at the other the cinematic detritus of the exploitation circuit – films believed to be cinematic trash, paracinema or B-movies perceived to have no artistic merit and little cultural value. Historically, these markets have been separated, based largely on preconceived valorisations and processes of cultural distinction. But in recent years there has been an increased convergence of the markets that, while being commercially driven, has seen distributors work to reinforce, extend and challenge traditional notions of what might constitute the cinematic canon. This chapter will examine the role that distributors have played in maintaining and extending what for different groups are considered important and canonical films, exploring the role that technology has played in these processes and what these transformations mean for the video nasties.

The Politics of Canon Formation

Paul Schrader has argued that the film canon is 'based upon criteria that transcend taste' (2006: 34), and that whether a film appealed to a particular viewer or critic or not was a largely inconsequential concern, arguing instead that every effort should be made to separate out 'personal favourites from those movies that artistically defined film history' (ibid.). Here, inclusion is not a subjective matter that is influenced by industrial motivation or by personal or popular taste, but instead, simply, that there are important canonical films that unequivocally represent the cinema's greatest accomplishments. While it is tempting to imagine a singular mutually agreed canon of important film, readings such as Schrader's ignore the selection processes that must inevitably take place just so that people might navigate the sheer volume of film available and which have served to elevate these 'important films' as canonical masterpieces of cinema in the first place. Janet Staiger cautions against imagining that these selection processes are somehow free from political motivation and suggests that whether films were grouped for efficiency, so that we might better navigate a body of work; grouped as a means classifying them to determine typicality and a set of generalised characteristics; or grouped through a process of evaluative selection, through which the best work is held up as an exemplar of artistry, they are often revealing of the hegemonic struggles that are taking place in these cultures around the interests of individuals or institutions. Staiger argues that 'with selection usually comes a politics of inclusion and exclusion', whereby 'some films are moved to the centre of attention; others, to the margins' (1985: 8). Historically, what constituted that centre within academic writing was broadly in line with Schrader's belief in a canon that elevated the best of cinema, and that imagined a canon free from political bias and with criteria for selection that transcended personal and popular taste formations.

Moreover, for some, these valorisations have extended beyond the type of film to include the mode of exhibition, usually to privilege the *cinematic* experience. Writing for *The New York Times* in 1996, Susan Sontag bemoaned the loss of the experiential qualities of cinema in a lament to 'cinema's glorious past', in which she invoked the icons of cinema's golden age. The Lumière brothers, Melies, Feuillade, D. W. Griffith, Dziga Vertov, Pabst, Murnau, Rossellini and Bertolucci were all presented here as the ghosts of cinema's once glorious past, before a systematic industrial decline. While much of Sontag's eulogy is concerned with the tensions between industry and art or recalling with nostalgia 'the feverish age of movie-going' in the 1960s and 1970s, the resounding message is (as she describes it) a waning in 'the distinctive cinephilic love of movies that is not simply love of, but a certain taste, in films'(1996, online). Sontag admits that outwardly this type of cinephilia may appear 'snobbish' but then extends this snobbery beyond mere valorisations of the types of film to considerations of the medium itself, suggesting 'to see a great film only on television isn't to have really seen that film' (ibid.). This distinction of the theatrical versus home viewing experience, perhaps borne out of a life spent in New York – a thriving metropolis where the 'worthy' cinema that Sontag prized so much was routinely available in the cinemas – refuses to acknowledge films which for a variety of reasons were never widely exhibited theatrically. This privileging of the cinematic experience prevents the elevation of films whose success was dependent upon the opportunities made available by the home viewing experience, with Mark Betz dismissing Sontag's account as the 'rarified, quasi-religious theatrical experience of the filmic relic' of Sontag's youth (2010: 131–2). Sontag's eulogy would prove to be premature when only a year later the introduction of DVD would begin to destabilise traditional notions of cinephilia and would help to consolidate the idea of the cinephile that was not explicitly reliant on the theatrical space.

Cinephilia's evolution had been incremental, and as early as 1991 scholars were introducing terms like 'videophilia' (Tashiro 1991: 7) or 'telephilia' (Price 2004: 36) to account for the increased influence of the small screen and the effect that this was having on traditional notions of what might constitute cinephilia. Marijke De Valck and Malte Hagener introduced the concept of 'videosyncrasy' to describe the modern cinephile's ability to move easily between 'different technologies, platforms, and subject positions in a highly idiosyncratic fashion that nevertheless remains connective and flexible enough to allow for the intersubjective exchange of affect, objects and memories' (2005: 14). For these authors, where videophilia, telephilia, or indeed cinephilia might imply a hierarchical structure to technology with priority given to one specific medium over another, and even though they are also keen to define cinephilia as an umbrella term that can be applied to all screen media, De Valck and Hagener suggest 'videosyncrasy' as an appropriate term as it may enable a levelling of all media under one all-encompassing category with little sense of a hierarchy determined by either technology or means of exhibition. However, semantics aside, it is clear that the availability of film through home media technology has altered traditional notions of cinephilia, and that increasingly, contemporary constructions of cinephilia are becoming reliant upon consumer culture and the ownership and curation of film.

'The New Media Aristocrats'

The home entertainment market has been shaped by the opportunities afforded by technological innovation and the demands of early adopters in the marketplace – those who Barbara Klinger has referred to as 'the new media aristocrats' (2006: 17). Klinger suggests that the introduction of digital technology brought with it an impression of quality which has helped to define the home as a site for media consumption (2006: 18), and that this created a distinction between older and more established analogue technologies and cast them as inferior or 'lowbrow' in relation to the new superior 'highbrow' experience offered by digital. DVD (digital versatile disc) was explicitly promoted on those terms, with an early trailer heralding its arrival by attempting to align the technology explicitly with the superior cinematic experience. The trailer begins:

> This is DVD ... the picture is twice as sharp as VHS, the sound is infinitely clearer, it looks and sounds as if you are at the movies, but you can experience it at home. Not to mention, you can watch it in widescreen, listen to audio commentary, choose from features like director's notes, behind the scenes footage, trailers and more ... see how good a movie at home can be.

Ironically, this trailer was most frequently screened as an advertisement that played prior to the main feature on VHS cassettes as an encouragement to consumers to adopt the new technology, so the viewer could not actually 'see how good the movie (on DVD) could be'. Whilst the trailer could never be truly indicative of the quality of DVD; it did help to create a set of clear expectations for anyone thinking of adopting the new platform. These promotions clearly attempted to align the format to the cinematic experience, and to the cinematic space and helped DVD (and subsequently Blu-ray) to become associated with the kind of cinephilia that had previously eluded VHS. Though the superior quality and pseudo-cinematic experience of the digital home media formats of DVD and Blu-ray is now an accepted aspect of the format, it wasn't always a foregone conclusion, with James Kendrick suggesting that in the early days of DVD there was a battle to legitimise the home theatre experience. Prior to DVD, home theatre enthusiasts throughout the late 1980s and the 1990s had typically opted for Laserdiscs, a format on which films 'were almost always presented in their original aspect ratios, thus aligning the viewing experience at home more closely with the theatrical experience' (Kendrick 2005: 60).

By way of comparison, films presented on video (be they VHS, Beta, or V2000) rarely offered widescreen presentations as standard, and even when widescreen masters were available, they would invariably be adapted to fit the native aspect ratio of standard television. To achieve this, distributors would reformat their films, removing the black bars on the top and bottom of the image, which could be accomplished in one of two ways. For films that had been recorded in full frame with an aspect ratio of 1.33:1 (the 4:3 aspect ratio of standard televisions), the transition was less problematic. This was the standard aspect ratio of film and was essentially compatible with that of television. To make these films compatible for theatrical exhibition they would undergo a process known as 'soft matte', whereby the projection would be masked top and bottom to achieve the familiar widescreen appearance and a theatrical aspect ratio of 1.85:1 or 1.66:1. When these films came to be transferred to video, since they already had a standard aspect ratio of 4:3 and were naturally compatible with the native aspect ratio of standard television, distributors simply took the decision not to mask the frame and instead deliver the image as full screen. The dominant perception from the industry was that the average consumer preferred a full-screen presentation over the reduced frame of a widescreen presentation on video. Indeed, so pervasive was this belief that if a film was not available as an open matte print, distributors would employ a process known as 'pan and scan' to deliver a full-frame print. This process had been developed for broadcast television in which an editor would scan parts of the original widescreen image based upon what they deemed to be the most important parts of that shot. They would then copy or 'scan' this subsection, and when the point of interest changed or moved to another part of the frame, they would 'pan' the scanner across the image and scan again. While the pan and scan process ensured full-screen presentation, it also radically changed the composition of the shot and would prove to be hugely contentious for anyone with more than a passing interest in film. Steve Neale describes the process as 're-compos[ing] films made in and for widescreen formats [. . .] by reframing shots, by re-editing sequences and shots, and by altering the pattern of still and moving shots used in the original film' (1998: 131). As one might expect, neither of these processes was welcomed by home theatre enthusiasts, who were typically trying to recreate the theatrical viewing space. James Kendrick suggests that for the majority of home theatre enthusiasts 'the theatrical viewing space [was] the ultimate arbiter of authenticity, and, therefore, the closer their home environments come to re-creating that space, the more legitimate it becomes as a place to view films properly' (2005: 65).

This privileging of the cinematic space mirrors Sontag's belief that 'to see a great film only on television isn't to have really seen that film' (1996, online), however the desire to achieve theatrical accuracy highlighted by Kendrick is revealing of the tensions that exist between the idea of film as an art form, with a set of expectations governing the presentation of that film, and film as platform that is dependent on technological innovation, and the occasional incompatibility between these two facets of the medium. To illustrate this, Kendrick explores the reception of the releases of Stanley Kubrick by a group of home theatre enthusiasts. Kubrick's later films

> were all shot open-matte with an aspect ratio of 1.33:1 and were projected in U.S. theatres in a standard matted 1.85:1. On their transferral to home video, Kubrick insisted, that rather than matte these films, that they were shown as open matte presentations and fill the entire frame/television screen. (Bracke cited in Kendrick 2005: 64)

However, the cinematic space brings with it a series of expectations that govern the presentation of film and Kubrick's decision to present these later films as full-frame open matte presentations became the cause of considerable criticism, with some bold enough to suggest that 'Kubrick did not fully understand the implications [of this decision] and that he died before being able to fully appreciate the development of high-definition televisions that allow for widescreen aspect ratios and still fill the screen' (ibid.). Kendrick suggests that this conflict over the legitimacy of the presentation is an 'issue of authorial versus technological intent (the director's artistic vision versus the medium's technological properties as the primary determinant of film form)' (2005: 65). Nevertheless, the way that form has been dictated by the technological expectations of the medium is beginning to inform what constitutes the canonical film, with the expectation that important film is presented in particular ways.

This is perhaps most evident in the work of directors without the status of Kubrick, for example, the Italian director Lucio Fulci. Fulci is regarded by many as an important cult director. He is noted for the extremity of his films and is often referred to as 'The Godfather of Gore'.

Of the seventy-two films on the DPP's video nasty list, three belonged to Fulci: *Zombie Flesh Eaters* (1979), *The Beyond* (1981), and *The House by the Cemetery* (1981), and Fulci's 1982 film *The New York Ripper* was rejected by the BBFC and refused a certificate outright. While Kubrick's status as an auteur is undeniable, Fulci has garnered a considerable reputation for the violence of his films and is often given only tertiary consideration in a hierarchy that tends to favour other the masters of Italian horror such as Dario Argento or Mario Bava. However, despite Fulci apparently occupying the opposite end of the cinematic spectrum to Kubrick, the UK VIPCO DVD releases of Fulci's *The Beyond* and *City of the Living Dead* were subject to the same expectations and greeted by the same criticisms as the films of Kubrick. The most vocal criticisms of these releases objected that the films were presented as full-frame pan and scan prints and that they were not displayed in the correct aspect ratio. These criticisms became synonymous with VIPCO and helped to consolidate the idea they were not as invested in the films as the fans were. These criticisms are significant as they illustrate how the market was beginning to change for the cult film in the UK with the advent of DVD in the late 1990s/early 2000s, and also of the shift between Raiford Guins's gore object/art object binary.

It is also demonstrative of a technological misunderstanding that has dogged VIPCO for many years. Mattei's Nipple, a blogger at *The VIPCO blog*, has challenged the dominant belief that the company specialised in releasing trimmed pan and scan prints, arguing that in most cases these releases were the full-frame presentation and were reflective of the same open matte processes as the films of Kubrick. The idea that VIPCO were consistently releasing pan and scan prints is usually invoked as a way of disparaging the company and suggesting that they were not as concerned about quality of the films as the audience that was buying them. Mattei's Nipple suggests that the only VIPCO releases that were pan and scan were the Screamtime collection editions of *The Beyond*, *The House by the Cemetery* and *Mountain of the Cannibal God* (1978) and the Cult Classics edition of *Gremloids* (1984). However, the belief that VIPCO were not as invested in the films as their audience was not unfounded. In line with the expectations of the format, VIPCO routinely released films that they claimed had been digitally remastered only for it later be revealed that they had not. The most notorious example of this was *City of the Living Dead*, which displayed damage typical of damage to magnetic tape suggesting that the company had simply transferred the film from their old VHS master copy (Figure 8.1).

THE ART OF EXPLOITATION 151

Figure 8.1 Screengrabs from VIPCO's DVD release of *City of the Living Dead* illustrating damage typical of magnetic tape.

Through all of these negotiations what is perhaps most significant is that in most cases fans were accepting of the cuts that VIPCO had been required to make, aware that the company were subject to the demands of the BBFC. What they were less accepting of was a lack of care and attention paid to the overall presentation of the films, and this is crucial in understanding how the idea of the video nasty had evolved over time. Where an emphasis on violence and gore had previously defined the video nasties, the expectations of DVD were beginning to reshape the marketplace, and these ideas were being eroded. Superseded by a sense of quality that was initially derived from the expectations of the medium but that slowly began to reframe the video nasties by adopting the language and aesthetic of important canonical cinema.

It is impossible to discuss the contemporary marketplace for DVD and Blu-ray without acknowledging the debt of gratitude that all contemporary 'boutique' DVD labels owe to the Criterion Collection, a company which Barry Schauer suggests 'has come to symbolize quality in-home video' (2005: 32). Beginning in 1983, Criterion released films exclusively on Laserdisc, following the wider format trend of using each film's original aspect ratios and mimicking the theatrical experience at home. Often seen as the technological forebear of the DVD format, the capability of Laserdisc to incorporate bonus features like production stills, making-of documentaries, audio commentaries, cut scenes and alternative endings would become a staple of DVD, where the variety of bonus features soon became standard and would quickly define 'quality' releases on the new digital format. Criterion was the first to incorporate these elements as the staples of their brand in the 1980s, but Schauer has commented that this did not attract mainstream consumers, with Laserdisc only ever appealing to a 'niche audience of cinephiles and academics who were attracted to the format's superior picture and sound as well as its ability to hold special features' (2005: 32).

While these cinematic extras were fundamental in creating a sense of quality around the product, equally important was an allusion toward the cinematic, which came from the films that were chosen for inclusion in the collection. The company drew together masterpieces of world cinema from directors like Michelangelo Antonioni, Sergei Eisenstein, Ingmar Bergman, Federico Fellini, Akira Kurosawa, François Truffaut and Yasujirō Ozu – the accepted masters of contemporary cinema. The catalogue was inspired by the company's partnership with Janus Films, a theatrical distributor that introduced American audiences to many classics of cinema and who now license their catalogue to Criterion. James Kendrick has argued that through the films they have selected, the Criterion Collection demonstrated an eclecticism in its catalogue with releases that have resisted 'restraints of politics, taste, geography, and time' (2001: 124), but he concedes that the company has demonstrated a bias toward established canonical titles and auteurs such as Ingmar Bergman. This perspective is mirrored in Schauer's belief that 'the Criterion Collection privileges the European and Japanese art cinema of the 1950s and 1960s', often 'at the expense of other national cinemas, genres, and eras' (2005: 32). This concentration on the established luminaries of contemporary cinema has helped reinforce the sense of a valuable product and draws attention to the curatorial role that the Criterion Collection performs and the ways in which this has worked to reinforce a canon of films that was first established in the art-house cinema of the 1950s, 1960s and 1970s.

Elevating the Gore Object

A company whose output exists at the opposite end of the cinematic spectrum to the Criterion Collection is Arrow Video, a company that specialises in releasing classic, cult and horror films. Yet, despite the contrast with the catalogue of Criterion, Arrow Video shares a branding and distribution strategy with them, which puts them in stark contrast to other well-known independent video nasty distributors such as VIPCO, despite carrying many of the same films, including the video nasties *The Driller Killer*, *The Burning* (1981), *Zombie Flesh Eaters* and *The Slayer*. Arrow's products are defined by an attention to detail and the quality of their restorations, something that has led to the company being described as the 'The Criterion of Shit Movies' (Bickel 2016). Much of this can be attributed to the care taken with the restorations of their cult releases, but it is also due to the company's decision to incorporate extensive and often originally produced supplementary materials like production stills, making-of documentaries, audio commentaries, cut scenes and alternative endings as part of the whole DVD or Blu-ray package. Kate Egan has argued that supplementary materials of this kind 'serve as "historical portraits"', that provide the distributor with the opportunity to reframe a film as an important part of cinematic history (2007: 186). In the cult film market, Arrow stands at the forefront of this reframing process, rehabilitating films as valuable and important that would have historically been described through a flurry of hyperbolic excess. So recognised is the company that it could be legitimately argued that the simple act of releasing a film in their catalogue serves to elevate a film and single it out as an important and canonical film, distancing it from other cult cinema. In this way, the distributor can be seen to be performing a curatorial role in which the decision to include films in their catalogue begins a reappraisal process that is then reinforced by these 'historical portraits', each of which serves to communicate the significance and artistry of any given film directly. There are other less obvious signifiers of value and authenticity found within Arrow's curation practices that are also working to reframe these films as important, such as their use of dubbing and subtitling in a catalogue that contains many foreign-produced films, especially Italian horror.

The translation processes that all foreign-language cinema must undergo in order to be understood outside the country of origin has historically been loaded with value judgments and cultural distinctions, and while these are primarily technical processes, they can tell us much about the value being placed on the film being translated. Subtitling typically costs between 'a tenth and a twentieth as much as dubbing', so there are clearly obvious economic benefits to subtitling (Ivarsson 2009: 3). However, historically, if a film was believed to have popular appeal, then it would be dubbed to ensure that the film generated maximum returns. In a similar discussion, and drawing on Koichi Iwabuchi's work, David Church suggests that Italian horror producers aimed to market '"culturally odourless" products', that concealed their cultural origins (2015: 4).

If the market was less certain or the film was considered as niche, then it would likely be subtitled, thereby reducing production costs and maximising profits. Over time, and in a practice that is particularly visible in Western markets, the process of subtitling has become associated with a particular type of marginal film, namely the foreign-language drama or the art film, and, because of this association, the subtitle itself has become imbued with an implicit cultural value that has come to function as a marker or signifier to the inherent value of any given film. Similarly, and in spite of the increased cost associated with the process, over time, dubbing has become associated with another kind of film: films which are often genre productions, and therefore considered less prestigious, films that are routinely repackaged and dubbed into the destination language to ensure a broad demographic appeal to ensure maximum return. Miller has argued that this can be considered as simply a matter of determining the most appropriate process for particular types of film, and that films that are 'largely narrative or action scenes work well with a dubbed track, while if it's a more cerebral production subtitling may be better' (cited in Dean 1987: 38). However, I would argue that no matter how appropriate these processes might be, Miller's distinction also works to reinforce entrenched cultural valorisations of the dubbed 'action' film, as somehow less valuable than the 'cerebral' art-house film.

Often these distinctions can be compounded by a familiar reliance on auteurism, in which established foreign-language titles are presented as the work of an auteur, and then, because of the value placed upon them, they are presented with subtitled dialogue as the most authentic representation of the director's vision. This, of course, ascribes a value to the subtitle, but it also assumes that there is an absolute translation and does not acknowledge that both the process of subtitling and the process of dubbing are ultimately a negotiation, based upon the constraints of the medium, and that relies on a degree of adaptation, what has become known as constrained translation. Jorge Díaz Cintas suggests that in the case of subtitling, constrained translation can be most easily understood as physical constraints inherent in the 'physical delivery of the written message', a message that is governed by the 'width of the screen that usually only allows for a total of 35 characters per line in a maximum of two lines' (2010: 33). In contrast, the primary constraints when dubbing are a need to ensure that 'the target language message [. . .] follow[s] the original movement of the lips' (ibid.). However, the dialogue being spoken rarely matches seamlessly with a literal translation, so to ensure that the subtitled text or audio dub remains in harmony and continues to remain synchronised with the visuals appearing on the screen, a process of adaptation must occur.

The fidelity of this process of adaptation is often the subject of much debate; however, often overlooked within this conversation is the implicit cultural value attributed to the subtitle and, as a direct result, the perceived lack of value in a film that has been dubbed rather than subtitled. Antje Ascheid suggests that when a film becomes considered as 'an artistically valuable "authored original"' (1997: 34), then subtitling becomes intertwined with its distinction as high art over a film perceived to be of low cultural value. However, for much of the Italian film industry, particularly for the popular films created to appeal to the international film market, no such remediation can take place as these films were not produced in one consistent language. Italian producers famously used post-synchronised audio tracks as standard practice (see Frayling 2012: 68), and this meant that location audio was not retained, and often not even recorded. Actors would deliver their performance in their own language, and then they would deliver the performance again in the studio in order to record the sound. These tracks would later be synched and applied to the visual component as part of the post-production process. The significance of this is that there is no one language to these films and, therefore, no authentic 'authored original' to rehabilitate. Even the original Italian versions of these films are composed of multiple dubbed elements, which raises interesting questions over how we construct and navigate value in relation to 'popular' foreign-language cinema that was produced in this way.

Similarly, Laurie Cubbison has observed that as East-Asian cinemas major exports, kung fu and anime movies are more likely to be dubbed for international markets. Cubbison also suggests that, outside of these genres, most foreign-language films tend to be subtitled and would therefore be marketed as art cinema (2005: 46). While I would argue that there is a large body of European foreign language cinema that is neither kung fu nor anime but is also dubbed and, as such, has historically sat outside of art cinema, there is no denying that the vast majority of film exported from Asia is routinely dubbed on its entry into foreign markets. However, this is something that is beginning to change as digital media has begun to offer a plurality of experience that cinema, and then video, could not. There have been recent releases of *Lady Snowblood* (1973) by both Arrow Video and Criterion; even the perennial pseudo video nasty *Shogun Assassin* (1980) has been released by Eureka Entertainment (another label specialising in releasing canonical cult film), and Criterion have released a box set of the series from which *Shogun Assassin* was drawn, the Lone Wolf and Cub. While this version does not include the *Shogun Assassin* cut, it nevertheless illustrates the increasing overlaps between the sectors. Although these films are indelibly associated with the exploitation market – and would have historically been presented with dubbed audio tracks to ensure a broad appeal – they are increasingly being presented as 'authored originals' in subtitled versions. While these are often secondary versions, with the 'authentic' dubbed version taking priority, the decision to incorporate both versions nevertheless demonstrates the shift in the perceived value of these films that has taken place, and illustrates that the conversation has shifted from one that discursively constructed these films as valuable because of their extremity and their difference to the mainstream, but that now constructs them as culturally significant and valuable in their own right.

The significance of these reappraisals cannot be overestimated, and this is a phenomenon that is not limited to Asian cinema. In fact, similar reappraisals are increasingly evident across a wide range of cult film releases. Recently, both Arrow Video and Shameless Screen Entertainment have begun the lengthy process of restoring footage to cult European releases. However, as this footage was usually omitted from the English language versions prior to the films being dubbed, these sequences never received a dubbed English language translation. The inherent difficulties in sourcing the original actors, or even finding impersonators to voice the characters, have meant that distributors have begun incorporating these scenes as subtitled sequences in otherwise dubbed English-language versions. This is a practice that most visible in Arrow Video's release of Argento's *Deep Red* (1975), and while the experience of viewing subtitled sequences within a film that is otherwise dubbed into English can often appear jarring, incongruous or disjointed, the decision to incorporate these sequences tells us much about the rehabilitation of these films in the past thirty years and the importance of releasing these valuable cinematic entries as 'authored originals'.

This sense of the authored original is something that would have historically been reserved for worthy canonical art cinema, a form which has been historically resistant to generic categorisation, though David Bordwell has argued that what we understand as 'art cinema' is itself now a 'distinct mode of film practice, possessing a definite historical existence, a set of formal conventions, and implicit viewing procedures' and, as such, could be considered a genre in its own right (1979: 716). Indeed, even films that had explicit genre associations, such as Akira Kurosawa's *Seven Samurai* (1954) as an action-adventure, or Ingmar Bergman's *The Virgin Spring* (1960) as a rape/revenge narrative, have been elevated as canonical world cinema or art cinema, before the application of any generic associations derived from the narrative. This negotiation is significant because it illustrates the elevation of art cinema above everyday traditional generic classification, but also, in doing so, it reinforces a binary distinction based upon the perception of genre cinema as somehow lesser than film that falls outside of generic categorisation.

However, what is increasingly evident in the distribution practices of both Arrow Video and Criterion is that for them at least, these binaries are beginning to collapse. In a marketplace which was once defined by cultural distinction, distributors are increasingly demonstrating what Joan Hawkins referred to as a 'levelling of cultural hierarchies and abolition of binary categories' (2000: 8). This levelling has seen both sectors – as exemplified by Criterion and Arrow – extending their respective catalogues into what would have previously been understood as the other's territory, while still seeking to position these new additions as canonical. So while Criterion has released Federico Fellini's *8½* (1963), it is now equally comfortable releasing 1950s schlock sci-fi *The Blob* (1958). Similarly, while Arrow's mainstay is cult and exploitation, it also has an imprint, Arrow Academy, that releases the canonical films of the art-house such as Fassbinder's *The Marriage of Maria Braun* (1979) or Vittorio De Sica's *Bicycle Thieves* (1948). While the decision to extend their catalogues is largely economically driven, because of the curatorial role that these companies perform as prestige 'boutique' labels they can also be seen to be contributing to the formation of an economic canon. These labels increasingly function as cultural intermediaries and tastemakers, curating collections that allow for the reappraisal of films that are then considered important by virtue of the treatment they have received, just to be part of that catalogue. While these appraisals can incorporate ideas that have traditionally been employed in the elevation of canonical cinema, mobilising the figure of the auteur, or framing films as important through historical portraits, they are not limited to just this. Increasingly, significance is being constructed through the technical specifications of a release as much as paratextual material that celebrates the artistry of a release. In this way, distributors can be seen to be actively contributing to an ever-evolving canon, and should not be regarded as passive agents that merely facilitate audiences' access to film, but more as curators who are invested in contributing to the formation of a new 'economic canon'. While much of the motivation to re-release these films is commercially motivated, the reappraisals that these releases have afforded has had a tangible effect on the sector and has provided a new language with which to describe these films that now considers them as important artistic works and not simply trash cinema that is to be dismissed.

Curating the Art Object

This sense of a shift in value that these films have undergone is perhaps best seen in a trailer produced by Arrow Video to promote their catalogue. It illustrates how the company are presenting their films, and demonstrates the importance placed upon paratextual materials, and the ways in which this material is crucial in helping to position their product as a valuable curated piece of art in its own right. The trailer begins fairly traditionally, foregrounding the figure of the auteur as a means of positioning their product as important:

> The most dedicated label for fans of cult film in the world! Brings you films from cult directors including George A. Romero, Lucio Fulci, Mario Bava, Lamberto Bava, Takashi Miike, Ernest Pintoff, Richard Wenk, Nico Mastorakis, Kinji Fukasaku, J. Michael Muro, Herschell Gordon Lewis, Charles E. Sellier Jr., Brian De Palma and more!

It then continues by foregrounding the films themselves, but here the emphasis is placed on the fact that the films are digitally restored, rather than enumerating the entirety of films contained in their catalogue. Only then, after the restoration process has been emphasised, is any emphasis given to the fact the many of the releases are available uncut in the UK for the first time: 'Digitally restored presentations . . . Inferno, City of the Living Dead, Available uncut for the first time in the UK . . . Deep Red, Inferno, Island of Death.' And then the remainder of the trailer is spent enumerating the paratextual material that accompanies their releases:

> A choice of sleeve art for every title (up to 5 sleeve art options). Bonus elements in every title can include; double-sided fold-out posters; collector's booklets; collector's comics' original artwork postcards, audio recollections, interviews with crew, the history of Italian horror, directors cuts, commentaries, documentaries, interviews and Q&A sessions, multiple language and audio options, newly created subtitle tracks including English, alternative versions of the feature, newly restored material, expert's notes, never seen before, newly commissioned bonus features, publicity vault: trailers, tv ads, stills, promo artwork, radio ads, transcripts and more!

The emphasis here is clearly on the package, and frames the releases as significant through the abundance of supplementary materials available. This text is accompanied by visuals that begin with the logo for the company presented in the 8-bit aesthetic of the original video distributors, before flickering into high definition. This precedes a showreel of clips culled from their films and edited together to the song 'Devil's Stompin' Ground' by the band Southern Culture on the Skids. These elements are then cut together in rapid succession without title or introduction. There is an expectation that the audience will have knowledge of the films as important cinematic milestones and that they will recognise their significance. What becomes increasingly clear is that the emphasis here is not upon the films themselves; indeed, anyone unfamiliar with the films used in the trailer might find the advertisement exclusionary and frustrating, with very little indication of the films that are being screened. Instead the emphasis is on the product and the art of Arrow Video itself. It is about the company's approach and its emphasis on quality and on the paratextual framing of the films as important. The trailer closes with the legend: 'for true connoisseurs of cult cinema', again speaking explicitly to a collector's market, and to an audience that is already familiar with the films and understands their importance (Figure 8.2).

These are, to borrow Antje Ascheid's term, releases that are constructed as 'an artistically valuable "authored original"', but the emphasis here is as much on the product, and on the brand, as it is about the films

Figure 8.2 Arrow Video's release of *The City of the Living Dead* illustrating the prestige packages of Arrow. © Arrow Films. Reprinted with permission.

themselves (1997: 34). These are collector's editions that are often only available in limited runs, a factor that has also helped to reinforce a sense of the artisanal qualities that the company brings to the films. A simple YouTube search reveals over 2,000 videos of fans discussing their own Arrow Video collections. Many follow the same format, typically lasting for around fifteen minutes during which time the fans will take their DVDs off the shelves and discuss their love of the label and when and why they started collecting. Accounts typically prioritise the artwork of the releases, the supplementary materials and the diversity of the films available; moving through DVDs and Blu-ray, collectors introduce Steelbooks, box sets and 'windowed releases'. A vlogger calling himself Logan Toxic suggests that for him 'it's hard to pick which one is their best release, because all of them are superb releases' (Logan Toxic 2016), reinforcing a sense that, for Logan at least, this is not necessarily about individual films but rather the specificities of the product. This is something that can be seen again and again. Vlogger Spidergeek's review of his collection prioritises the artwork, something that can be seen in his review of *The Bride of Re-animator* (1990). He says that the release 'is just fantastic, I love the artwork on that' (Spidergeek 2016), but he admits that his collection includes films that he despises. Of the film *Hellgate* (1989) he says 'I had it, watched it, hated it, sold it', but then admits that he 'bought it back again because [he] wanted to complete the collection', suggesting that he loves the artwork on the cover, 'but the movie is just fucking awful' (Spidergeek 2016).

This is largely a canon based upon personal consumption and is in many respects a celebration of the brand and of the artistry of the product more than it is a legitimate celebration of the artistry of any given film. Arrow's own curation has helped to elevate the mass-produced to the level of art, reinforcing the idea of an economic canon that is determined by their catalogue and by their treatment of the films, more than the films themselves. Something which has helped reinforce this idea is planned obsolescence, releasing films for intentionally limited runs or for a deliberately limited time period. Arrow Video's blog, Arrowvideodeck, details the variety of reasons that their releases might go out of print, suggesting that firstly, a particular version may be superseded by an alternative release, something which is often the case with releases that incorporate special packaging (Arrow Video 2013: online). These releases are only ever intended to be available for a limited period before they are replaced by a standard edition. Occasionally, an older version may be superseded by a newer restoration that is based upon a better negative or master. Another reason relates directly to the licensing of the films, and how long that the company has arranged to retain the rights to distribute any given film. They suggest that while they endeavour to retain the rights to all of their back catalogue, licences may sometimes lapse due to circumstances beyond their control and that this would lead to a film becoming out of print. The article takes care to detail the variety of reasons that a version of a film may no longer be available and closes with a list of titles that are either no longer available or that have limited availability. While the article is informative, detailing the inner workings and processes of the company, it also reinforces a sense that these products are valued and are in high demand as collector's items.

Arrow has released many of the original video nasties; however, with the cassettes still in circulation and commanding increasingly high prices, it is difficult to construct a sense of authenticity around a contemporary mass-produced product. Limited edition runs may create a sense of scarcity but in order to be truly successful a product needs to appear authentic. Sharon Zukin has argued that for an object to appear authentic, it needs to belong to either the 'historically old', or to the 'creatively new' (2010: xiii), and only then can it be considered to be valuable. For the video nasties to be accepted and valued as authored originals, they must belong to the 'historically old' – that is the original VHS, Betamax or V2000 releases of the video nasties, what Kate Egan called 'origin objects' (2007: 158) – or they must belong to the 'creatively new' – films such as the releases of Arrow that construct their authenticity through digital restoration and historical portraits that all work to reinforce the artistry of the product.

It is not insignificant that for many of their releases Arrow has called upon the services of illustrator Graham Humphreys. His work acts as an intertextual link to the past, reaching back to the original video nasties, and to *The Evil Dead* sleeve and poster that Humphreys developed for Palace. Moreover, Humphreys himself demonstrated perfectly the remediation that had taken place in the British marketplace when in 2015, he appeared on the Channel 4 television programme *Four Rooms*. The format of the show was simple: guests would bring along their valuable and collectable items and would enter four different rooms, to receive four different offers, from one of four different dealers for the lots that they had brought with them. Humphreys had brought with him two original paintings: the original painting for *The Evil Dead 2* (1987) and the original painting for *A Nightmare on Elm Street*, hoping to achieve £10,000 from each of the paintings in order to finance the production of a deluxe coffee table book of his work and to facilitate the curation of gallery exhibition that would act as a retrospective of his work and through which he could promote the book. While the dealer in the first room did not recognise the value in the lot and was not prepared to come close to Humphreys' £20,000 target, in the second room was entrepreneur and gallery owner Alex Proud. Proud was a lot more receptive to Humphreys' goal, and, after some negotiation, Humphreys walked away with a tokenistic £1000 for the two paintings, but with an agreement that the Proud Group would not only publish a book of Humphreys work but that they would also develop the gallery exhibition with which to promote it. *Drawing Blood: 30 Years of Horror Art* was published by Proud Publishing Limited on Halloween, 31 October 2015, with the release timed to coincide with an exhibition which ran from 29 October until 22 November at the Proud Gallery in Camden, London. The book was released in a limited edition run of 500 books which retailed for £150, and that gave those that bought the book entry to the official launch party of the exhibition on Wednesday 28 October 2015 at Proud Camden. The invitation, as you would expect of any gallery show, focused on the 'skill and imagination' of Humphreys, and billed the exhibition as 'an inside look into the most celebrated films of the genre with this extraordinary collection of original artwork by the last master of horror art' (Proud Galleries 2016). The rehabilitation of Humphreys' work, from the 'lurid' pulp packaging of *The Evil Dead*, a film that had featured so prominently in the moral panic, to the production of a deluxe coffee table book and prestigious gallery show, marks the transition that has taken place over the last thirty years. Humphreys has worked for Palace and for VIPCO, distributors that were both known for releasing the video nasties originally on video, and he has been instrumental in the repositioning of these films in the contemporary era, in the work that he has produced for Arrow Video and Shameless Screen Entertainment. Framing Humphreys as 'the last master of horror art', the Proud Gallery is not only acknowledging his skill and imagination but also the fact that the industry has changed significantly since these paintings were first commissioned. With many modern designers preferring the ease, convenience and flexibility of computer-generated imagery, these paintings are increasingly relics of a time and of an industry that does not exist anymore, and with the exhibition and book signalling the final passage of the video nasties from an object that was once feared into legitimate artistic remnant, there is a growing sense that these remediations are signalling a profound shift in the marketplace and in how we understand exploitation cinema. In 2016, Arrow Video published *Cult Cinema: An Arrow Video Companion* (Nield 2016), which was in part illustrated by Humphreys, and detailed Arrow's releases to date and reprinted the artwork and the liner notes. The book is divided into five sections: the opening chapter features seven essays on key cult movies followed by sections devoted to directors, actors, genres (and subgenres) and distribution, which 'examines how different methods of seeing a film, from travelling shows to DVDs, has allowed cult movies and their audiences to flourish' (2016: 7). In this, Arrow has assumed the role of custodian, archivist and preservationist, and in doing so has begun to acknowledge the shift in perceived value that has taken place around these films. While Arrow's book and the rehabilitation of Humphreys' illustrations into the Proud Gallery are a signifier of the transition that has been made, in July 2010, as part of 'The Project for The Dictionary of Received Ideas', the artist Darren Banks exhibited another. 'The Palace Collection' was a project that drew upon Marcel Duchamp's theory of the 'readymades', found objects that were originally mass-produced, industrially manufactured objects, repurposed as art to question the very notion of art. The most notorious of Duchamp's readymades was a urinal, turned on its side and titled *Fountain* (1917). *The Palace Collection* was eleven horror videos: *Basket Case* (1982), *Brain Damage* (1988*)*, *Carnival of Souls* (1962), *Creepers* (1985), *Demon Night* (1988), *Dream Demon* (1988), *Edge of Sanity* (1989), *The Evil Dead II* (1987), *The Hills Have Eyes* (1977), *Trick or Treat* (1986) and *Vampire at Midnight* (1988), films that had originally been released by Palace and that were illustrated by Graham Humphreys. The cassettes were accompanied by a six-minute manipulation of the opening ident for Palace Pictures, transformed into a pulsing visual collage and arranged together in a living-room-like space. Here, the audience could interact with the environment, they could play the films on the television and videocassette recorder provided, and Banks suggested that the installation was designed to ask us to remember the 'just forgotten' and the 'recently redundant', arguing that The Palace Collection 'negotiate[d] collective horror history', and the 'effects of new technology, and ideas of the collection' (Coleman 2010). He argued that by 'viewing Palace Picture videos as ephemera' the installation challenged the preciousness of this collection by placing it on public display as a useable resource. However, irrespective of Banks's motivations, placing horror videos in a gallery space that mimics a living room is a transformative process that collapses any lingering sense of these films as dangerous. It removes all sense of the illicit and rehabilitates these objects into art.

The End of Exploitation

Many contemporary accounts of engagement with the video nasties articulate a sense of disappointment on watching at the lack of extremity of the films themselves, with many noting that aside from a handful of what are often incredibly violent exceptions, the vast majority of the video nasties were fairly innocuous and nowhere near as nasty as they had been portrayed to be. Whether that misrepresentation was in the press or in the official promotional material is, in many ways, inconsequential to the legacy of the video nasties; what is perhaps more important is how these disparities have been negotiated. In her analysis of the promotional strategies of the 1930s and 1940s, and what is now considered to be the golden age of exploitation, Amanda Ann Klein argues that 'advertising for exploitation films promised an experience they did not necessarily deliver', referring to the hyperbolic 'come-ons' typical in the promotion of this type of film (2011: 7). Similarly, Eric Schaefer suggest that throughout this period, 'an exploitation film could be completely misrepresented by the advertising and could disappoint spectators', but that 'the ballyhoo that preceded it was part of the overall entertainment experience, a fact which the audience recognised and appreciated and in which they were complicit' (1999: 111). In many ways, the video nasties have become victims of the same kind of misrepresentation. The hyperbolic claims of the press about the threat that these films posed created a set of expectations that was based entirely on the notoriety of the films. However, I would argue that unlike Schaefer's observations about classical exploitation cinema, here the audience were not always complicit, but they have learned to negotiate these deceptions and construct value and significance in other, more conventional ways, and through a process of subcultural gentrification.

British sociologist Ruth Glass coined the term 'gentrification' in 1964 to describe an influx of affluent middle-class residents into what had previously been poor working-class neighbourhoods in central London. This arrival facilitated the socio-economic transformation of the area, but in the process forever altered the social strata and physical characteristics of the environment. Jeremy Bryson suggests that the process of typically 'involves the reinvestment of capital after a period of disinvestment, the production of an aestheticized landscape, and lower-class displacement followed by middle-class replacement' (2013: 578). While both of these descriptions are explicitly concerned with society as a whole, the transformation of the video nasties and of cult cinema more generally can be seen to have followed the same trajectory, with previously marginal films rehabilitated into valuable artistic objects. What remains to be seen is whether these two conceptions can exist side by side, or whether one will ultimately invalidate the other, and an understanding of the video nasties as illicit, excessive or transgressive will be replaced by artistically important, culturally significant and commercially valuable.

More than ten years ago, Julian Petley suggested that it was unlikely that the BBFC would ever relax their regulations enough to release the contentious video nasties *The House on the Edge of the Park* and *SS Experiment Camp* in their original uncut form, or even that *The Driller Killer* could be distributed with its original artwork (2009: 272).

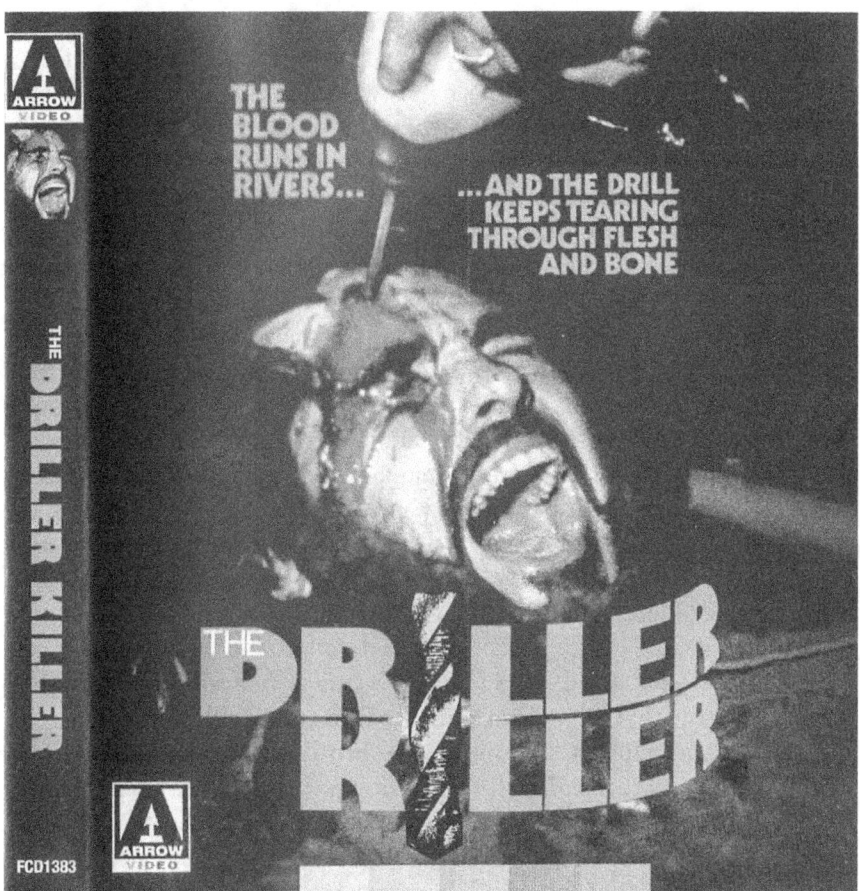

Figure 8.3 Arrow Video's 2016 release of *The Driller Killer* using the original VIPCO artwork. © Arrow Films. Reprinted with permission.

However, since that time, *SS Experiment Camp* has been passed uncut, with the BBFC suggesting that 'despite the questionable taste of basing an exploitation film in a concentration camp, the sexual activity itself was consensual and the level of potentially eroticised violence sufficiently limited', and that 'scenes that had once exercised the authorities when the work was released on video in the early '80s did not contravene the Board's strict policy' (BBFC 2005). *The House on the Edge of the Park* is now available with only forty-two seconds cut from its overall running time, and, perhaps most surprisingly, since 2016, and courtesy of Arrow Video, *The Driller Killer* was made available as a limited-edition Steelbook featuring the original gory packaging that had once been credited with creating the moral panic (Figure 8.3). (While all of this illustrates the ways in which attitudes have changed, video nasty *Love Camp* 7 (1969) was still refused a certificate in March of 2020 on the grounds that the sexually abusive material represented in the film was too pervasive for cuts to offer an effective solution.) As is typical of Arrow's releases, the film was bursting with supplementary materials that helped to frame it as culturally significant. The film itself was presented in a brand new 4K restoration drawn from the original camera negative of the never-before-seen pre-release version and the theatrical cut. It featured an audio commentary by director and star Abel Ferrara that was moderated by Brad Stevens, author of *Abel Ferrara: The Moral Vision* (2004), recorded especially for this release. Also recorded exclusively for this release are *Laine and Abel: An Interview with the Driller Killer*, a brand-new interview with Ferrara himself, and *Willing and Abel: Ferraraology 101*, a visual essay guide to the films and career of Ferrara by academic Alexandra Heller-Nicholas. Alongside the extras that were developed exclusively for this release is the 2010 feature-length documentary portrait *Mulberry St*, exploring the New York location that has played a key role in the life and work of Abel Ferrara, and the trailer. These digital materials were accompanied by a collector's booklet that featured new writing by Michael Pattison and Brad Stevens.

As already discussed, these supplementary materials serve as historical portraits that help to reframe the film as valuable and significant, and they begin to hint at the discursive shift that has taken place. Upon its release, the picture editor for *The Guardian*, Rowan Righelato, made a case for the film's rehabilitation, in which he suggested that the film was 'far from a mere video nasty'. For Righelato, the film had a cultural value far beyond that generic label with his suggestion that it was a 'gory gem [that] shatters our complacency and forces us to confront our moral choices' (2016). Righelato compares Abel Ferrara to Van Gogh and describes him as 'a truly visionary artist whose genius is destined to be ignored in his own lifetime' (ibid.). This reappraisal assigns a value to *The Driller Killer* that is not based upon its violence or its obscenity, or on the belief that this is the archetypal video nasty. Instead, Righelato's appraisal is based upon his belief that *The Driller Killer* is a visionary artistic statement, a valuable canonical film from an auteur director, and while Righelato is quick to make a distinction between *The Driller Killer* and the other video nasties, it is nevertheless a similar impulse to valorise that informs almost all reappraisals of these films. Between Righelato's reappraisal and Arrow's repackaging, it would seem as if the gentrification of the video nasties is complete, elevated from cinematic depths of exploitation trash and rehabilitated into respectable canonical works of art.

Writing in 1993, Peter Hutchings said of the Hammer horror film that 'rendering the films worthy and respectable would be doing them a disservice. More, it would be like forcing them into the light and watching helplessly as they crumble into dust' (1993: 187). The video nasties now exist across a spectrum of media forms with a plurality of meanings in which they are simultaneously denigrated as trash and exploitation while being celebrated as worthy and canonical cinematic entries; however, as the language that was once used to describe these films is gradually being eroded and replaced by the language of cinephilia and the curatorial practices of distribution labels, it remains to be seen whether 'rendering the films worthy and respectable [will] be doing them a disservice', and whether they will 'crumble into dust'.

CHAPTER 9

Conclusion: The Golden Age of Exploitation?

On 14 March 2006, the last major Hollywood movie to be released on video was released in the UK. The film was David Cronenberg's *A History of Violence* (2005), and although entirely coincidental, Cronenberg and his film would provide a fitting epitaph to the format that had popularised and commercialised film as a viable form of home entertainment. Not only had video's introduction been a curiously violent and troubled affair, but Cronenberg's seminal work *Videodrome* (1983) had offered a visceral satirical commentary on the corrupting effects of watching violence and sadomasochism on screen – a narrative that was underpinned by the same concerns as those that had informed the video nasties moral panic. In the US, just a few months after the film's release, Diane Garrett, the features editor for *Variety* magazine provided a poetic obituary to the failing format entitled 'An Obituary: VHS Dies of Loneliness at Age 30' (Garrett 2006). It ran as follows:

> The home-entertainment format lived a fruitful life. After a long illness, the ground-breaking home-entertainment format VHS has died of natural causes in the United States. The format was 30 years old. No services are planned. The format had been expected to survive until January, but high-def formats and next-generation videogame consoles hastened its final decline. [. . .] VHS is survived by a child, DVD, and by Tivo, VOD and DirecTV. It was preceded in death by Betamax, Divx, mini-discs and laserdiscs. Although it had been ailing, the format's death became official in this, the video biz's all-important fourth quarter. Retailers decided to pull the plug, saying there was no longer shelf space. As a tribute to the late, great VHS, Toys 'R' Us will continue to carry a few titles like 'Barney,' and some dollar video chains will still handle cassettes for those who cannot deal with the death of the format.

While Garrett's obituary to the format was timely, it would ultimately prove to be premature, and while chains like Toys 'R' Us did initially carry the last of the dwindling stock, in recent years there has been a rekindled interest in the format with a steady growth in grass-roots movements that are run by an enthusiastic community of collectors. In the US, documentaries like *Adjust Your Tracking: The Untold Story of the VHS Collector* (Kinem and Peretic 2013) and *Rewind This!* (Johnson 2013) have done much to revive interest in the ailing format, raising interesting and important questions about how and what we might preserve from over thirty years of home entertainment, with many concerned that many of the films that were made available on video were actually made on video, and as such may never receive a release on one of the new digital formats. In August 2015, Yale University library announced that it was leading that charge with the digitisation and preservation of nearly 3,000 videocassettes, among them numerous horror and exploitation titles, while in the UK interest in video has never really gone away.

The video nasties moral panic and the removal of the videos from the shelves, inadvertently made collectables of these cassettes and created a market that still exists today. This marketplace has ensured that these cassettes have retained their value and continued to become more and more valuable as the years have progressed. This is a market created by censorship, and to some degree, the willingness of fans to accept the rhetoric of tabloid journalism as an accurate representation of both the industry and the films. Interest in the video nasties continues to grow and received a significant boost in 2010 with the success of the documentary *Video Nasties: Moral Panic, Censorship & Videotape* (West 2010a), while the documentaries *Rewind This!* and *Adjust Your Tracking: The Untold Story of the VHS Collector* have helped to create an awareness of the growing interest in video and the sense of nostalgia that surrounds it. The director of *Rewind This!*, Josh Johnson, suggested that 'video shaped who [he was] more than any other presence in [his] life', even going onto argue that 'the video revolution democratised media in a profound way' (Beanland 2013). However, for all the importance that Johnson places on the format, the dominant perception seems to be of a redundant and obsolete low-budget format with very little value in the contemporary marketplace. So persistent is this idea that even the journalist conducting the interview with Johnson, Christopher Beanland, frames it as a discussion of the 'fag end of film – the videotape' (ibid.) and doing so expresses what is perhaps the dominant view of the waning format. However, the perception of video as somehow of lesser importance than subsequent formats has value to those still invested in the technology, and to the genres of film that continue to thrive among collectors. In the same article, Beanland interviewed British video collector Dale Lloyd, known widely as Viva VHS, who reminisced about his own experience of video, growing up in the West Midlands. Lloyd suggests that although video was seeing a resurgence, he did not think that this would lead to a widespread re-adoption of the format in the way that had been witnessed with vinyl, attributing vinyl's renaissance to the format's superior sound. Lloyd was keen to make a distinction between his own fandom and any wider resonance of the format in popular culture, though he did suggest that 'some movies, mainly low budget 1980s horror [movies], just work better with a bit of grain', going on to argue that 'Hi-Def isn't as scary' (ibid.). However, while Lloyd was keen to caution about the wider appeal of video in the digital age, his belief is an increasingly common perspective and is something that is mirrored in director Neil Marshall's suggestion that although video is widely considered to be a low-end format, the 'low-res, grubby, grainy, crackly, scratchy image' [. . .] lends 'an edge to those films that doesn't exist anymore' (West 2010). While Marshall was talking explicitly about the video nasties, this is true all kinds of exploitation film; whether that is drawing on the aesthetic of grindhouse cinema or related explicitly to subgenres like the *Giallo* or the *Poliziotteschi*, the appeal of that grubby, grainy, crackly image increasingly serves as a signifier for a particular type of film from a particular period.

In recent years the low-resolution aesthetic of video has become a generic signifier for the 1980s, a universal visual shorthand that is employed in a number of very different ways. This is a practice that can be seen in the branding of Arrow Video and their application of an analogue aesthetic as a part of their ident which invokes the rudimentary graphics of those early distributors and in doing so acts as a generic indicator for the type of film that the company specialises in. Here, it evokes Britain's 'golden age of exploitation' and recalls the pre-certification period and the era of the video nasty nostalgically. However, the aesthetic of video has a universal quality that can be seen mobilised in just as many mainstream places. The title sequence for the ABC sitcom *The Goldbergs* (2013–) uses home video as a way of nostalgically evoking the 1980s, with 'home video footage' routinely seen to be tracking or overlaid with graphics typical of the format. Just as 8mm and Super 8mm was once the aesthetic that was used to evoke the 1960s on film and television in shows like *The Wonder Years*, home video is now the aesthetic of the 1980s. This aesthetic is now available as a filter on smartphones giving self-produced contemporary digital media content a 'retro' feel. Popular apps employ the idea of video culture as a way to mobilise ideas of nostalgia and therefore align a new product and an old idea. This is an alignment that can also be seen in an advertising campaign that was developed by the London based advertising agency WCRS for Sky Movies Marketing division. Developed in 2012 for BSkyB, the agency dressed the electricity showrooms in Shoreditch to look like a video shop as Kate Winslet walked through row after row of videocassettes and talked nostalgically about her experience of going to the video shop in her youth. She began:

> Video shops, I remember spending so much time just looking, trying to choose. Did I feel like laughing, crying, falling in love? And how do you pick just one? Imagine if you had your very own movie store at home, just for you.

The ad closes with the voice of Michael Gambon informing the viewer that they could 'now rent over 1000 movies instantly through [their] Sky + HD Box, with Sky Store' (Jack Bayley, *Sky Store with Kate Winslet*, 2012), the implication being that the convenience and accessibility of Sky offers a comparable and in many ways superior experience to the inconvenience of the video shop: an experience in which the consumer is not limited to just one videocassette, but instead has access to thousands of films on demand. Traces of video are mobilised in lots of different places, in different ways, and for different purposes, but there are few that draw so well on the image of the video shop itself as a site of nostalgia. However, while the convenience of Sky's platform appeals to a great number of people, for many in the UK the nostalgic remembrance of video and the video shop lies not in its convenience (or lack thereof), but rather in a sense that this early culture offered a glimpse into an X-rated alternative to the homogeneous mainstream.

Many companies have begun to capitalise on this sense of nostalgia by offering limited edition VHS releases, to accompany their new Blu-ray releases. This is a strategy that has been employed successfully by Magnet Releasing with the film *V/H/S* (2012), but also by Severin Films with the American release of the British video nasty *Exposé* (1976). Similarly, the American distributor Wizard, on recognising the potential for profit from re-releases of cult video, claimed that they had found hundreds of big-box VHS cassettes in a warehouse more than thirty years after their original release. Among these titles were the video nasties *I Spit on Your Grave*, *SS Experiment Camp* and *Zombie Flesh Eaters*. However, it was later revealed that these cassettes were not original releases that had been lost in storage, but that the company were simply reproducing the cassettes in order to capitalise on the unexpected video boom years after its bust (Slasher Index 2013: online). Daniel Herbert has observed that although these companies are contributing to the de-formatting of video by also releasing movies on DVD and Blu-ray, they are nevertheless endeavouring 'to redefine VHS as a platform, making it a signifier of subcultural authenticity' (2017: 9).

While I dispute some of the romanticism of the 'golden age of exploitation' narrative, it is impossible to ignore the nostalgia that the period holds for many and how this nostalgia continues to inform both ideas about the video industry in the UK and contemporary culture. In his work on the *Giallo*, Oliver Carter has argued that 'the VHS is important here as it remains the primary medium on which many *Gialli* were made available for home viewing' (Carter 2018: 155), but while many films were certainly first introduced on home video, it does not *remain* the dominant mode of consumption, having been steadily replaced by DVD and Blu-ray. William Proctor argues that companies such as Arrow and 88 Films 'have been producing and distributing Italian cult cinema objects in boutique formats at an accelerated pace, and the availability of *gialli* and Italian horror etc. has never been so healthy' (Proctor 2019: online). So much so, that Shameless Screen Entertainment's Halloween sale was renamed 'Gialloween'. So, perhaps what Carter is highlighting above all else is how pervasive the desire to believe the myth of the golden age of exploitation is, despite being easily challenged. It is possible that the rhetoric of the golden age is linked to an anti-consumerist sentiment because of the fact that these films circulated illegally as a result of a sustained programme of censorship. However, this is difficult to measure empirically, and it is far more likely that the films that were circulating illegally were films that were either commercially available or had been commercially available before being removed in the wake of censorship. At the time of writing, Arrow has 485 releases across a range of exploitation subgenres that include the video nasties and the *Giallo*. Shameless Screen Entertainment have sixty-three releases that are almost exclusively Italian film from this period, and 88 Films have 225 films, many of them Italian and with subcategories for the *Giallo* and *Poliziotteschi*. That is 773 titles from just three British distributors. In 1982 and at the height of the video boom, and before a sudden decline in the face of censorship, the entire video industry commercially released only 2107 videos. To put that in context, VIPCO, one of the most notorious distributors associated with the video nasties moral panic, released only sixty-eight films in the entirety of their existence in the precertification period and many of those were family films.

This romanticism for the period disguises the commercial imperative that underpinned all of these historic releases and denies the commodification process that has subsequently taken place. In a discussion of grindhouse cinema, David Church suggests that the flexibility of the term as an overarching generic label can be attributed to its function as a 'highly sellable commodity', and that what was often pitched as a 'struggle for (sub)cultural capital surrounding their genrified films now exposes itself as the struggle for economic capital that it always was' (2011). Similarly, although the video nasties were in many ways an accident that evolved into an overarching generic label, their rehabilitation into legally sellable commodity reveals the struggle for economic capital that has always underpinned the category, and that only now, after a long struggle for (sub)cultural capital, has contributed to a golden age for exploitation.

APPENDIX I

Video Nasty Artwork Analysis

Title	Photographic	Painted	Novelty	Genre	Brand names	Realism	Authenticity	Spectacle	Narrative	Stars	Creators	Affect
Absurd		×						×		×	×	
Anthropophagous: The Beast	×			×				×		×	×	
Axe		×		×				×		×	×	
The Beast in Heat		×		×				×				
The Beyond	×			×				×		×	×	
Blood Bath		×		×				×				
Blood Feast		×	×	×				×	×	×	×	×
Blood Rites	×			×								
Bloody Moon		×		×				×				
The Bogey Man	×							×		×	×	
The Burning	×			×	×			×		×	×	
Cannibal Apocalypse		×			×			×	×	×		
Cannibal Ferox		×	×					×		×	×	
Cannibal Holocaust		×		×	×			×				
The Cannibal Man		×		×				×		×	×	
Cannibal Terror	×				×			×	×			
Contamination	×							×		×	×	
Dead and Buried		×		×	×			×			×	
Death Trap		×			×			×		×	×	

APPENDIX I

Title	Photographic	Painted	Novelty	Genre	Brand names	Realism	Authenticity	Spectacle	Narrative	Stars	Creators	Affect
Deep River Savages		×						×			×	
Delirium	×				×							
The Devil Hunter		×			×			×		×		
Don't Go in the House	×				×			×				
Don't Go in the Woods... Alone!		×			×			×		×		
Don't Go Near the Park	×			×	×			×		×	×	
Don't Look in the Basement		×			×			×				
Don't Ride on Late Night Trains		×	×		×			×	×			
The Driller Killer	×				×	×		×		×	×	
The Evil Dead		×		×	×						×	
Evilspeak		×									×	
Exposé	×			×	×			×		×	×	
Faces of Death		×			×	×		×		×		
Fight for Your Life	×				×			×				
Andy Warhol's Frankenstein	×				×			×		×	×	
Forest of Fear		×										
Frozen Scream	×			×	×						×	
Funhouse – Carnival of Terror		×			×			×			×	
Gestapo's Last Orgy		×			×							
The House by the Cemetery		×			×			×		×	×	
House on the Edge of the Park		×			×					×		
Human Experiments	×							×		×	×	
I Miss You Hugs and Kisses	×				×			×		×	×	
Inferno		×			×			×			×	
Island of Death	×				×			×		×	×	
I Spit on Your Grave		×			×			×		×	×	
Killer Nun	×				×			×		×	×	
The Last House on the Left		×	×		×			×				×

(Continued)

Title	Photographic	Painted	Novelty	Genre	Brand names	Realism	Authenticity	Spectacle	Narrative	Stars	Creators	Affect
The Living Dead	×				×					×	×	
Love Camp 7		×						×	×			
Madhouse	×									×	×	
Revenge of the Bogey Man		×		×	×							
Shogun Assassin		×		×	×			×		×	×	
The Slayer	×				×			×		×	×	
Snuff		×						×				
SS Experiment Camp		×			×			×				
Tenebrae		×			×			×		×	×	
Terror Eyes	×				×			×		×	×	
The Toolbox Murders		×			×			×				×
Mardi Gras Massacre		×			×			×				
Nightmare Maker	×				×			×				
Nightmares in a Damaged Brain	×							×		×	×	
Night of the Bloody Apes		×						×				
Night of the Demon		×			×			×				
Possession		×			×			×		×	×	×
Pranks		×			×							
Prisoner of the Cannibal God		×			×			×		×		
Unhinged		×			×							
Visiting Hours		×			×			×				
The Werewolf and the Yeti	×				×			×				
The Witch that Came from the Sea	×				×			×				
Women Behind Bars		×			×			×				
Xtro	×				×			×				
Zombie Creeping Flesh		×			×			×		×	×	
Zombie Flesh Eaters		×			×			×		×		
TOTALS	28	46	2	12	60	2	0	61	4	37	38	4

APPENDIX II

Department of Public Prosecutions (DPP) 39: Films Prosecuted under the Obscene Publications Act in 1984

Title	Video label/ Catalogue number	Country of origin	Production year	Release year	Director
Absurd	MEDUSA CAT MC002	ITALY	1981	November 1982	Joe D'Amato
Anthropophagous: The Beast	VFP CAT VFP001	ITALY	1980		Joe D'Amato
Axe	VRO (VIDEO NETWORK) CAT VN0004	UNITED STATES	1977	January 1982	Frederick R. Friedel
The Beast in Heat	JVI (JAVED VIDEO INTERNATIONAL) CAT JVI006	ITALY	1977		Luigi Batzella
Blood Bath	HOKUSHIN CAT VM75	ITALY	1971	February 1983	Mario Bava
Blood Feast	ASTRA	UNITED STATES	1963	May 1982	Herschell Gordon Lewis
Blood Rites	SCORPIO CAT SVP101	UNITED STATES	1967	March 1983	Andy Milligan
Bloody Moon	INTERLIGHT CAT ILV107	WEST GERMANY	1980	November 1981	Jesus Franco
The Burning	THORN EMI CAT TVA9008362	UNITED STATES	1980	October 1982	Tony Maylam
Cannibal Apocalypse	REPLAY CAT R1015	ITALY/ SPAIN	1980	1983	Antonio Margheriti
Cannibal Ferox	REPLAY CAT R1016	ITALY	1981	August 1982	Umberto Lenzi
Cannibal Holocaust	GO CAT GO121	ITALY	1980	March 1982	Ruggero Deodato
The Cannibal Man	INTERVISION CAT A-A0348	SPAIN	1972	November 1981	Eloy de la Iglesia
Devil Hunter	CINEHOLLYWOOD CAT V1590	SPAIN/ FRANCE/ WEST GERMANY	1980	November 1981	Jesus Franco

(*Continued*)

Title	Video label/ Catalogue number	Country of origin	Production year	Release year	Director
Don't Go in the Woods	VRO (VIDEO NETWORK) CAT VN0012	UNITED STATES	1981	March 1982	James Bryan
The Driller Killer	VIPCO CAT VIP029	UNITED STATES	1979	February 1982	Abel Ferrara
Evilspeak	FILMTOWN (VIDEOSPACE) CAT FT02	UNITED STATES	1981	August 1983	Eric Weston
Exposé	INTERVISION CAT A-AE0201	GREAT BRITAIN	1975	1980	James Kenelm Clarke
Faces of Death	ATLANTIS CAT AVP601	UNITED STATES	1979	September 1982	John Alan Schwartz
Fight for Your Life	VISION-ON CAT VOV016	UNITED STATES	1977	1982	Robert A. Endelson
Flesh for Frankenstein	VIPCO CAT VIP046	ITALY/ FRANCE	1973	November 1982	Paul Morrissey, Antonio Margheriti
Forest of Fear	MONTE CAT MON1	UNITED STATES	1979	November 1982	Charles McCrann
Gestapo's Last Orgy	VFP CAT VFP004	ITALY	1976	1983	Cesare Canevari
The House by the Cemetery	VAMPIX (VIDEOMEDIA) CAT HVM1027	ITALY	1981	January 1983	Lucio Fulci
The House on the Edge of the Park	SKYLINE (VIDEOFORM) CAT CL003	ITALY	1980	October 1982	Ruggero Deodato
Island of Death	AVI CAT AVI003	GREECE	1976	November 1982	Nico Mastorakis
I Spit on Your Grave	ASTRA CAT WV016	UNITED STATES	1978	January 1982	Meir Zarchi
The Last House on the Left	REPLAY Cat R1013	UNITED STATES	1972	June 1982	Wes Craven
Love Camp 7	MARKET	UNITED STATES	1968		Lee Frost
Madhouse	MEDUSA CAT MC006	UNITED STATES	1981	January 1983	Ovidio G. Assonitis
Mardi Gras Massacre	MARKET	UNITED STATES	1978		Jack Weis
Night of the Bloody Apes	IFS (IVER FILM SERVICES) CAT FF30218	MEXICO	1968	January 1983	René Cardona
Night of the Demon	IFS (IVER FILM SERVICES) CAT FF30173	UNITED STATES	1980	June 1982	James C. Wasson
Nightmares in a Damaged Brain	WOV2000 CAT XF140	UNITED STATES	1981	May 1982	Romano Scavolini

APPENDIX II

Title	Video label/ Catalogue number	Country of origin	Production year	Release year	Director
Snuff	ASTRA/ UNKNOWN	ARGENTINA	1976	1982	Michael Findlay (archive footage) (uncredited) Horacio Fredriksson (archive footage) (uncredited) Simon Nuchtern (new footage) (uncredited)
SS Experiment Camp	GO CAT GO118	ITALY	1976	January 1982	Sergio Garrone
Tenebrae	VIDEOMEDIA CAT HVM1032	ITALY	1982	June 1983	Dario Argento
The Werewolf and the Yeti	CANON CAT CV005	SPAIN	1975	April 1983	Miguel Iglesias
Zombie Flesh Eaters	VIPCO CAT VIP024	ITALY	1979	December 1980 Cut November 1981 Uncut	Lucio Fulci

APPENDIX III

The DPP 'Dropped' 33: Films Listed in the Department of Public Prosecutions List but not Prosecuted under the Obscene Publications Act

Title	Video label/ Catalogue number	Country of origin	Production year	Release year	Director
The Beyond	VAMPIX (VIDEOMEDIA) CAT HVM1021	ITALY	1981	March 1982	Lucio Fulci
The Bogey Man	VIPCO CAT VIP014	UNITED STATES	1980	November 1981	Ulli Lommel
Cannibal Terror	MODERN FILMS (MOUNTAIN) CAT MD10	FRANCE/ SPAIN	1980	October 1981	Alain Deruelle (as A. W. Steeve), Olivier Mathot (uncredited), Julio Pérez Tabernero (uncredited)
Contamination	VIP (VIDEO INDEPENDENT PRODUCTIONS) CAT VIP001	ITALY/ WEST GERMANY	1980	July 1982	Luigi Cozzi
Dead & Buried	THORN EMI CAT TVA 901286 2	UNITED STATES	1981	April 1983	Gary Sherman
Death Trap	VIPCO CAT VIP035	UNITED STATES	1976	July 1982	Tobe Hooper
Deep River Savages	DERANN CAT FDV305	ITALY	1972	November 1982	Umberto Lenzi
Delirium	VTC CAT VTC1022	UNITED STATES	1979	March 1982	Peter Maris
Don't Go in the House	ARCADE (VIDEOSPACE) CAT AV007	UNITED STATES	1979		Joseph Ellison
Don't Go Near the Park	HOME VIDEO PRODUCTIONS (Intervision) CAT A-AE0429	UNITED STATES	1979	May 1982	Lawrence D. Foldes
Don't Look in the Basement	CRYSTAL (DERANN) CAT FCV604	UNITED STATES	1973	February 1983	S. F. Brownrigg
The Evil Dead	PALACE CAT PVC2018A	UNITED STATES	1982	February 1983	Sam Raimi
Frozen Scream	HOME VIDEO PRODUCTIONS (INTERVISION) CAT A-AE0433	UNITED STATES	1981	1983	Frank Roach

APPENDIX III 181

Title	Video label/ Catalogue number	Country of origin	Production year	Release year	Director
The Funhouse	CIC VIDEO CAT VHA1058	UNITED STATES	1981	June 1983	Tobe Hooper
Human Experiments	JAGUAR (WORLD OF VIDEO 2000) CAT XF121	UNITED STATES	1979	August 1981	Gregory Goodell
I Miss You Hugs and Kisses	INTERCITY CAT ICV111	UNITED STATES	1978	April 1982	Murray Markowitz
Inferno	20TH CENTURY FOX CAT 1140-50	ITALY	1980	September 1982	Dario Argento
Killer Nun	TECHNO FILM (FLETCHER) CAT V111	ITALY	1978	April 1981	Giulio Berruti
Late Night Trains	VIDEO WAREHOUSE (WORLD OF VIDEO 2000) CAT GF506	ITALY	1974	1979	Aldo Lado
The Living Dead at *Manchester Morgue*	VIP (VIDEO INDEPENDENT PRODUCTIONS) CAT VIP002	SPAIN/ ITALY	1974	June 1982	Jorge Grau
Nightmare Maker	ATLANTIS CAT AVP702	UNITED STATES	1981	Unknown	William Asher
Possession	VTC CAT VTC1031	FRANCE/ WEST GERMANY	1981	September 1982	Andrzej Zulawski
Pranks	CANON CAT CV002	UNITED STATES	1981	June 1982	Stephen Carpenter, Jeffrey Obrow
Prisoner of the Cannibal God	HOKUSHIN CAT VM27	ITALY	1978	November 1980	Sergio Martino
Revenge of the Boogeyman	VTC CAT VM27	UNITED STATES	1978	February 1984	Bruce Starr Ulli Lommel
The Slayer	VIPCO CAT VIP036	UNITED STATES	1981	June 1982	J. S. Cardone
Terror Eyes	GUILD CAT GH201	UNITED STATES	1980	February 1983	Ken Hughes
The Toolbox Murders	HOKUSHIN CAT VM61	UNITED STATES	1977	November 1981	Dennis Donnelly
Unhinged	AVATAR (CBS/ FOX) CAT 6238-50	UNITED STATES	1982	April 1983	Don Gronquist
Visiting Hours	CBS/FOX CAT 1171-50	CANADA	1981	November 1983	Jean-Claude Lord
The Witch Who Came From the Sea	CANON CAT CV005	UNITED STATES	1975	September 1982	Matt Cimber
Women Behind Bars	GO CAT GO128	BELGIUM/ FRANCE	1975	May 1982	Jesus Franco
Zombie Creeping Flesh	MERLIN (VCL) M264D	ITALY			Bruno Mattei (as Vincent Dawn) Claudio Fragasso (uncredited)

APPENDIX IV

DPP Section 3 Titles: Films which were Liable for Seizure and Forfeiture under Section 3 of the Obscene Publications Act, 1959, but not Prosecution

Title	Video label/ Catalogue number	Country of origin	Production year	Release year	Director
Abducted Alternative Titles *Schoolgirls in Chains* *Let's Play Dead*	Astra CAT WV022	UNITED STATES	1973	November 1982	Don Jones
Aftermath	World of Video 2000	UNITED STATES	1980	Unknown	Steve Barkett
Black Room, The	Alpha (Intervision) CAT A-A0453	UNITED STATES	1981		Elly Kenner Norman Thaddeus Vane
Blood Lust	Derann CAT DV130	SWITZERLAND	1976	1981	Marijan Vajda
Blood Song	IFS (Iver Film Services) CAT FF30174	UNITED STATES	1974	August 1982	Alan J. Levi
Blue Eyes of the Broken Doll, The	Canon CAT CV003	SPAIN	1973	October 1982	Carlos Aured
Brutes and Savages	Derann CAT DV103	UNITED STATES	1975	1980	Arthur Davis
Cannibal	Derann CAT DV133	ITALY	1976	August 1981	Ruggero Deodato
Cannibals	Cinehollywood V1000 ———————— Serpent (IDS) CAT 002	FRANCE	1980	November 1981 ———— Unknown	Jesús Franco
Chant of Jimmie Blacksmith, The	Walton CAT WLG17 ———————— Odyssey (CBS/FOX) CAT 6431-50	AUSTRALIA	1978	August 1982 ———— 1984	Fred Schepisi

APPENDIX IV 183

Title	Video label/ Catalogue number	Country of origin	Production year	Release year	Director
Child, The	VRO (Video Network) CAT VN0002 Prestige Star CAT A117	UNITED STATES	1976	1981 Unknown Unknown	Robert Voskanian
Christmas Evil	IFS (Iver Film Services) CAT FF30177	UNITED STATES	1980	December 1982	Lewis Jackson
Communion	VCL CAT P219D	UNITED STATES	1976	August 1982	Alfred Sole
Dawn of the Mummy	FilmTown (VideoSpace) CAT FT01	UNITED STATES/ITALY	1981	1983	Frank Agrama [Farouk Agrama]
Dead Kids	IFS (Iver Film Services) CAT FF30171	NEW ZEALAND, AUSTRALIA	1981	July 1982	Michael Laughlin
Death Weekend	Vampix (Videomedia) CAT HVM1025	CANADA	1976	June 1982	William Fruet
Deep Red	Techno Film (Fletcher) CAT V188	ITALY	1975	October 1982	Dario Argento
Demented	Media CAT M179	UNITED STATES	1980	1983	Arthur Jeffreys
Demons, The	GO CAT A102 GO CAT GO116	FRANCE/ PORTUGAL	1972	1981	Clifford Brown [Jesús Franco]
Don't Answer the Phone!	Jaguar (World of Video 2000) CAT XF132	UNITED STATES	1979	November 1981	Robert Hammer
Enter the Devil	Inter-Ocean CAT IOV059	UNITED STATES	1972	February 1983	Frank Q. Dobbs
Erotic Rites of Frankenstein, The	GO CAT GO117	SPAIN, FRANCE	1972	1981	Jess Franco [Jesús Franco]
Evil, The	VFO (Video Network) CAT VN0008 Video Film Organisation CAT VN0008 VRO (Video Network)	UNITED STATES	1978	October 1982 Unknown Unknown	Gus Trikonis
Executioner, The	VTI HELLO CAT H18 ACTIVE	UNITED STATES	1974	Unknown July 1982 July 1983	Duke Mitchell

(*Continued*)

Title	Video label/ Catalogue number	Country of origin	Production year	Release year	Director
Final Exam	Embassy CAT EV1618 Embassy CAT ELV1618	UNITED STATES	1981	January 1983 1984	Jimmy Huston
Foxy Brown	Guild CAT GH125	UNITED STATES	1974	May 1982	Jack Hill
Friday the 13th	Warner CAT PEV 61172 Warner CAT WEV 61172	UNITED STATES	1980	1983 June 1982	Sean S. Cunningham
Friday the 13th Part 2	CIC CAT VHE2035 CIC CAT LVG2035	UNITED STATES	1981	November 1982 1983	Steve Miner
GBH (Grievous Bodily Harm)	World of Video 2000 CAT XFV180	GREAT BRITAIN	1983	March 1983	David Kent-Watson
Graduation Day	IFS (Iver Film Services) CAT FF30167	UNITED STATES	1981	May 1982	Herb Freed
Happy Birthday to Me	RCA/Columbia Pictures CAT CVT10108 RCA/Columbia Pictures 42011	CANADA	1980	1983 Unknown	J. Lee Thompson
Headless Eyes	Sapphire (AVI) CAT SV100	UNITED STATES	1971	April 1983	Kent Bateman
Hell Prison	KM CAT A012	ITALY, SPAIN	1979	1982	
Hills Have Eyes, The	Jaguar (World of Video 2000) CAT XF122	UNITED STATES	1977	April 1981	Wes Craven
Home Sweet Home	Media CAT M177	UNITED STATES	1980	August 1982	Nettie Pena
Inseminoid	Brent Walker CAT BW07	GREAT BRITAIN	1980	November 1981	Norman J. Warren
Invasion of the Blood Farmers	Rainbow (Mountain) CAT MVT2009 CAT N8	UNITED STATES	1972	November 1981 Unknown	Ed Adlum
Killing Hour, The	L.U. Productions (World of Video 2000) CAT XF143 Ariel CAT AFV84-011	UNITED STATES	1982	March 1983 1984	Armand Mastroianni
Last Horror Film, The	Alpha (Intervision) CAT A-A0469	UNITED STATES	1982	June 1983	David Winters

APPENDIX IV 185

Title	Video label/ Catalogue number	Country of origin	Production year	Release year	Director
Last Hunter, The	Inter-Light CAT ILV108 Intervision CAT A-A0476	ITALY	1980	November 1981 1983	Anthony M. Dawson [Antonio Margheriti]
Love Butcher, The	Intervision CAT A-A0144	UNITED STATES	1975	1979	Mikel Angel Don Jones
Mad Foxes, The	Merlin (VCL) CAT M249D	SWITZERLAND, SPAIN	1980	May 1982	Paul Gray [Paul Grau]
Mark of the Devil	Intervision CAT A-A0343	West Germany	1969	November 1981	Michael Armstrong
Martin	Hello CAT H14	UNITED STATES	1976	July 1982	George A. Romero
Massacre Mansion	VIPCO CAT VIP059	UNITED STATES	1975	June 1983	Michael Pataki
Mausoleum	FilmTown (VideoSpace) FT03	UNITED STATES	1982	October 1983	Michael Dugan
Midnight	Alpha (Intervision) CAT A-A0451	UNITED STATES	1980	March 1983	John Russo
Naked Fist	VRO (Video Network) CAT VN0009 Video Film Organisation CAT VN0009 Prestige	UNITED STATES, PHILIPPINES	1981	1982 Unknown Unknown	Cirio H. Santiago
Nesting, The	VIPCO CAT VIP043	UNITED STATES	1980	October 1982	Armand Weston
New Adventures of Snow White, The	Mountain CAT VCSS 2/044	WEST GERMANY, UNITED STATES	1970	1980	Rolf Thiele
Night Beast	VIPCO CAT VIP052	UNITED STATES	1982	1983	Don Dohler [Donald M. Dohler]
Night of the Living Dead	Alpha (Intervision) CAT A-A0356 Intervision CAT H07	UNITED STATES	1968	July 1981 1979	George A. Romero
Nightmare City	VTC CAT VTC1199 VTC CAT VTC1006	ITALY, SPAIN	1980	Feb 84 June 82	Umberto Lenzi
Oasis of the Zombies	Filmland CAT FV101	SPAIN, FRANCE	1981		A. M. Frank [Jesús Franco]
Parasite	Entertainment in Video CAT EVV1002	UNITED STATES	1982	1983	Charles Band

(*Continued*)

Title	Video label/ Catalogue number	Country of origin	Production year	Release year	Director
Phantasm	VCL CAT P096D	UNITED STATES	1978	April 81	Don Coscarelli
Pigs	IFS (Iver Film Services) CAT FF30176	UNITED STATES	1972	November 82	Marc Lawrence
Prey	Vampix (Videomedia) CAT HVM1017	GREAT BRITAIN	1977	May 81	Norman J. Warren
Prom Night	Embassy CAT ELV2049	CANADA	1980	1983	Paul Lynch
Rabid	Alpha (Intervision) CAT A-A0354	CANADA	1976	July 1981	David Cronenberg
Rosemary's Killer	Entertainment in Video CAT EVV1006	UNITED STATES	1981	October 1983	Joseph Zito
Savage Terror	Go CAT Go127	INDONESIA	1979	1982	Sisworo Gautama Putra
Scanners	Guild CAT GH084	CANADA	1980	August 1981	David Cronenberg
Scream for Vengeance!	Intervision) CAT A-A0376	UNITED STATES	1979	1982	Bob Bliss
Shogun Assassin	VIPCO	JAPAN, UNITED STATES	1980	1981	Robert Houston Kenji Misumi
Street Killers	Astra CAT WV021	ITALY	1977	October 1982	Sergio Grieco
Suicide Cult	Mega Films CAT MGA101	UNITED STATES	1977		Jim Glickenhaus
Superstition	VTC CAT VTC1036	UNITED STATES	1982	December 1982	James W. Roberson
Suspiria	Thorn EMI CAT TVB 900265 2	ITALY	1976	August 1982	Dario Argento
Terror	Hokushin CAT VM51	GREAT BRITAIN	1978	August 1981	Norman J. Warren
Texas Chain Saw Massacre, The	IVER FILM SERVICES CAT FF30022	UNITED STATES	1974	November 1981	Tobe Hooper
Thing, The	CIC CAT VHA1062	UNITED STATES	1982	July 1983	John Carpenter
Tomb of the Living Dead	Horror Time CAT A14HT	PHILIPPINES, UNITED STATES	1968	January 1983	Eddie Romero Gerardo De Leon
Toy Box, The	TCX CAT TCX802	UNITED STATES	1970	November 1981	Ron Garcia
Werewolf Woman	Cinehollywood CAT V1770	ITALY	1976	November 1981	Rino Di Silvestro

Title	Video label/ Catalogue number	Country of origin	Production year	Release year	Director
Wrong-Way	Inter-Ocean CAT IOV05	UNITED STATES	1972	November 1981	Ray Williams
Xtro	Spectrum (PolyGram) CAT 790648 2	Great Britain	1982	May 1983	Harry Bromley Davenport
Zombie Holocaust	VTC CAT VTC1110	ITALY	1980	September 1983	Frank Martin [Marino Girolami]
Zombies: Dawn of the Dead	Alpha (Intervision) CAT A-A0358	UNITED STATES	1978	July 1981	George A. Romero
Zombies Lake	Modern Films (Mountain) CAT MD09	Spain, France	1980	November 1981	J. A. Laser [Jean Rollin] Julian de Laserna

Bibliography

Admin (2013), 'Horror genres and sub-genres', *Horror on Screen*, <http://www.horroronscreen.com/2013/06/10/horror-genres> (last accessed 19 October 2016).

Altman, R. (1998), *Film/Genre*, London: British Film Institute.

Armin (2013), 'New logo and identity for the Academy of Motion Picture Arts and Sciences', <http://www.underconsideration.com/brandnew/archives/new_logo_and_identity_for_the_academy_of_motion_picture_arts_and_sciences_by_180la.php#.V3TSCbgrJaQ> (last accessed 27 January 2017).

Arrow Video (2013), 'Out of print – what and why?', *Arrow Video Deck*, 25 June, <http://arrowvideodeck.blogspot.co.uk/2013/06/out-of-print-what-and-why_25.html> (last accessed 26 November 2016).

Ascheid, Antje (1997), 'Speaking in tongues: voice dubbing in the cinema as cultural ventriloquism', *The Velvet Light Trap*, (40): 32.

Ascher, S. and E. Pincus (2007), *The Filmmaker's Handbook: A Comprehensive Guide for the Digital Age*, New York: Plume.

Author unknown (1981), 'Rating guide for anxious parents', *Popular Video*, September, p. 18.

Author unknown (1982a), 'DPP ponders the case against "horror" videos', *Video Business*, mid-June, 2(9): 1.

Author unknown (1982b), 'Wrecking the pirates', *Video Business*, September, 2: 45

Author unknown (1982c), 'Outlawing the sadism-pushers', *Daily Mail*, 1 July, p. 6.

Author unknown (1983a), 'Gold & Sons', *Video Business*, 14 February, p. 64.

Author unknown (1983b), 'The rape of our children's minds', *Daily Mail*, 30 June, p. 6.

Author unknown (1993), 'For the sake of all our kids . . . burn your video nasty', *The Sun*, 28 November, p. 1.

Author unknown (2019), 'UK cinema admissions and box office', *Cinemauk*, <https://www.cinemauk.org.uk/the-industry/facts-and-figures/uk-cinema-admissions-and-box-office/annual-admissions/> (last accessed 19 November 2019).

Barber, Sian (2011), *Censoring the 1970s: the BBFC and the Decade That Taste Forgot*, Newcastle: Cambridge Scholars.

Barker, Martin (1984), *Video Nasties: Freedom and Censorship in the Media*, London: Pluto Press.
Barker, Martin and J. Petley (1997), *Ill Effects The Media/Violence Debate*, New York: Routledge.
Bates, Laura (2016), 'Chokeholds and headless women: Hollywood's poster problem', *The Guardian*, 8 June, <https://www.theguardian.com/lifeandstyle/2016/jun/08/chokeholds-and-headless-women-hollywoods-poster-problem> (last accessed 10 June 2016).
Bazin, André (1960), 'The ontology of the photographic image', *Film Quarterly*, 12(4): 4–9, California: University of California Press.
BBFC (2005), 'Annual Report', bbfc.co.uk, <https://bbfc.co.uk/sites/default/files/attachments/BBFC_AnnualReport_2005.pdf> (last accessed November 2019).
BBFC (2019), 'BBFC VRA Submission Guide 2019', <https://bbfc.co.uk/industry-services/video/submission-guide> (last accessed November 2019).
Beanland, C. (2013), 'It's a spool world: a new film is paying tribute to the legacy – and afterlife – of VHS', The Independent, 24 April, <http://www.independent.co.uk/life-style/gadgets-and-tech/features/its-a-spool-world-a-new-film-is-paying-tribute-to-the-legacy-and-afterlife-of-vhs-8586841.html> (last accessed 3 December 2016).
Belsky, Marcia (2016), 'About', 'The headless women of Hollywood', < https://headlesswomenofhollywood.com/About> (last accessed November 2019).
Benson-Allott, Cætlin (2013), *Killer Tapes and Shattered Screens: Video Spectatorship from VHS to File Sharing*, Berkeley and Los Angeles: University of California Press.
Berra, John (2009), *Declarations of Independence: American Cinema and the Partiality of Independent Production*, Chicago: University of Chicago Press.
Betz, M. (2010), 'In Focus: cinephilia, introduction', *Cinema Journal*, 49(2): 131–2.
Bickel, C. (2016), '"The Criterion of shit movies": Arrow Videos lionization of lowbrow', <http://dangerousminds.net/comments/the_criterion_of_shit_movies_arrow_videos_lionization_of_lowbrow> (last accessed 2 September 2016).
Black, Gregory D. (1996), *Hollywood Censored: Morality Codes, Catholics, and the Movies*, Cambridge: Cambridge University Press.
Bordwell, David (1979), 'The art cinema as a mode of film practice', *Film Criticism*, 4: 56–64. Reprinted in Catherine Fowler (ed.) (2002), *The European Cinema Reader*, New York: Routledge, pp. 94–102.
Brewster, Francis, Harvey Fenton and Marc Morris (2005), *Shock! Horror!: Astounding Artwork from the Video Nasty Era*, Guildford: FAB Press.
Brookey, Robert Alan (2007), 'The format wars: drawing the battlelines for the next DVD', *Convergence*, 13(2): 199–211.
Brooks, Andree (1982), 'Debunking the myth of P. T. Barnum', *New York Times*, 3 October, <http://www.nytimes.com/1982/10/03/nyregion/debunking-the-myth-of-pt-barnum.html> (last accessed 27 April 2014).

Bryce, Allan (1998), *The Original Video Nasties: From Absurd to Zombie Flesh-eaters*, London: Stray Cat Publishing.
Bryce, Allan (2001), *Video Nasties 2: Strike Up the Banned: A Pictorial Guide to the Movies that Bite!*, London: Stray Cat Publishing.
Bryson, Jeremy (2013), 'The nature of gentrification', *Geography Compass* 7/8: 578–87.
BVA (1986), British Videogram Association Status Report 1986, London: BVA.
Calboli, I. (2014), 'Overlapping copyright and trademark protection: a call for concern and action', *University of Illinois Law Review*, Slip Opinions, pp. 25–34, Research Collection School Of Law, <http://ink.library.smu.edu.sg/sol_research/1709/> (last accessed 19 October 2016).
Carroll, Nathan (2005), 'Unwrapping archives: DVD restoration demonstrations and the marketing of authenticity', *The Velvet Lightrap*, (56, Fall): 18–31.
Carter, Oliver (2018), *Making European Cult Cinema: Fan Enterprise in an Alternative Economy*, Amsterdam: Amsterdam University Press.
Cettl, R. (2014), *American Film Taglines*, Washington: CreateSpace Independent Publishing Platform.
Cherry, Brigid (2009), *Horror*, London: Routledge.
Chibnall, Steve and Brian McFarlane (2009), *The British 'B' Film*, London: BFI.
Chippendale, P. (1982), 'How high street horror is invading the home', *Sunday Times*, 23 May.
Church, David (2011), 'From exhibition to genre: the case of grind-house films', *Cinema Journal*, 50(4): 1–25.
Church, David (2015), 'One on top of the other: Lucio Fulci, Transnational Film Industries, and the retrospective construction of the Italian horror canon', *Quarterly Review of Film and Video*, 32(1): 1–20. DOI: 10.1080/10509208.2013.780935.
Clepper, Catherine (2016), '"Death by fright": risk, consent, and evidentiary objects in William Castle's rigged houses', *Film History: An International Journal*, 28(3): 54–84.
Clover, Carol J. (1987), 'Her body, himself: gender in the slasher film', reprinted in Barry Keith Grant (ed.), *Film Genre Reader III* (2003), Austin: University of Texas Press.
Coleman, Caryn (2010), 'Darren Banks: the Palace Collection', <https://carynco-leman.com/darren-banks-the-palace-collection/> (last accessed 17 February 2020).
Conboy, Martin (2005), *Tabloid Britain: Constructing a Community Through Language*, London: Routledge.
Connett, David (1992), 'Thousands of horror video films seized in raids', *The Independent*, 8 May.
Cook, Pam (1976), 'Softcore as serialized (and feminized)', *Screen*, 17(2): 122–7.
Cubbison, Laurie (2005), 'Anime fans, DVDs, and the authentic text', *The Velvet Light Trap*, (56): 5–57.
Dawe, T. (1982), 'This poison being peddled as home "entertainment"', *Daily Express*, 26 May, p. 7.

Dean, R. (1987), 'The subs and dubs divide', *TV World*, 10: 38–9.

Derann (2014), 'History', <www.derann.com> (accessed 2014).

De Valck, Marijke and Malte Hagener (2005), 'Down with cinephilia? Long live cinephilia? And other videosyncratic pleasures', in Martijn de Koning, Marijke de Valck and Malte Hagener (eds), *Cinephilia: Movies, Love and Memory*, Amsterdam: Amsterdam University Press, pp. 11–24.

Díaz Cintas, J. (2010), 'Dubbing or subtitling: the eternal dilemma', *Perspectives: Studies in Translatology*, 7(1): 31–40, <http://www.tandfonline.com/doi/abs/10.1080/0907676x.1999.9961346> (last accessed 26 July 2016).

Dickinson, Kay (2007), 'Troubling synthesis: the horrific sights and incompatible sounds of video nasties', in J. Sconce (ed), *Sleaze Artists: Cinema at the Margins of Taste, Style, and Politics*, Durham, NC: Duke University Press, pp. 167–88.

Doherty, Thomas (2002), *Teenagers and Teen Pics: The Juvenilization of American Movies in the 1950s*, Philadelphia: Temple University Press.

Dolan, Des (1982), 'That's marketing baby!', <http://www.go-video-ltd.co.uk/72.html> (last accessed November 2019).

Donald, Chris (ed.) (1991), *Viz: The Big Pink Stiff One*, London: John Brown Publishing.

Dover, Clare (1982), 'Children in video peril', *Daily Express*, 12 October, p. 5.

Edelstein, D. (2006), 'Now playing at your local multiplex: torture porn: why has America gone nuts for blood, guts and sadism', *New York Magazine*, <http://www.wwrsd.org/cms/lib04/NJ01000230/Centricity/Domain/230/Now%20Playing%20at%20Your%20Local%20Multiplex%20-%20Torture%20Porn.docx> (last accessed 19 October 2016).

Egan, Kate (2007), *Trash or Treasure: Censorship and the Changing Meanings of the Video Nasties*, Manchester: Manchester University Press.

Elder, R. B. (2007), 'Hans Richter and Viking Eggeling: the dream of universal language and the birth of the absolute film', *Avant-Garde Film*, 23: 1–53, <http://booksandjournals.brillonline.com/content/books/b9789401200035s002> (last accessed 19 October 2016).

Evry, Max (2014), 'The strange saga of Spookies', *The Dissolve*, <https://thedissolve.com/features/oral-history/788-the-strange-saga-of-spookies/> (last accessed 24 February 2017).

Ferman, James (1979), Letter, Sir Thomas Hetherington / Department of Public Prosecutions, 6 June, reprinted in *Saló, or The 120 Days of Sodom* [Blu-ray liner notes]. London: BFI.

Frayling, Christopher (2012), *Sergio Leone: Something To Do With Death*, St Paul: University of Minnesota Press.

Garret, Diane (2006), 'An obituary: VHS dies of loneliness at age 30', *Variety*, 4 November, <http://variety.com/2006/digital/news/vhs-30-dies-of-loneliness-1117953955/> (last accessed 30 November 2016).

Gelder, Ken (2000), 'Introduction to Part 10', in Gelder (ed.), *The Horror Reader*, London and New York: Routledge: pp. 311–13.

Gibbs, S. (2015), 'Betamax is dead, long live VHS', *The Guardian*, 10 November, <https://www.theguardian.com/technology/2015/nov/10/betamax-dead-long-live-vhs-sony-end-prodution> (last accessed 3 February 2017).

Glass, Ruth (1964), *London: Aspects of Change*, London: MacGibbon and Kee.

Graham, D. (1982), 'Video film kids beat the X-cert', *Daily Star*, 7 May, p. 13.

Gray, Ann (1992), *Video Playtime: The Gendering of a Leisure Activity*, London and New York: Routledge.

Grant, Barry Keith (1986), 'Introduction', in Grant (ed.), *Film Genre Reader*, Austin: University of Texas Press.

Gregory, D. (2005), *Ban the Sadist Videos!*, London: Anchor Bay UK.

Guins, Raiford (2005), 'Blood and black gloves on shiny discs: new media, old tastes, and the remediation of Italian horror films in the United States', in Steven J. Schneider and Tony Williams (eds), *Horror International*, Detroit: Wayne State University Press.

Gunning, Tom (1986), 'The cinema of attraction[s]: early film, its spectator and the avant-garde', in Wanda Strauven (ed.) (2006), *The Cinema of Attractions Reloaded*, Amsterdam: Amsterdam University Press, p. 387.

Gunning, Tom (2004), 'What's the point of an index? Or faking photographs', in Karen Beckman and Jean Ma (eds), *Still/Moving: Between Cinema and Photography*, Durham, NC: Duke University Press, 2008, pp. 23–40.

Hall, Kevin A. (2019), 'Iver Film Services – a detailed history', <www.iverfilmservices.co.uk/company-history.html> (last accessed November 2019).

Hamill, L. (2000), 'The introduction of new technology in the household', *Personal Technologies*, 4(1): 54–69.

Harding, Vivien (1983), 'The men who grow rich on bloodlust'. *Daily Mail*, 4 August, p. 19.

Hawkins, Joan (2000), *Cutting Edge: Art-Horror and the Horrific Avant-Garde*, St Paul: University of Minnesota Press.

Hayward, John (1982), 'From discs to "nightmares" in video', *Video Business*, 2(13, September): 36.

Hayward, A. (2006), 'David Maloney, director of Doctor Who chillers', *The Independent*, 9 August, <http://www.independent.co.uk/news/obituaries/david-maloney-411226.html> (last accessed 23 January 2017).

Hearn, Marcus (2010), *The Art of Hammer*, London: Titan Books.

Heffernan, Kevin (2004), *Ghouls, Gimmicks, and Gold: Horror Films and the American Movie Business 1953–1968*, Durham, NC: Duke University Press.

Hellman, Heikki and Martti Soramäki (1985), 'Economic concentration in the videocassette industry: a cultural comparison', *Journal of Communication*, 35(3, September): 122–34, <https://doi.org/10.1111/j.1460-2466.1985.tb02453.x>.

Hellman, Heikki and Martti Soramäki (1994), 'Competition and content in the U.S. video market', *Journal of Media Economics*, 7(1): 29–49.

Herbert, Daniel (2017), 'Nostalgia merchants: VHS distribution in the era of digital delivery', *Journal of Film and Video*, 69(2): 3. DOI:10.5406/jfilmvideo.69.2.0003.

Hills, Matt (2002), *Fan Cultures*, London and New York: Routledge.
Hills, Matt (2005), *The Pleasures of Horror*, London and New York: Continuum.
Hindley, Brian (1993), 'European venture: VCRs from Japan', in David Greenaway and Brian Hindley, *What Britain Pays for Voluntary Export Restraints*, Thames Essay no. 43, London: Trade Policy Research Centre, 1985: p. 37.
House of Commons (2012), 'Video killed the cinema's star', London: Reports, <http://www.parliament.uk/documents/commons/lib/research/olympic-britain/olympicbritain.pdf#page=125> (last accessed 3 February 2017).
House of Lords (1982), Local Government (Miscellaneous Provisions) Bill, <http://hansard.millbanksystems.com/lords/1982/mar/15/local-government-miscellaneous-1#S5LV0428P0_19820315_HOL_396> (last accessed 3 February 2016).
Humphreys, Graham (2015), *Drawing Blood: 30 Years of Horror Art*, London: Proud Galleries.
Hunt, Leon (1998), *British Low Culture: From Safari Suits to Sexploitation*, London: Routledge.
Hunter, I. Q. (2013), *British Trash Cinema*, London: BFI.
Hutchings, Peter (1993), *Hammer and Beyond: The British Horror Film*, Manchester: Manchester University Press.
Hutchings, Peter (2004), *The Horror Film*, London: Routledge.
Hutchings, Peter (2012), 'The limits of European horror', in Patrica Allmer, Emily Brick and David Huxley (eds), *European Nightmares: Horror Cinema in Europe Since 1945*, New York: Columbia University Press: pp. 13–23.
Impey, Jason (2019), 'Interview with Mike Lee', The Untold Story of VIPCOs Vaults of Horror (forthcoming).
Ivarsson, Jan (2009), 'The history of subtitles in Europe', in Gilbert Chee Fun Fong and Kenneth K. L. Au (eds), *Dubbing and Subtitling in a World Context*, Hong Kong: Chinese University Press, pp. 3–13.
Jackson, John (1984), 'Pony maniac strikes again', *Daily Mirror*, 3 January, p. 5.
Jackson, Neil (2002), '*Cannibal Holocaust*, realist horror and reflexivity', *Postscript*, 21(3): 32–45.
James, Brian (1983), 'We must protect our children NOW', *Daily Mail*, 25 February, p. 6.
Jancovich, Mark, Antonio Lázaro Reboll, Julian Stringer and Andy Willis (eds) (2003), *Defining Cult Movies: The Cultural Politics of Oppositional Taste*, Manchester: Manchester University Press.
Jenkins, Henry (1992), *Textual Poachers: Television Fandom and Participatory Culture*, London and New York: Routledge.
Jenkins, Henry, Sam Ford and Joshua Green (2013), *Spreadable Media: Creating Value and Meaning in a Networked Culture*, New York and London: New York University Press.
Johnson, Josh (2013), *Rewind This!*, USA: Imperial PolyFarm Productions.
Kattelman, Beth (2011), 'We Dare You to See This!': Ballyhoo and the 1970s horror film', *Horror Studies*, 2(1, June): 61–74.

Kendrick, James (2001), 'What is the Criterion? The Criterion Collection as an archive of film as culture', *Journal of Film and Video*, 53(2/3, Summer/Fall): 124–39

Kendrick, James (2005), 'Aspect ratios and Joe Six-Packs: home theater enthusiasts' battle to legitimize the DVD experience', *The Velvet Light Trap*, (56): 58–70.

Kerekes, David and David Slater (2000), *See No Evil: Banned Films and Video Controversy*, Manchester: Critical Vision/Headpress.

Kinem, Dan M. and Levi Peretic (2013), *Adjust Your Tracking: The Untold Story of The VHS Collector*, USA: Romark Entertainment.

Klein, Amanda Ann (2011), *American Film Cycles: Reframing Genres, Screening Social Problems, and Defining Subcultures*, Austin: University of Texas Press.

Klinger, Barbara (2006), *Beyond the Multiplex: Cinema, New Technologies, and the Home*, Berkeley: University of California Press.

Kotler, Philip (1991), *Marketing Management: Analysis, Planning, Implementation and Control*, 7th edn, Englewood Cliffs, NJ: Prentice Hall.

Koven, Mikel (2006), *La Dolce Morte: Vernacular Cinema and the Italian Giallo Film*, North Carolina: Scarecrow Press.

Lamberti, Edward (2012), *Behind the Scenes at the BBFC: Film Classification from the Silver Screen to the Digital Age*, London: Palgrave Macmillan.

Lardner, James (1987), *Fast Forward: Hollywood, the Japanese, and the VCR Wars*, London: W. W. Norton.

Logan Toxic (2016), 'My entire Arrow video Blu-ray movie collection', YouTube, <https://www.youtube.com/watch?v=ZlTPNG61yrU&t=87s> (last accessed 25 November 2016).

Maguire, David (2018), *I Spit on Your Grave*, New York: Wallflower Press.

Maltby, Richard (1995), 'The Production Code and the Hays Office', in Tino Balio (ed.), *Grand Design: Hollywood as a Modern Business Enterprise 1930–1939*, Berkeley: University of California Press, pp. 37–72.

Maltby, Richard (2012), 'The Production Code and the mythologies of "pre-Code" Hollywood', in Steve Neale, *The Classical Hollywood Reader*, London: Routledge, pp. 237–48.

Martin, John (2007), *Seduction of the Gullible : The Truth Behind the Video Nasty Scandal*, Nottingham/Rome: Procrustes Press.

McDonald, Paul (2007), *Video and DVD Industries*, London: British Film Institute.

Mee, L. (2013), 'The re-rape and revenge of Jennifer Hills: gender and genre in *I Spit on Your Grave*', *Horror Studies*, 4(1): 75–89.

Meikle, Denis (1996), *A History of Horrors: The Rise and Fall of the House of Hammer*, Maryland: Scarecrow Press.

Merrin, Tom (1983), 'Children turned on by TV horror', *Daily Mirror*, 24 November, p. 7.

Meyers, Ric (2011), *For One Week Only: The World of Exploitation Films*, Guilford, CT: Erini Press.

Miles, T. (1983a), 'Fury over the video rapist', *Daily Mail*, 28 June, p. 1.

Miles, T. (1983b), 'Charity shock from the "king" of the nasties', *Daily Mail*, 16 July, p. 2.
Miles, T. (1983c), 'Sadism for six-year-olds', *Daily Mail*, 24 November, p. 1.
Moore, Demi (2019), *Inside Out*, New York: Harper.
Moretti, Franco (2001), 'Planet Hollywood', *New Left Review*, May/June, <https://newleftreview.org/II/9/franco-moretti-planet-hollywood> (last accessed 14 October 2016).
Neale, Steve (1990), 'Questions of genre', *Screen*, 31(1, Spring): 45–66, <https://doi.org/10.1093/screen/31.1.45> (last accessed 29 February 2002).
Neale, Steve (1998), 'Widescreen composition in the age of television', in Steve Neale and Murray Smith (eds), *Contemporary Hollywood Cinema*, London: Routledge, pp. 130–41.
Neale, Steve (2000), *Genre and Hollywood*, London: Routledge.
Neighbour, Richard (1983), 'Hooking of the video junkies', *Daily Mail*, 13 August, p. 6.
Newman, Kim (1984), 'The video nasty list', *Monthly Film Bulletin*, London: British Film Institute.
Newman, Kim (1996), 'Journal of the plague years', in Karl French (ed.), *Screen Violence: an Anthology*, London: Bloomsbury.
Nicholson, M. (1981), 'Tape ads must be decent', *Video Review*, (April): 67.
Nield, Anthony (2016), *Cult Cinema: An Arrow Video Companion*, London: Arrow.
Nowell, Richard (2011), *Blood Money: A History of the First Teen Slasher Film Cycle*, London and New York: Continuum.
Pautz, M. (2002), 'The decline in average weekly cinema attendance: 1930–2000', *Issues in Political Economy*, vol. 11.
Pearse, Justin (1999), 'Matrix DVD breaks "extras" barrier', *ZDNet*, <http://www.zdnet.com/article/matrix-dvd-breaks-extras-barrier/> (last accessed 15 October 2016).
Pearson, A. (1994), 'Mary, Mary, quite contrary', *The Independent*, 28 May, <http://www.independent.co.uk/arts-entertainment/television--mary-mary-quite-contrary-1439331.html> (last accessed 3 February 2016).
Petley, Julian (1984a), 'A nasty story', *Screen*, 25(2): 68–74.
Petley, Julian (1984b), 'Two or three things I know about the video nasties', *Monthly Film Bulletin*, 51(610): 350–2.
Petley, Julian (2005), '*Cannibal Holocaust* and the pornography of death', in Geoff King (ed.), *The Spectacle of the Real – From Hollywood to Reality TV and Beyond*, Bristol: Intellect, pp. 173–85.
Petley, Julian (2007), 'Review of Kate Egan, *Trash or Treasure? Censorship and the Changing Meaning of the Video Nasties*', *Journal of British Cinema and Television*, 6(2): 272.
Petley, Julian (2009), 'Kate Egan, Trash or Treasure? Censorship and the Changing Meaning of the Video Nasties (Manchester: Manchester University Press, 2007), *Journal of British Cinema and Television*, Edinburgh: Edinburgh University Press.

Petley, Julian (2011), *Film and Video Censorship in Britain*, Edinburgh: Edinburgh University Press.
Petley, Julian (2012), '"Are We Insane ?", The "Video Nasty" Moral Panic', *RSA Revues*, 43(1): 35–57, <http://rsa.revues.org/839> (last accessed 2 February 2016).
Porter, Michael E. (1980), *Competitive Strategy: Techniques for Analyzing Industries and Competitors*, New York: Free Press. Republished with a new introduction 1998.
Pound, Kaylin (2016), 'Did you notice this one thing women on movie posters have in common?', *Elitedaily.com*, <https://www.elitedaily.com/envision/issues-movie-posters-headless-women/1472152> (last accessed November 2019).
Price, Brian (2004), 'Cinephilia versus telephilia', *Framework: The Journal of Cinema and Media*, 45(2), <http://digitalcommons.wayne.edu/framework/vol45/iss2/4> (last accessed 26 July 2016).
Prince, Stephen (2003), *Classical Film Violence: Designing and Regulating Brutality in Hollywood Cinema, 1930–1968*, New Jersey: Rutgers University Press.
Proctor, William (2019), 'On *Making European Cult Cinema*', Confessions of an Aca-Fan, 21 April, <http://henryjenkins.org/blog/2019/4/17/fancademia-on-the-continuing-perception-of-fan-studies-as-celebrating-resistance-and-cult-media-studies-as-valorizing-trash-cinema-by-william-proctor-part-ii> (last accessed 6 June 2019).
Quandt, James (2004), 'Flesh and blood: sex and violence in recent French cinema', *Artforum*.com, <https://www.artforum.com/print/200402/flesh-blood-sex-and-violence-in-recent-french-cinema-6199> (last accessed November 2019).
Radewagen, T. and S. Zielinski (1984), 'Video software 1984 – strukturen des markets und tendenzen des angebotes', *Media perspekiven*, 5: 372–88.
Renowden, G. (1982), 'The secret video show', *Daily Mail*, 12 May, p. 12.
Righelato, Rowan (2016), '*The Driller Killer* and the humanist behind the blood and sickening crunch', *The Guardian*, 30 November, <https://www.theguardian.com/film/filmblog/2016/nov/30/the-driller-killer-humanist-abel-ferrara-moral-choices?CMP=share_btn_tw> (last accessed 2 December 2016).
Romney, Jonathan (2014), 'The Girl Can't Help It', *Film Comment*, 50(2): 26–31.
Rothman, Wilson (2009), 'The dirty backstabbing mess called Betamax vs VHS', Gizmodo.com.au, <http://www.gizmodo.com.au/2009/07/the-dirty-backstabbing-mess-called-betamax-vs-vhs/> (last accessed: 3 February 2017).
Russell, David J. (1998), 'Monster roundup: reintegrating the horror genre', in Nick Browne (ed.), *Refiguring American Film Genres*, Berkeley: University of California Press, pp. 233–54.
Samuelson, P. (2006), 'The generativity of Sony v. Universal: the intellectual property legacy of Justice Stevens', *Fordham Law Review*, 74: 1831, <http://scholarship.law.berkeley.edu/facpubs/1463> (last accessed 3 February 2017).

Schaefer, Eric (1999), *Bold! Daring! Shocking! True: A History of Exploitation Films, 1919–1959*, Durham, NC: Duke University Press.

Schauer, B. (2005), 'The Criterion Collection in the new home video market: an interview with Susan Arosteguy', *The Velvet Light Trap*, 56: 32–5.

Schofield, J. (2003), 'Why VHS was better than Betamax', *The Guardian*, 25 January, <https://www.theguardian.com/technology/2003/jan/25/comment.comment> <last accessed 3 February 2017).

Schrader, Paul (2006), 'Cannon fodder: as the sun finally sets on a century of cinema, by what criteria do we determine its masterworks?', <http://paulschrader.org/articles/pdf/2006-FilmComment_Schrader.pdf> (last accessed 1 September 2016).

Sconce, Jeffery (1995), '"Trashing the Academy": taste, excess, and an emerging politics of cinematic style', *Screen*, 36(4, Winter): 371–93.

Sheridan, Simon (2011), *Keeping the British End Up: Four Decades of Saucy Cinema*, Richmond: Reynolds and Hearn.

Sklar, Robert (1975), *Movie-Made America: A Cultural History of American Movies*, New York: Random House.

Slasher Index (2013), 'Charles Band's bogus wizard video VHS releases – THE EVIDENCE', vhscollector.com, <https://vhscollector.com/articles/charles-bands-bogus-wizard-video-vhs-releases-evidence> (last accessed 19 November 2019).

Slater, Jay (2002), 'Flesh-eating mother', *Darkside Magazine*, August–September: 6–10.

Smith, Sarah J. (2005), *Children, Cinema and Censorship: From Dracula to the Dead End Kids*, London: I. B. Tauris.

Sontag, Susan (1977), *On Photography*, New York: Penguin.

Sontag, Susan (1996), 'The decay of cinema', *New York Times*, 25 February, <https://www.nytimes.com/books/00/03/12/specials/sontag-cinema.html> (last accessed 1 July 2016).

Sony (1982), *The Guide to Beta Outlets*, Middlesex: Marketing Drive.

Spidergeek (2016), 'Complete Arrow Video Blu-ray collection', YouTube, 27 April, <https://www.youtube.com/watch?v=coexIHrZwqk> (last accessed 25 November 2016).

Staiger, Janet (1985), 'The politics of film canons', *Cinema Journal*, 24(3): 4–23.

Staiger, Janet (1988), 'Standardization and differentiation: the reinforcement and dispersion of Hollywood's practices', in David Bordwell, Janet Staiger and Kristin Thompson (1988), *The Classical Hollywood Cinema: Film Style and Mode of Production to 1960*, London and New York: Routledge.

Stanley, Richard (2002), 'Dying light: an obituary for the great British horror movie', Steve Chibnall and Julian Petley (eds), *British Horror Cinema*, London: Routledge, pp. 183–95.

Starr, Marco (1984), 'J. Hills is alive: a defence of *I Spit on Your Grave*', in Martin Barker (ed.), *The Video Nasties: Freedom and Censorship in the Media*, London: Pluto Press, pp. 48–55.

Stevens, Brad (2004), *Abel Ferrara: The Moral Vision*. London: FAB Press.

Strauven, Wanda (ed.) (2006), *The Cinema of Attractions Reloaded*, Amsterdam: Amsterdam University Press.

Sun Reporter (1982), 'Fury over video nasties: the merchants of menace "Get Off"', *The Sun*, 1 September, p. 5.

Szulkin, David A. (2000), *Wes Craven's Last House on the Left: The Making of a Cult Classic*, 2nd edn, Surrey: FAB.

Tashiro, Charles Shiro (1991), 'Videophilia: what happens when you wait for it on video', *Film Quarterly*, 45(1): 7–17.

The Soft Machine Operator (2002), 'Zombie Dullards', <https://www.amazon.co.uk/Zombie-Flesh-Eaters-3-DVD/product-reviews/B00006CY93/ref=cm_cr_othr_d_paging_btm_1?ie=UTF8&reviewerType=all_reviews&pageNumber=1> (last accessed 1 August 2018).

Tudor, Andrew (1973), 'Genre', in Barry Keith Grant (ed.), *Film Genre Reader III* (2003), Austin: University of Texas Press, pp. 3–11.

Upton, Julian (2016), 'Electric Blues: the rise and fall of Britain's first pre-recorded videocassette distributors', *Journal of British Cinema and Television*, 13(1): 19–41.

Valenti, Jack (1982), 'Testimony of Jack Valenti, President, Motion Picture Association of America, Inc.', Hearing, 12 April (Serial No. 97), <https://cryptome.org/hrcw-hear.htm> (last accessed 26 January 2017).

Vasey, Ruth (1997), *The World According to Hollywood, 1918–1939: How Hollywood Homogenized the World*, Wisconsin: University of Wisconsin Press.

Vaughn, Stephen (1990), 'Morality and entertainment: the origins of the Motion Picture Production Code', *Journal of American History*, 77(1): 39–65.

Waddell, Calum (2016), *Cannibal Holocaust*, Leighton Buzzard: Devil's Advocates/Auteur Publishing.

Wade, Graham (1980), 'Soho goes video'. *Television and Home Video*, May: 31–5.

Wainscott, Ronald H. (1997), *The Emergence of the Modern American Theater, 1914–1929*, New Haven, CT and London: Yale University Press.

Walker, Johnny (2017), 'Video nicies: rethinking the relationship between video entertainment and children in Britain during the early 1980s', *Historical Journal of Film, Radio and Television*, 37(4): 630–48.

Wark, Angus (2017), *Library Question – Answer [Question #12200463]*. [email].

Wasser, Federick (2001), *Veni, Vidi, Video: The Hollywood Empire and the VCR*, Texas: University of Texas Press.

West, Jake (2010a), *Video Nasties: Moral Panic, Censorship & Videotape*, London: Nucleus Films.

West, Jake (2010b), *Video Nasties: The Definitive Guide* [Documentary], London: Nucleus Films.

West, Jake (2014), *Video Nasties: The Definitive Guide 2*, London: Nucleus Films.

White, Christopher (1983), 'The video nasty killer', *Daily Mail*, 13 July, p. 1.

Williams, Linda (1991), 'Film bodies: gender, genre, and excess', *Film Quarterly*, 44(4, Summer): 2–13. DOI: 10.2307/1212758.

Wilson, David M. (1982), 'Letters and video queries', *Television and Home Video*, p. 59.
Wilson, Matt (2017), '1982-83 Annual Report', Advertising Standards Authority [email].
Wingrove, Nigel and Marc Morris (1998), *The Art of the Nasty*, London: FAB Press.
Wingrove, Nigel and Marc Morris (2009), *The Art of the Nasty*, 2nd edn, London: FAB Press.
Wolpin, Stewart (1994), 'The race to video', *Invention and Technology: The Magazine of Innovation*, 10(2), <https://www.inventionandtech.com/content/race-video-1> (last accessed November 2019).
Zeisler, Andi (2008), *Feminism and Pop Culture*, New York: Seal Press.
Zukin, Sharon (2010), *Naked City: The Death and Life of Authentic Urban Places*, Oxford: Oxford University Press.

Index

Abbott, Norman, 10, 17, 26
Adjust Your Tracking: The Untold Story of the VHS Collector, 169
Adventures of Choppy and the Princess, 12
Advertising Standards Authority (ASA), 8, 14–16, 26, 30
Aguirre: Wrath of God, 101
Alphaville, 130
And God Created Woman, 65
American Werewolf in London, An, 124
Andy Warhol's Frankenstein, 107, 130, 175
Ann Summers, 43–4
Arrow Video, 114, 153, 156–61, 163, 165–6, 170, 172
Astra Video, 9, 12, 22, 141
Audition, 123

Ballyhoo, 59–60, 67–9, 74, 77, 86–8, 91, 113, 164
Barker, Martin, 7, 72
Barnum, P. T., 59, 67, 74, 76, 87
Basket Case, 101
Bazin, André, 117
Beast in Heat, 78–81, 174, 177
Bed Hostesses, 65

Best Little Whorehouse in Texas, The, 131
Betamax, 33, 35–9, 42, 128, 161
Betamax Case, The, 35, 51
Beyond, The, 109, 150, 174
Bicycle Thieves, 157
Blob, The, 157
Blood Feast, 12, 54, 61, 78, 88, 174, 177
Blood Rites, 54, 174, 177
Bloody Moon, 84, 96, 174, 177
Bogeyman, The, 65
Breen, Joseph, 19, 21
Brewster, Francis, 3, 137
Bride of Re-animator, The, 160
Bright, Graham, 12, 27, 54–5, 134
British Board of Film Classification (BBFC), 2, 8–9, 11–13, 15–17, 24–6, 29–30, 47–9, 50–1, 54, 62–63, 66, 80–1, 87, 103, 106, 110–12, 126, 131, 141, 150–1, 164–5
British Videogram Association (BVA), 10–11, 15–17, 23–4, 26, 29–30, 50–1, 114
Bryce, Allan, 1–3, 108, 111, 137

Cabinet of Dr. Caligari, The, 103
Cabin Fever, 124
Caged Women, 65
Cannibal, 65
Cannibal Ferox, 109, 174, 177
Cannibal Holocaust, 8, 10, 15, 30, 109, 130, 174, 177
Cannibal Man, The, 78, 174, 177
Castle, William, 68, 74
Cataclysm, 131
Catholic Legion of Decency, 19, 21
Chien Andalou, Un, 130
Child's Play 3, 133
Chippendale, Peter, 8–10, 95
Cinematograph Act, The, 9
City of the Living Dead, 109, 132, 150–1, 158–9
Color Me Blood Red, 90
Company of Wolves, The, 102
Conservative Party, 9, 12, 24–7, 29, 48, 51, 54
Cramps, The, 91
Criterion Collection, 153–7
Critters, 124
Crying Game, The, 102

Daily Mail, The, 2, 8, 54, 95
Darkside Magazine, 3, 109, 111, 137
Day The World Ended, The, 61
Deadly Spawn, The, 108
Death Trap, 11, 108, 174, 180
Deep Red, 156, 183
Department of Public Prosecutions (DPP), 2, 11, 45, 54, 81, 84, 108, 131, 150, 177
DER, 37
Derann, 22, 40–1, 53, 180, 182

Devil Rides Out, The, 79
Devil's Rejects, The, 123
Driller Killer, The, 8–9, 11, 15, 30, 76–7, 84–6, 107, 153, 164–6, 175
Dickinson, Kay, 7
Dirty Dancing, 24
Dolan, Des, 10, 22, 24, 71–2, 80
Dolly Dearest, 133
DVD, 5–6, 16–17, 35, 52, 70, 96–7, 109, 111, 113–20, 128, 137, 144, 147–8, 150–3, 160, 168, 171–2

Egan, Kate, 72, 106, 112, 121, 125–7, 129, 153, 161
8½, 157
Electric Blue, 14, 46, 56
Evil Dead, The, 17, 70, 77, 88–99, 91, 101, 161–3, 175, 180
Exorcist, The, 8, 131–2, 137
Exposé, 66–7, 171

Fab Press, 128
Faces of Death, 76
fanzines, 130–1
Ferman, James, 26, 47, 84, 103
Fenton, Harvey, 3, 137–8
Fitzcarraldo, 101
Flavia the Heretic, 141
Flesh Gordon, 8
Fly, The, 124
For Your Eyes Only, 83
Four Dimensions of Greta, 64
Four-Sided Triangle, The, 65
Fright Night, 124

Garden of Eden, The, 60, 62–3
Giallo, 116, 140–1, 170–2
Gold, Barrie, 46, 108, 114

Goldbergs, The, 170
Goldmember, 83
Go Video, 9–10, 22, 24, 71, 80, 99
Great Train Robbery, The, 73
Gregory, David, 10, 17, 30, 46, 88, 101
Gremlins, 124
Groove Tube, The, 108
Guins, Raiford, 116–17, 119–20, 139, 143, 150

Hamilton-Grant, David, 13, 63–4, 86–7
Hammer Film Productions, 54–5, 58, 66–8, 79, 134, 166
Henry: Portrait of a Serial Killer, 123
Hill, Rev. Dr Clifford, 12, 21, 27, 29, 95
History of Violence, A, 168
Homicidal, 68
Hostel, 123
Hot Sex in Bangkok, 65
House By The Cemetery, The, 109, 150, 175, 178
House of Commons, 34
House of Lords, 9, 25, 27
House on Haunted Hill, The, 68
House on the Edge of the Park, The, 140, 164–5, 178
Humphreys, Graham, 91, 161–3

I am Curious (Yellow), 65
Ichi The Killer, 123
I Miss You Hugs and Kisses, 78, 175
Impey, Jason, 22
Interview with the Vampire, 102
Invasion of the Body Snatchers, 61
Irréversible, 123
Island of Mutations, 65

I Spit On Your Grave, 9, 12, 27, 30, 77–9, 82–3, 96, 118, 123, 141, 171, 175, 178
Iver Film Services, 40–2, 100–2, 178, 182–4, 186

Jackson, Neil, 7
Jane Fonda's Workout, 45
JVC, 33–4, 37–9

Kill Bill: Vol. 2, 114
Killer Nun, 103, 140–1, 175, 181
Kingpin, 83
Kingsman: The Secret Service, 83
Kruger, Peter, 9–10, 30

Lady Snowblood, 156
Last House on the Left, The, 61, 90, 123, 176, 178
Late Night Trains, 78, 140, 175, 181
Lee, Mike, 57, 110
Life of an American Fireman, 73
Living Dead at Manchester Morgue, The 65
Lloyd, Peter, 9
Love Camp 7, 54, 81, 106, 175, 178
Love Variations, 63–4

M, 103
Maguire, David, 7
Maltby, Richard, 20, 24, 51
Man Bites Dog, 123
Maniac, 131
Man's Epic Magazine, 81
Mardi Gras Massacre, 78, 176, 178
Marriage of Maria Braun, The, 157
Martin, John, 9–11, 14–15, 80, 137

Matrix, The, 114
Matsushita Electric Company, The (Panasonic), 33, 36–7
Mausoleum, 131
Mee, Laura, 7
Mephisto, 101
Miracle Decision, The, 60
Miracle Film Productions, 24, 64–5
Mom and Dad, 60, 93
Mona Lisa, 102
Monthly Film Bulletin, 128
Morris, Marc, 3, 56, 85, 137–8
Mother's Day, 131
Motion Picture Association of America (MPAA), 17–18, 51–2, 68
Motion Picture Production Code, The, 18, 20–2, 24
Mummy, The 67
Myers, Martin, 24

Naked, 83
National Viewers' and Listeners' Association (NVLA), 10, 21, 24–9, 55
Neighbour, Richard, 8
Nesting, The, 108, 185
Newman, Kim, 3, 55, 72, 128
New York Ripper, The 131
Nightbeast, 108, 185
Nightmares in a Damaged Brain, 13, 87–8, 176, 178
Nightmare on Elm Street, A, 161
Night of the Bloody Apes, 54, 100, 109, 176, 178
Night of the Demon, 100, 109, 176, 178
Night Porter, The, 80
Nosferatu, 103, 130

Obscene Publications Act, The (OPA) 9, 11, 13, 30, 38, 44, 46, 81, 111, 140, 177
Old Dark House, The, 68
Oppidan Film Productions, 64–5, 87

Palace Pictures, 17, 88, 101–2, 108, 161–3, 180
Panasonic *see* Matsushita Electric Company, The
Pan Book of Horror series, 85–6
Parliamentary Group Video Enquiry (PGVE), 12, 21, 24, 27, 29
Peeping Tom, 55
Pete's Dragon, 23
Petley, Julian, 7–8, 54–5, 72, 125–6, 135, 164
Pet Semetary, 133
Phantom Carriage, The, 103, 105
Plan 9 From Outer Space, 101
Powell, Nik, 101
Pre-Cert Forum, 42, 44, 85, 129
Prisoner of the Cannibal God, 78, 176, 181
Production Code, The *see* Motion Picture Production Code, The
Psychic Killer, 65
Psycho, 40
Psycho II, 133

Quatermass Xperiment, The, 65

Radio Rentals, 37, 39, 47
Raiders of the Lost Ark, 70
RCA, 32–3, 36–8
Redemption, 102–7, 110, 114, 117, 119–20
Reefer Madness, 60, 93–4
Renowden, Gareth, 8

Repulsion 130
Rewind This!, 169

Salò: or 120 Days of Sodom, 80–1, 130
Salon Kitty, 80, 105
Sarnoff, David, 32–3
Saw, 123
Scars of Dracula, The, 41
Scum, 8, 133
Seven Samurai, 157
Shameless Screen Entertainment, 140–2, 156, 162, 172
Sheena, Queen of the Jungle, 78
Shogun Assassin, 107–8, 114, 156, 176, 186
Sklar, Robert, 19–20
Slayer, The, 107–8, 153, 176, 181
Slaughterhouse Five, 86
Snuff (film), 9, 176, 179
snuff movies, 129
Society, 124
Sontag, Susan, 118, 146, 149
Sony, 33–8, 42, 53
Sony U-Matic, 33–4
Spookies, 108
SS Experiment Camp, 8–9, 14–16, 77–81, 164–5, 171, 176, 179
Starr, Marco, 7
Straw Dogs, 131
Sweet and Sexy, 64–5
Szulkin, David A., 7

Tartan Video, 102, 118, 125
Taste of Fear, 67–8
TCX, 44, 186
Television and Home Video Magazine, 14, 43–4
Television and Video Retailer Magazine, 7, 9, 14–15

Texas Chainsaw Massacre, The, 8, 16, 41–2, 84, 100, 131, 133, 137
Thatcher, Margaret, 27
13 Ghosts, 68
3:10 to Yuma, 83
Tingler, The, 68
Toolbox Murders, The, 65, 78, 84, 176, 181
To The Devil A Daughter, 79

Uncle Tom's Cabin, 73
Under The Bed, 64

Valenti, Jack, 17–18, 21
Vampyre, 103
Vampyros Lesbos, 105
VHS, 34, 36–9, 42, 113, 117–18, 128, 147–8, 150, 161, 168–9, 171–2
V/H/S, (film), 171
Video Business Magazine, 46, 71
Videodrome, 168
Video Nasties: Moral Panic, Censorship and Videotape, 169
Video Packaging Review Committee (VPRC), 111–12
Video Recordings Act (VRA), 1, 3, 7, 12–13, 17, 20–4, 29, 51–2, 109, 120, 126, 129
Video Review, 14
Vipco, 9, 11, 22, 42, 47–8, 57, 65, 85, 99–100, 102, 107–14, 116–17, 120, 150–1, 153, 162, 165, 172, 178–81, 185–6
Virgin Spring, The, 157
Visions of Ecstasy 103
Viz, 133

Waddell, Callum, 7
Wages of Sin, The, 60, 63, 93
Washing Machine, The, 130
Wasser, Frederick, 33, 36, 39–40, 43
Weekend, 130
Werewolf and the Yeti, The, 130, 176, 179
West, Jake, 9, 11, 30, 55, 169–70
Which Video?, 8
Whitehouse, Mary, 10, 12, 21, 25–8
Whitelaw, Willie, 25
Wingrove, Nigel, 56, 85, 137
Women Behind Bars, 78, 176, 181
Women in Love, 63

Wonder Years, The, 170
World of Video 2000, 13, 42, 86–8, 181–4
Woolley, Stephen, 17, 26, 101, 108

X The Unknown, 66

Zombie Creeping Flesh, 24, 65, 167, 181
Zombie: Dawn of the Dead, 113, 187
Zombie Flesh Eaters, 8, 65, 107–8, 110–13, 137, 150, 153, 171, 176, 179
Zombie Flesh Eaters 3, 112–13

EU representative:
Easy Access System Europe
Mustamäe tee 50, 10621 Tallinn, Estonia
Gpsr.requests@easproject.com

www.ingramcontent.com/pod-product-compliance
Lightning Source LLC
Chambersburg PA
CBHW071842230426
43671CB00012B/2046